*On the third day he
in accordance with the Scriptures;
he ascended into heaven
and is seated at the right hand of the Father.
He will come again in glory
to judge the living and the dead,
and his kingdom will have no end.*

*We believe in the Holy Spirit,
the Lord, the giver of life,
who proceeds from the Father [and the Son],
who with the Father and the Son
is worshipped and glorified,
who has spoken through the prophets.
We believe in one holy catholic
and apostolic Church.
We acknowledge one baptism
for the forgiveness of sins.
We look for the resurrection of the dead,
and the life of the world to come.*

Amen.

The APOSTLES' CREED

I believe in God, the Father almighty,
creator of heaven and earth.

I believe in Jesus Christ,
God's only Son, our Lord,
who was conceived by the Holy Spirit,
born of the Virgin Mary,
suffered under Pontius Pilate,
was crucified, died, and was buried;
he descended to the dead.
On the third day he rose again;
he ascended into heaven,
he is seated
at the right hand of the Father,
and he will come to judge
the living and the dead.

I believe in the Holy Spirit,
the holy catholic Church,
the communion of saints,
the forgiveness of sins,
the resurrection of the body,
and the life everlasting.   *Amen.*

Book of
COMMON ORDER
of the
CHURCH OF SCOTLAND

To
Terry

from

West Church

Mens Fellowship

30th. April 2000

Book of
COMMON ORDER
of the
CHURCH OF SCOTLAND

SAINT ANDREW PRESS

EDINBURGH

First published in 1994 by
SAINT ANDREW PRESS
121 George Street, Edinburgh EH2 4YN

on behalf of the
PANEL ON WORSHIP
of the CHURCH OF SCOTLAND

Second edition (emended) 1996

ISBN 0 7152 0721 0

British Library Cataloguing in Publication Data
A catalogue record for
this book is available
from the British Library

ISBN 0715207210

This book has been set in 10 pt Times Roman.

Book design by Mark Blackadder.
Typesetting by Lesley A Taylor.
Calligraphy by John McWilliam.
Printed and **bound** by BPC Wheatons Ltd.

Contents

CONTENTS

Preface

At a time of ceaseless change in the way churches understand and participate in worship, to publish a book of Common Order may seem a courageous act. Liturgical and gender language, the understanding of worship leadership, the theology of preaching and of the sacraments – all are in flux, a restlessness which may be a sign more of the Spirit's indwelling than absence.

Whatever else God calls us to, we are called to worship, to do so together, and to do so in the promised company of Jesus Christ. It is in worship that our lives are expressed before God and informed and converted by God's Word. It is in worship that through song, prayer, and preaching, our theology is formed, our discipleship encouraged, and our spirits nourished. It is in worship that we reach out to touch the hem of Christ's garment and find that, instead of touching the hem, we are being offered the grace of God by word of mouth and gift of hand.

The Church of Scotland, since the Reformation, has provided publications such as this to aid the corporate experience of worship. These books have never been prescriptive, making 'this and this only' mandatory on ministers and congregations. Rather, in a tradition which reveres both freedom *to* worship and freedom *in* worship, three things are offered:

Firstly, orders of service, which may be followed verbatim.

Secondly, patterns of prayer and devotion, which can be used as models to be emulated or starting points for development.

Thirdly, a wealth of resources, which can be mined and re-mined for many years to come.

This is a **common** book, because it belongs to all the people of God. In the reformed understanding, worship is not the right or rite of an ordained caste, but is the duty, joy, and prerogative of all believers. *Common Order* includes services where congregational participation is encouraged, and a Daily Office for use by individuals or small groups wherever they may gather for prayer. The book also reflects the common heritage of prayer and devotion of the whole Church, drawing from the orthodox wellsprings of liturgy and from the lay heritage of Celtic spirituality originating in these shores.

It is also a book of **order**. In worship we engage as the Body of Christ in an encounter with almighty God. This engagement should never become a rambling incoherence of well-meaning phrases and gestures. It should exhibit that deliberate and historical patterning of sentiment and expression which befits the meeting of the sons and daughters of earth with the King of kings. Further, in public worship, as distinct from personal devotions, it is important that the whole congregation sense a purpose and direction in their representation before God. They should never be placed in the position of being spectators at a performance which is entirely dependent on the aesthetic, emotional, and spiritual whims of its leaders.

This in no way precludes or denies the inspiration and direction of the Holy Spirit. The enemy of the Spirit is not form but anarchy.

Thanks are due to those who compiled this book – the members of the Panel's Liturgical Committee, its successive Conveners, Andrew J Scobie and Graeme T Longmuir, and Charles Robertson, the Honorary Secretary of the Panel who acted as the Committee's secretary and the book's chief editor. It is their hope and prayer that their labours will be rewarded by the increase of serious, enthusiastic, and joyful participation of all God's people in the shared privilege of worshipping together the One who has made us to find fulfilment in his service, to whom be praise and glory in the Church and in Christ Jesus for ever.

JOHN L BELL
Convener, Panel on Worship

Introduction

In 1987, the General Assembly accepted a motion proposed by Dr Herron and seconded by Professor Whyte to 'instruct the Panel on Worship without delay to proceed with the production of a new *Book of Common Order*'. In the discussion that preceded this decision, it was made clear that any new book should follow the 1940 rather than the 1979 model.

In pursuing its task, the Panel's Liturgical Committee kept in mind two elements that have always in some degree marked worship as Scottish and presbyterian: the notion that public worship is a converting ordinance, with the outsider always in mind; and that it is at the same time an edifying ordinance, with the role of building up the Church, the Body of Christ. It is hoped that the directness of the language, the biblical content, and the wide range of material offered, go some way to expressing and meeting these two concerns.

Consideration for inclusive language is given throughout the book. Language about *people* is inclusive: *mankind,* for example, becomes *all* or *all people*, *the family of man* becomes *the human family* or *humankind.* In prayers and in rubrics, pronouns are italicized, and in the Form and Order for Holy Baptism, for example, the italicized pronoun used throughout is *she.*

In addressing or speaking of God, male-dominated language has been avoided wherever possible. Traditional metaphors like *Father, Judge, King* remain, but they are used sparingly, as are references to God's might and power. This does not always make for elegant composition, but it is an honest attempt to fulfil an undertaking given to the General

Assembly in 1986 and in 1988 to use inclusive language wherever possible, though not to the extent of altering Scripture or
changing classical texts.

The *you* form, and not the *thou* form, is used for addressing
God. This seemingly simple change affects syntax, grammar,
and vocabulary, and increases the obligation to ensure that the
language used is fresh, clear, and relevant.

Care has been taken to make the speaking of the prayers as
easy and as rhythmical as possible, so that during acts of worship there should be no unnecessary strain either in saying or in
hearing them. They are set out not in prose paragraphs, but in
short lines, like verse. This lay-out means that the book is larger
than it otherwise might have been; the space taken up by short
lines is obviously greater than that occupied by paragraphs.
The ideal has been that the prayers should reflect such a pitch
of simplicity, dignity, and beauty that ministers will at once
adopt the new book, and the Church at large welcome and own it.

The Table of Contents reflects the Panel's aim to provide
as comprehensive a book as possible, building on the 1940
book's breadth of material. It begins with a short section of
Preparation for Worship, with prayers for the minister and
prayers with the choir. There follow five *Orders of Service for
Morning Worship* and five for *Evening Worship*. An attempt
has been made to provide freshness and variety in the services:
the Fourth Morning Service, for instance, contains material
from the Celtic tradition; and an innovative note has been
struck in the Evening Services.

*Forms and Orders for the Sacraments and Ordinances of
the Church* begins with *Holy Baptism*, for which only one
Form and Order has been provided, adapted for children and
for adults. The insights of the French Reformed Church's
Liturgy, which were first made accessible to the Church in a
booklet by the Panel in 1986, are retained; and the image of
burial with Christ in the water of baptism is given a heightened
place. *The Service of Public Profession of Faith* is also a
Service of Confirmation and Admission to the Lord's Supper.

It accords baptism its central and fundamental role in the life and worship of the Church and in the experience of the individual Christian. In the Service of Baptism, provision has been made for a candidate to be confirmed and admitted to Holy Communion; and the Confirmation Service is so arranged as to allow Baptism before Confirmation.

There are five *Forms and Orders for Holy Communion.* The 1940 *Book of Common Order* was especially rich in its provision of eucharistic material, keeping the Sacrament of the Lord's Supper central and fundamental; even where there was no Action, services were constructed to be eucharistic in their form and order.

The new book shares this emphasis on the Sacrament. The attempt has been made to strike a positive note, echoing the dynamic joy of the presence of Christ and reflecting the boundless energy of his Spirit.

The principal Order follows a more or less classical pattern and offers three Thanksgiving or Eucharistic Prayers, thus allowing for variety and frequency of celebration. Each one of these is different in character: the first follows the classical pattern in structure and language; the second is drawn from our own Reformed tradition, from the *Genevan Service Book*; and the third comes from the world Church (English Language Liturgical Consultation).

The second Order reflects the Celtic tradition; the third is a shorter Order to be used at a second Service or other similar occasion; the fourth is for use when children communicate; and the fifth is for use at home or in hospital. This section of the book concludes with the *Proper Prefaces* and a short selection of Prayers for use at different points in the Service of Holy Communion.

Three Orders of Service are offered for *Christian Marriage,* the first and last following respectively the 1940 and 1979 books, and the second adopting a eucharistic pattern. The Marriage Vows have been changed to allow for a *giving* before *taking,* and the suggestion has been made in the rubrics that the procedures commonly followed at weddings, whereby, for example, the man waits in the church for the woman to arrive, or the man makes the vows first, need not always be followed. *Orders for the Blessing of a Civil Marriage*, and for *Thanksgiving for Marriage* (*with the Renewal of Marriage Vows*) complete this section.

In addition to appropriate Forms and Orders for various *Funeral Services*, a comprehensive collection of material is offered in the hope that ministers and people alike will find resources that are helpful in the various circumstances of bereavement.

Among the Occasional Services, such as Orders for the *Admission of Elders*, for *Remembrance Day*, and for the *Dedication of a Church*, there are three new Services: a *Covenant Service*, a *Service of Healing*, and an *Order for the Blessing of a New Home*.

Prayers for the Seasons of the Christian Year follows directly the pattern of the 1940 book, as do the sections on *Prayers for Occasional Use*, such as Harvest, New Year, Elections; *Prayers for Specific Graces*, such as patience, hope, cheerfulness; *Specific Intercessions*; and *Additional Prayers for Public Worship* – five prayers each for Confession, Thanksgiving, Intercession, and Dedication of the Offerings.

A short *Daily Service* is provided for use in the parish church, thus recovering a practice of the Reformation; and a Form of *Daily Devotion for Morning and Evening* is offered for personal use.

Ascriptions of Glory and *Benedictions*, usually in the language of the *Revised English Bible*, which is used throughout the book, are followed by a short section of Readings for *Pastoral Visitation*.

The lectionary chosen to accompany the book is the *Revised Common Lectionary*, which runs on a three year cycle, and is used in most of the English-speaking churches in the west. A few adjustments have been made to it, such as the provision of Old Testament Lessons alongside readings from the Apocrypha. Appropriate Scripture Sentences and Collects of the Day have also been supplied.

The Index at the back of the book, while by no means exhaustive, is intended to alert the users of the book to opportunities which do not lie on the surface. For example, the section on Dedication of a Church and on Church Furnishings, may not be used very often, but it contains much valuable material which is appropriate for many occasions and circumstances. The Index helps the diligent to seek them out.

A glance will show that not all the services are printed in full. In the Morning and Evening Forms and Orders, for instance, the first services are complete; reference should be made to them for later ones which do not appear so fully.

The rubrics and the layout are meant to make the services easy to follow and the book a pleasure to use, but sometimes a little reflection is required before they yield their full meaning. For example, *Hymn*, when it appears, is intended to cover not just hymns, but psalms and worship songs as well; and *Psalm* can mean a metrical version or a chant to be sung, or a psalm to be read antiphonally, responsorially, or together. Efforts have been made to achieve clarity for the more complicated rubrics, such as are found in the Baptism and Confirmation Services, and in the *Order for Thanksgiving for Marriage (with the Renewal of Marriage Vows)*, and in the Remembrance Day Service. It is assumed that careful and thorough preparation always precedes every service, and that the study of the rubrics is a necessary part of that preparation.

The new book is for the whole Church, not just for ministers. Provision has been made for the people to participate, either by offering a substantial part for them to say in the service or by making some of the material responsorial. The hope of the Panel is that this book will prove to be of service to the Church, and that its abundant variety of material will enrich the worship of the Church and enliven the devotion of the people of God.

CHARLES ROBERTSON
Honorary Secretary, Panel on Worship

Acknowledgments

Scripture quotations are from *The Revised English Bible,* 1989, Oxford University Press and Cambridge University Press, except where stated otherwise.

The Liturgical Texts come from *Praying Together,* The English Language Liturgical Consultation (ELLC), 1988, Canterbury Press, as does the main substance of the third Eucharistic Prayer, option *c*.

The *Revised Common Lectionary,* Consultation on Common Texts (CCT), 1992, Canterbury Press, appears here slightly modified.

Most of the Collects which accompany the Lectionary were originally prepared by the General Synod of the Anglican Church in Canada.

The *Order for a Covenant Service* is derived from *The Methodist Service Book,* Methodist Publishing House, 1984 reprint.

The Fourth Evening Service originated in *The Promise of His Glory,* Central Board of Finance of the Church of England, 1990.

The Collect for Tuesday in *The Daily Service* is taken from *The Daily Office, Revised,* Joint Liturgical Group, 1978, SPCK.

Many sources have contributed to the compilation of this book, and not all of them are now traceable. Individual members of the Committee prepared drafts, which were revised more or less drastically by the Committee, often resulting in final versions which looked little like the original drafts. Among the casualties of this sometimes protracted process was the identity of many of the sources: they could not be recalled, nor did there seem to be any way to track them down. The Panel wishes to record at once both its indebtedness to any who may recognize in this book rhythms and patterns, expressions and phrases, ideas and images which are their own, and its regret that it became impossible to ask permission or seek consent for their inclusion here. If, in addition, any infringement of copyright has been committed, it has been unintentional and unwitting, and the Panel trusts that it will be forgiven. The Panel and its publisher would be pleased to be notified about material which is used here but not acknowledged, and will rectify such omissions in future printings.

I
PREPARATION
for
WORSHIP

Before
Divine Service

FOR THE MINISTER

Sentences

1   God is spirit,
and those who worship him
must worship in spirit and in truth.

St John 4: 24

2   Send out your light and your truth
to be my guide;
let them lead me to your holy hill,
to your dwelling-place.
Then I shall come to the altar of God,
the God of my joy and delight.

Psalm 43: 3 - 4

3   Through your great love
I may come into your house,
and at your holy temple bow down in awe.
Lead me and protect me, Lord;
give me a straight path to follow.

Psalm 5: 7 - 8

4   God, create a pure heart for me,
and give me a new and steadfast spirit.
Do not drive me from your presence
or take your holy spirit from me.   *Psalm 51: 10*

5   I wait for the Lord with longing,
    I put my hope in his word.
    My soul waits for the Lord
    more eagerly than watchmen for the morning.

Psalm 130: 6

Prayers

6   God of grace and truth,
    without you I can do nothing as I ought.
    Clothe me with your Spirit,
    that with joy and reverence
    I may lead the worship of your people
    and worthily proclaim the gospel of your love
    to the glory of your name;
    through Jesus Christ my Lord.

7   You have shown us, O Lord, what is good.
    Help me to perform what you require:
    to do justly
    to love mercy,
    and to walk humbly with you,
    my Lord and my God.

8   Fill this day with grace, Lord Jesus Christ,
    that every thought, word, and deed
    may be acceptable to you,
    my rock and my redeemer.

9   Teach me, my God and King,
    to begin your work with faith,
    to continue it with obedience,
    to finish it in love;
    and to watch and wait in patience,
    knowing that your promises can never fail;
    through Jesus Christ.

10   Since I am coming to that holy room
          where with the choir of saints for evermore
          I shall be made thy music;
          as I come
          I tune the instrument here at the door,
          and what I must do *then*,
          think *here* before.

WITH THE CHOIR

The choir may say the Scripture Sentences.

1   ***I shall sing always***
           of the loving deeds of the Lord;
           throughout every generation
           I shall proclaim your faithfulness.

                                 Psalm 89: 1

           Lord of life and glory,
           help us fulfil our ministry
           with faithfulness and joy
           as we celebrate the mystery of your power
           and the triumphs of your grace;
           through Jesus Christ our Lord.

                                 Amen.

2   ***Sing to the Lord and bless his name,***
           day by day proclaim his victory.
           Majesty and splendour attend him,
           might and beauty are in his sanctuary.

                               Psalm 92: 2, 6

God of all joy,
fill our souls to overflowing
with the fullness of your grace,
that we may sing of your strength
in the sanctuary
and shed abroad your love in the world;
through Jesus Christ our Lord.   ***Amen.***

3   ***I shall praise God's name in song,
          and glorify him with thanksgiving.***

Psalm 69: 30

Gracious God,
you are worthy of praise.
All creation worships you;
the glorious company of heaven adores you;
throughout the world
the holy Church acclaims you.
Receive the praise we offer,
and inspire us by your Spirit
to sing in our hearts with grace
to the glory of your name;
through Jesus Christ our Lord.

Amen.

4   ***Sing a new song to the Lord,
          for he has done marvellous deeds.
          Acclaim the Lord, all the earth;
          break into songs of joy.***

Psalm 98: 1, 4

Eternal God,
the hosts of heaven
ceaselessly proclaim your praise.
Help us who serve you
in the worship of your house

to sing and make music
from our hearts to the Lord;
through our Saviour Jesus Christ.

Amen.

5   ***With psalms and hymns***
     and spiritual songs,
     sing from the heart in gratitude to God.

               Colossians 3: 16

God of all kindness,
we thank you for the many ways
your love comes into our lives.
You have filled our mouths with laughter
and our tongues with singing.
Accept our sacrifice of song
in your Church on earth,
and grant us a part in the music
of your Church in heaven;
through Jesus Christ our Lord.   *Amen.*

II
The
ORDER
of
PUBLIC WORSHIP

First
Morning Service

1   *The Bible is brought into the church.*
    The congregation stands.

2   CALL TO WORSHIP

    The minister says:

    Let all the earth acclaim God.
    Sing to the glory of his name.
    Come and see what God has done,
    let the sound of his praise be heard.
    Blessed is God
    who has not withdrawn from us
    his love and care.   *Psalm 66: 1, 2, 5, 8, 20*

    Let us worship God.

3   HYMN

4   SCRIPTURE SENTENCE

    The minister says the Sentence(s) appropriate to the
    day (pp 645 to 692); or a general Sentence such as:

    Blessed be the name of the Lord
    now and evermore.
    From the rising of the sun to its setting
    the Lord's name be praised!   *Psalm 113: 2 - 3*

5 PRAYERS

The minister says:

Let us pray.

Adoration

Worthy of praise from every mouth,
of confession from every tongue,
of worship from every creature,
is your glorious name,
Father, Son, and Holy Spirit,
one God for ever.
You created the world in your grace,
and by your compassion you redeemed it.
Heaven and earth are full of your praises:
glory be to you, O God most high.

Angels and archangels
and all the hosts of heaven worship you.
We are not worthy to praise you;
but, for your mercy's sake,
accept the praises of all your servants,
in this house and throughout the world;
through Jesus Christ our Lord.

Gracious Father,
your might is beyond measure,
your wisdom beyond knowledge,
your love beyond all telling.
You have put eternity into our hearts,
and made us hunger and thirst for you.
Satisfy the longings you have implanted
that we may find you in life,
and find life in you;
through Jesus Christ our Lord.   ***Amen.***

Confession

    Merciful God,
    you made us in your image,
    with a mind to know you,
    a heart to love you,
    and a will to serve you.
    But our knowledge is imperfect,
    our love inconstant,
    our obedience incomplete.
    Day by day we fail to grow into your likeness;
    yet you are slow to be angry with your children.
    For the sake of Jesus Christ,
    your Son, our Saviour,
    do not hold our sins against us,
    but in your tender love, forgive.

    Lord have mercy.
        Christ have mercy.
    Lord have mercy.

silence

    The almighty and merciful Lord
    grant you pardon
    and remission of all your sins,
    time for amendment of life,
    and the grace and comfort of the Holy Spirit.
                                Amen.

silence

Supplication

    God of love,
    your Son gave us a new commandment,
    that we should love one another,
    even as you love us,
    the unworthy and the wandering.

Give us a mind forgetful of past ill-will
and a heart to love one another;
through the same Jesus Christ,
your Son, our Saviour.   ***Amen.***

Collect of the day; or this Collect
Guide us, O Lord,
in all the changes of life,
that we may neither complain in adversity
nor boast in prosperity;
but with faith, hope, and love,
may follow your divine will;
through Jesus Christ our Lord.

                                        Amen.

6   HYMN

7   OLD TESTAMENT

The reader says:

Listen for the Word of God.

The Old Testament reading comes from
(*book*), chapter (*ab*), verse (*xy*).

8   PSALM

The Psalm may be sung or said.

9   EPISTLE

The reader says:

The Epistle reading comes from
(*book*), chapter (*ab*), verse (*xy*).

10   GOSPEL (*the congregation may stand*)

The reader says:

> The Gospel reading comes from
> (*book*), chapter (*ab*), verse (*xy*).

At the end of the readings, the reader says:

> May God bless to us
> the reading of his holy Word.   ***Amen.***

11   ALLELUIA *or* HYMN

12   PRAYER FOR ILLUMINATION

The minister says:

> Let us pray.

> Lord Jesus Christ,
> by the power of your presence
> open the mind of God to us,
> that in your light we may see light,
> and in your strength be strong.   ***Amen.***

13   SERMON

14   ASCRIPTION OF PRAISE

After the Sermon, the minister says:

> To God the Father,
> God the Son,
> and God the Holy Spirit,
> be glory and praise, now and for ever.   ***Amen.***

15 APOSTLES' CREED (*all standing*)

> *I believe in God, the Father almighty,*
> *creator of heaven and earth.*
> *I believe in Jesus Christ,*
> *God's only Son, our Lord,*
> *who was conceived by the Holy Spirit,*
> *born of the Virgin Mary,*
> *suffered under Pontius Pilate,*
> *was crucified, died, and was buried;*
> *he descended to the dead.*
> *On the third day he rose again;*
> *he ascended into heaven,*
> *he is seated*
> *at the right hand of the Father,*
> *and he will come to judge*
> *the living and the dead.*
>
> *I believe in the Holy Spirit,*
> *the holy catholic Church,*
> *the communion of saints,*
> *the forgiveness of sins,*
> *the resurrection of the body,*
> *and the life everlasting.*   *Amen.*

16 HYMN

17 INTIMATIONS

18 OFFERING

19 PRAYERS

The minister says:

Let us pray.

Thanksgiving
> God of wisdom and love,
> giver of all good things,
> we thank you for your loving-kindness,
> and for your constant care over all creation.
>
> We bless you for the gift of life,
> for your guiding hand upon us,
> and your sustaining love within us.
>
> We thank you for friendship and duty,
> for good hopes and precious memories,
> for the joys that cheer us,
> and the trials that teach us to trust in you.
>
> We bless you for Jesus Christ,
> your Son, our Saviour,
> for the living presence of your Spirit,
> for your Church, the body of Christ,
> for the ministry of Word and Sacrament
> and all the means of grace.
>
> In our weakness, you are our strength;
> in our darkness, light;
> in our sorrows, comfort and peace.
> From everlasting to everlasting
> you are our God,
> Father, Son, and Holy Spirit,
> one God, glorified for ever.

Amen.

Dedication
> In glad thanksgiving for your goodness,
> we offer you our gifts;

and pray for the power
to offer and present
our very selves to you,
a living sacrifice,
dedicated and fit for your acceptance;
through Jesus Christ our Lord.   **Amen.**

Intercession

Loving God,
you care for all your children;
you know each one and hear each prayer,
you know each house and see each need.
Give peace and love to those who call upon you,
and receive us into the kingdom of your light.

Bless your Church, here and everywhere.
Confirm your people in the faith of the Gospel,
inspire them with love for your house,
zeal in your service,
and joy in the well-being of your kingdom.

Bless your servant, Elizabeth our Queen.
Govern the hearts and minds
of the Queen's ministers and counsellors,
that they may fulfil their service
for the welfare of the people
and the glory of your name.

Bless the whole world with peace.
Kindle in the hearts of all people
the true love of peace,
and guide with your wisdom
the leaders of the nations,
that your kingdom may advance
until the earth be filled
with the knowledge of your love.

Bless with your comfort
all who are in trouble or pain.
Heal those who are sick;
support those who are dying;
console those who mourn;
supply the wants of those who are in need.
And be near to those
whom now we name in silence . . .

Bless our homes,
that love and joy may dwell there;
and keep those who are absent from us
within the protection of your love.

Commemoration of the Faithful Departed
Eternal God,
sinners find mercy in you and saints find joy.
You hold all souls in life;
the dead as well as the living are in your care.
We thank you for your people
of every age and place,
and for those dear to our own hearts,
who kept the faith on earth
and have entered into the joy
of your heavenly presence.

Inspire us by their example,
encourage us by their fellowship,
and bring us with them at the last
to glory everlasting.
through Jesus Christ our Lord.

Amen.

Our Father in heaven,
hallowed be your name,
your kingdom come,
your will be done,
on earth as in heaven.
Give us today our daily bread.
Forgive us our sins
as we forgive those who sin against us.
Save us from the time of trial
and deliver us from evil.
For the kingdom, the power,
and the glory are yours
now and forever.   *Amen.*

20   HYMN

21   DISMISSAL AND BLESSING

The minister says:

Go in peace and serve the Lord.

The minister blesses the people from God, saying:

The blessing of God almighty,
Father, Son, and Holy Spirit,
be with you all.   *Amen.*

Second
Morning Service

1   CALL TO WORSHIP

The Lord be with you.
And also with you.

Let us worship God

or

Grace and peace to you from God our Father
and the Lord Jesus Christ.

Let us worship God.

or

We come from scattered lives to this sanctuary,
to seek our unity in the Spirit,
to seek the grace of the Lord Jesus Christ,
to seek the peace of God the Father.

God's people have gathered:
let us worship him together.

2   HYMN

3   CALL TO PRAYER

The Lord is gracious and compassionate,
long-suffering and ever faithful.

The Lord is good to all;
his compassion rests upon all his creatures.

Psalm 145: 8 - 9

4   PRAYERS

Let us pray.

God our Father, *You made us and*
your love is at work in all that you have made.
Son of God, *You gave Your life for us ~ and*
in your likeness we are made new.
Holy Spirit, *You bring the Power of God into our human experience*
you touch our lives with hope.
Triune God, Receive our worship,
and claim us for your service,
set us free to honour you today.

You are the
Holy God, giver of light and grace,
We have sinned against you
and against our fellow men and women,
Sometimes through ignorance,
Sometimes through weakness,
and often through our own deliberate fault.

In so doing, We have belittled your love,
and betrayed your trust.
We bow before You to say that We are sorry, we are ashamed,
we repent of all our sins.
For the sake of your Son Jesus Christ,
who died for us,
please forgive us all that is past,
and lead us out from darkness
to walk as children of light. *who worship You with*
glad and generous hearts

silence

Jesus died and rose again for you:
In humble penitence,
accept his pardon,
receive his peace. *Amen.*

God and Father of our Lord Jesus Christ,
from you alone come everlasting joy and peace.
Fill us with joy in your promises,
and send us out to be bearers of your peace;
through your Son Jesus Christ our Lord.
Amen.

Collect of the day

5 HYMN

6 SCRIPTURE READINGS

7 HYMN

8 PRAYERS

Thanksgiving
Lord of life,
you have called us together
in the name of Jesus Christ:
in him, and through him, we praise you.

For the gift of your Son, our Saviour,
born a child,
growing to maturity,
teaching your truth,
healing the sick,
befriending sinners,
crucified at Calvary,
risen, ascended, and with us forever:
Lord, from our hearts we thank you.

For all that you offer us through Christ,
for the leading and strengthening
of the Holy Spirit,
for our baptism and growing in faith,
for the nourishment of Word and Sacrament,
for the fellowship of others in the Church,
living in this place and across the world:
Lord, from our hearts we thank you.

For those gifts of yours
which make us what we are,
for talents of mind and eye and hand,
for every opportunity to be of service,
for those who love us and cherish us,
for those whom we value
as neighbours and friends:
Lord, from our hearts we thank you.

Give us grace, we pray,
to accept your gifts joyfully
and to use them generously
to your glory and praise;
through Jesus Christ our Lord.   *Amen.*

Intercession
Gracious God,
rejoicing in your blessings,
trusting in your loving care for all,
we bring you our prayers for the world.

We pray for the created world:
for those who rebuild
where things have been destroyed;
for those who fight hunger, poverty, and disease;
for those who have power
to bring change for the better and to renew hope.

silence
In the life of our world
your kingdom come, O Lord,
your will be done.

We pray for our country:
for our Queen and her family;
for those who frame our laws
and shape our common life;
for those who keep the peace
and administer justice;
for those who teach,
those who heal,
all who serve the community.
silence
In the life of our land
your kingdom come, O Lord,
your will be done.

We pray for people in need:
those for whom life is a bitter struggle;
those whose lives are clouded
by death or loss,
by pain or disability,
by discouragement or fear,
by shame or rejection.
silence
In the lives of those in need
your kingdom come, O Lord,
your will be done.

We pray for those
in the circle of friendship and love around us:
children and parents;
sisters and brothers;
friends and neighbours;

and for those especially in our thoughts today.
silence
In the lives of those we love
your kingdom come, O Lord,
your will be done.

We pray for the Church
in its stand with the poor,
in its love for the outcast and the ashamed,
in its service to the sick and the neglected,
in its proclamation of the Gospel,
in this land, in this place.
silence
In the life of your Church
your kingdom come, O Lord,
your will be done.

Eternal God,
we give thanks to you
for the great community of faith
into which you have brought us:
for those who have kept safe our Scriptures,
gathered our songs,
built our sanctuaries,
and taught us to know and trust you.
Grant us grace in our day
to live as faithfully as they did,
and to provide as generously for our children,
until you bring us with all your people
into the fullness of your eternal joy;
through Jesus Christ our Lord,
to whom, with you, and the Holy Spirit,
be all praise and glory for ever.

Amen.

Our Father . . .

9   HYMN

10   SERMON

11   OFFERING

Prayer

Out of your providing, Lord,
we make this offering
brought from our daily living.
Sanctify your gift,
and bless the life from which it comes,
that with a cheerful spirit
and an ungrudging heart
we may be devoted to your service;
through Jesus Christ our Lord.

Amen.

12   HYMN

13   DISMISSAL AND BLESSING

Go in the peace of God.

The grace of the Lord Jesus Christ,
and the love of God,
and the fellowship of the Holy Spirit,
be with you all.

Amen.

Third
Morning Service

1 CALL TO PRAYER

Let all the earth acclaim the Lord!
Worship the Lord in gladness. *Psalm 100: 1*

2 PRAYERS

Let us pray.

Adoration
Lord God,
the wonders of your creation,
the splendour of the heavens,
the beauty of the earth,
the order and richness of nature,
all speak to us of your glory.
The coming of your Son,
the presence of your Spirit,
the fellowship of your Church,
show us the marvel of your love.
We worship and adore you,
God of grace and glory,
through Jesus Christ our Lord. **Amen.**

Confession
God of mercy, God of love,
in humbleness of heart
we confess our sins.

We forget to love and serve you,
and wander from your ways.
We are careless of your world,
and put its life in danger.
We talk of our concern for others,
but fail to match our words with action.

silence

Lord have mercy.
> **Christ have mercy.**
Lord have mercy.

silence

> **Merciful God,**
> **forgive us our sins**
> **and bring us to everlasting life,**
> **through Jesus Christ**
> **your Son, our Saviour.**   **Amen.**

Supplication
Heavenly Father,
be with us in every experience of life.
When we neglect you,
remind us of your presence;
when we are frightened,
give us courage;
when we are tempted,
give us power to resist;
when we are anxious and worried,
give us peace;
when we are weary in service,
give us energy and zeal;
for the sake of Jesus Christ our Lord.

                                        Amen.

> **Our Father . . .**

3 PRAYERS

Let us pray.

Thanksgiving
Loving God,
we give thanks for your goodness
and love towards us:
for the joy of home and family;
for the companionship
of friends and neighbours;
for the activities that fulfil our lives;
for the strength that supports us
and the love that surrounds us,
both when our joy is complete
and when it is touched by pain.

We give thanks for your Son Jesus Christ:
for the glory of his humble birth,
for the graciousness of his selfless life,
for the obedience and trust
that led him to the cross,
and for the triumph
of his resurrection and ascension.

We give thanks for your Holy Spirit
at work in your Church and in our hearts,
revealing your truth, renewing our lives,
and bringing us to your eternal kingdom.

Intercession
God of love and power,
We pray for your Church in this parish
and throughout the world,
that, through the courage and faith of your people,
your word may be preached and lived.

We pray for the Queen and those in authority,
that, in the fulfilling of their duties,
they may be guided by your Spirit
and upheld by your grace.

We pray for our community, our country,
and the nations of the world,
that, following the ways of truth and justice,
they may be free from bitterness and strife,
and by the power of your love, live in peace.

We pray for all who are in trouble,
that those who are sick may be cared for,
those who are lonely sustained,
those who are oppressed strengthened,
those who mourn comforted,
and that those who are close to death
may know their risen Lord.

We give thanks
for those who have died in the faith,
especially those known to us,
who have entered into the joy and peace
of your nearer presence.
Grant that we may follow their example,
and come to share with them
the glory of everlasting life,
through Jesus Christ our Lord,
who with the Father and the Holy Spirit
is worshipped and glorified for ever.

Amen.

4   DEDICATION OF THE OFFERING

Let us pray.

Blessed are you, Lord God,
from the first of time to the last.
Yours, Lord, is the greatness and the power,
the glory, the splendour, and the majesty;
for everything in heaven and on earth is yours.
Yours, Lord, is the sovereignty,
and you are exalted over all as head.
Wealth and honour come from you;
you rule over all.

Of your own we now give you,
for the good of your Church
and the glory of your name;
through Jesus Christ our Lord.   *Amen.*

5   COLLECT OF THE DAY

6   DISMISSAL AND BLESSING

The peace of God
which passes all understanding,
keep your hearts and minds
in the knowledge and love of God,
and of his Son Jesus Christ our Lord.

Go in the strength of God.

And the blessing of God almighty,
the Father, the Son, and the Holy Spirit,
be with you, and remain with you,
now and always.   *Amen.*

Fourth
Morning Service

1   <small>CALL TO WORSHIP</small>

> God is the King of moon and sun;
> God is the King of stars beloved.
> He knows our every need;
> he is the kindly God of life.

> Let us worship God.

2   <small>PRAYERS</small>

> Let us pray.

Invocation
> God of love,
> light a flame of love in our hearts to you,
> a flame of love to our families and friends,
> a flame of love to our neighbours,
> a flame of love to our enemies.

> Son of the loveliest Mary,
> light a flame of love in our hearts to all,
> from the lowliest thing that lives,
> to the Name that is highest of all.

Confession

    God of life,
    grant us your forgiveness.

    We have been heedless in our thoughts,
    cruel in our words,
    shameful in our actions.
    We are indifferent to a world made sad
    by want and wastefulness;
    we pass by on the other side
    when we see our neighbour in need;
    we wander from the way that leads to peace
    in paths of our own pleasing.

    God of life,
    grant us your forgiveness.

    silence

Supplication

    God of the new day and God of love,
    you created us and you have redeemed us.
    As you scatter the mist
    from the hills,
    banish the deeds of darkness
    from the sons and daughters of your light.
    Help us to know and believe
    that, as the children of your love,
    we are free to begin again;
    through Jesus Christ our Lord.

                               Amen.

    God and Jesus and Spirit of wholeness,
    as Three and as One,
    shield us and save us,
    possess us and aid us,

clear our path,
go before our souls
each step of the stormy world.   ***Amen.***

3   PRAYERS

Intercessions
      Let us pray for the Church,
      the world, and one another.

      For the Church we pray, the bright lamp of faith,
      her ministers and people, and this parish.
      May the King of angels protect her,
      keep her, and save her.

      For the world we pray, the creation of God,
      its land and sea, its peace and prosperity.
      May the Son of Mary move through all the earth,
      blessing it.

      For those who are ill we pray,
      and for those who suffer.
      May the Good Shepherd
      who knows and loves his sheep
      make them whole and well, active and content.

      For those who work we pray,
      and for all who weave
      the patterns of this world's life.
      May the King of grace
      give to their labour
      growth and kindly substance,
      until the day of gladness come.

      For those we love, and for ourselves we pray.
      May the guarding of God be theirs and ours,

until together we come
to the High King's house in heaven,
in the name of Father, Son, and Spirit Holy.

Amen.

Commemoration of the Faithful Departed
God of surprises,
in every age you have called men and women
from security to danger,
from comfort to hardship,
from silence to speaking-out:
we honour you and we honour them.

We remember with gratitude and wonder
the impetuous fisherman,
the despised tax-collector,
the zealous persecutor,
and all the other friends
and witnesses of Christ,
who lived out what they heard and saw
and wrote for us the story of his life.

We remember with gratitude and wonder
those courageous souls
who first brought the Gospel to our shores,
and braved wild northern seas,
defied rocks and skerries,
crossed moorland and mountain,
to offer Christ to our ancient peoples.

We remember with gratitude and wonder
holy men and women of later days,
who made Christ's presence bright
in word, and water, wine and bread;
and lit a flame of glory to his name
in places which became,

through praise and prayer,
beacons of hope and sanctuaries of his grace.

We remember with gratitude and affection
those who first led us to you,
parents, teachers, ministers,
men and women who worshipped with us;
and those we once loved here on earth.

We celebrate their faith-filled lives,
and pray that they may be
bright flames before us,
guiding stars above us,
smooth paths below us,
a sure defence behind us,
until we reach our home,
the court of Christ, the peace of heaven.

Amen.

4   DEDICATION

Let us pray.

Father, Son, and Spirit Holy,
we give you thanks and praise,
and dedicate to you
our thoughts, our words,
our gifts, our deeds,
the working of our hands,
the thinking of our minds,
the loving of our hearts.

Shield us this day
for the sake of Christ of the wounds.

Keep us from offence,
and compass us with your love
for ever and for evermore.   ***Amen.***

5   BLESSING

The guarding of the God of life be on you,
the guarding of the loving Christ be on you,
the guarding of the Holy Spirit be on you,
every day and night,
to aid you and enfold you,
each day, each night.   ***Amen.***

Fifth
Morning Service

1 PRAYERS

Let us pray.

Approach
Hidden God, we worship you.
By ourselves, we could not know you;
no human wisdom can discover you,
no argument lead to you,
no enterprise reveal you;
in the wealth of its knowledge
the world fails to find you.
But you came to search for us
in the frailty of a human life;
you trusted yourself to the fragile faith
of wavering disciples.

We praise you that in our very weakness
we can know you;
that stumbling blocks become stepping stones,
and the foolishness of the cross
the very truth that quickens us to life.

Confession
We confess, O God,
that we breathe the proud spirit of the world,
the spirit which scorns the way of weakness,
boasts of its cleverness,

clings to knowledge as a means of power,
and seeks to prove its worth by belittling others.

Lord have mercy.
   Christ have mercy.
Lord have mercy.

Supplication
   Hidden God,
   your wisdom unsettles our values
   and compels our love.
   Fill us with the desire to search for your truth,
   that being content to be fools for Christ's sake,
   we may transform the world.

                                             Amen.

2   INTERCESSION AND COMMEMORATION

   Let us pray.

   Almighty God,
   we pray for those
   locked in circumstances beyond their control,
   restrained by oppressors,
   and seeing no end to their captivity.
   May they discover hope
   buried in deepest suffering;
   through Jesus Christ,
   who shared the weakness and despair
   of human life,
   yet gave even death a new outcome
   and brought resurrection from a closed tomb.

   Lord in your mercy,
      Hear our prayer.

We pray for the Church,
set in the world
to show how people belong together
and how your gifts are given to be shared.
Grant that, as we feel
for the rejection and voicelessness of others,
we may meet Christ in them
and bear witness to his transforming love.

Lord in your mercy,
> **Hear our prayer.**

We pray for the communities
in which we live and work;
for people under stress
and unable to deal with their difficulties;
for those who seek comfort
in ways which bring no help;
for all who are fearful.
Give us grace to show by our concern and actions
how each is loved and valued by you.

Lord in your mercy,
> **Hear our prayer.**

We remember those now hidden from us
but at home with you.
We give thanks especially
for those who have strengthened our weak faith,
built up our trust in you,
and by their life have drawn us
into the life of Christ
who died in weakness and reigns in glory.

> **Amen.**

3   THANKSGIVING AND DEDICATION

Let us pray.

Hidden God,
we rejoice that we can know you in Jesus Christ,
who by eating with the outcast
broke down barriers,
by touching the leper
brought wholeness,
and by welcoming Mary Magdalene
proclaimed forgiveness.
We give thanks
that he accepted a drink of water
from a Samaritan woman,
gained strength
from a Roman soldier's faith,
and received help
from an African who carried his cross.

We give thanks that because of his example
prejudice no longer binds us,
fear has lost its power,
and all that makes us weak
has met its match in Christ.

We bring our offerings to you,
acknowledging that all your gifts
are given for our own growth
and for the service of humankind.

Receive them and our worship.
Accept us and show us the gifts
we do not know we have to offer,
in the strong name

and by the wisdom of Jesus Christ our Lord.

Amen.

Our Father . . .

4   DISMISSAL AND BLESSING

Your life lies hidden with Christ in God.
May you come to the full wealth of conviction
which understanding brings,
and grasp God's secret, which is Christ himself,
in whom lie hidden
all the treasures of wisdom and knowledge.

Go in peace.

And the blessing of God almighty,
the Father, the Son, and the Holy Spirit,
be with you all.

Amen.

First
Evening Service

1   *The Bible is brought into the church.*
     The congregation stands.

2   CALL TO WORSHIP

     The minister says:

> It is good to give thanks to the Lord,
> to sing psalms to your name, Most High,
> to declare your love in the morning
> and your faithfulness every night.
>
> *Psalm 92: 1 - 2*

> Let us worship God.

3   HYMN

4   SCRIPTURE SENTENCE

     The minister says:

> May my prayer be like incense set before you,
> the lifting up of my hands
> like the evening offering.
>
> *Psalm 141: 2*

5   PRAYERS

The minister says:

Let us pray.

Adoration

Lord God of Hosts, who is like you?
Your strength and faithfulness, Lord,
are all around you.
The heavens are yours,
the earth is yours also;
you formed the world
and all that is in it.
Your throne is founded
on righteousness and justice;
love and faithfulness
are in attendance on you.

Happy the people
who have learnt to acclaim you,
who walk in the light
of your countenance!
In your name they rejoice
all day long;
your righteousness
will lift them up.
Blessed be the Lord
for ever and ever.

Confession

Eternal God,
we honour you,
Father, Son, and Holy Spirit.
You are worthy to be praised
by voices that are pure

and by faces filled with light.
But as the sun sinks to its setting
and the twilight of the evening comes,
we discern the darkness,
around us, and within.
We have not loved what you commanded,
nor desired what you promised.
Our wills have been unruly,
our affections unsettled.
And amid the passing changes of the world,
our hearts have not been fixed on you
where true joys are to be found.

Lord have mercy.
   Christ have mercy.
Lord have mercy.

silence

The almighty and merciful Lord
grant you pardon,
and remission of all your sins,
time for amendment of life,
and the grace and comfort of the Holy Spirit.
                                   Amen.

Supplication
   Almighty God,
   teach us to live as always in your presence,
   and to fold our hearts in your peace.
   Help us to rest on the strong love of Christ,
   and by the power of his Spirit
   keep us from sinning,
   free us from worry,
   and guide us in the way we should go;
   through Jesus Christ our Lord,

who lives and reigns
with you and the Holy Spirit,
one God, now and for ever.   ***Amen.***

6   HYMN

7   SCRIPTURE READINGS

The reader says:

Listen for the Word of God.

The Old Testament reading comes from
(*book*), chapter (*ab*), verse (*xy*).

The New Testament reading comes from
(*book*), chapter (*ab*), verse (*xy*).

At the end of the readings, the reader says:

May God bless to us
the reading of his holy Word.   ***Amen.***

8   HYMN

9   PRAYER FOR ILLUMINATION

The minister says:

Let us pray.

Consecrate us, O God, by the truth;
your word is truth.
Guide our minds by your Spirit,
that we may understand your word,
learn your will,

> and follow more closely
> in the steps of Christ our Lord. **Amen.**

10   SERMON

11   ASCRIPTION OF PRAISE

The minister says:

> And now to God: Father, Son, and Holy Spirit,
> be glory and praise, now and for ever.
>
> **Amen.**

12   HYMN

13   INTIMATIONS

14   OFFERING

15   PRAYERS

The minister says:

> Let us pray.

Thanksgiving
> We praise you, O God;
> we give you thanks,
> the God of nature and the God of grace,
> and the giver of all good.

> For the world you have made
> with its wonderful landscapes,
> its changing seasons,
> its teeming life;
> for the life you have given us

You are [handwritten]

We Thank You. [handwritten]

with its opportunities and responsibilities,
its routines and delights;
for the history we have inherited,
with its treasures of art and science
and its variety of ordinary human goodness;
for the joy and care of our homes;
for the food we eat,
the friendships we cherish,
and the health we enjoy;
for all the bounty of your providence,
we praise you,
and bless your holy name.

We praise you that at the appointed time
you sent your Son, born of a woman,
to live and work in our world,
to seek and save the lost,
to suffer and die on the cross,
to rise victorious over death,
and to rule at your right hand for ever.

We thank you that you sent your Holy Spirit
to the Church and to the world,
to lead us into truth,
to point the way to goodness,
to increase among all people
the spirit of sympathy and understanding.

Make us worthy of your goodness.
Open our hearts to love and praise you,
and inspire us always to live for your glory;
through Jesus Christ our Lord,
who lives and reigns
with you and the Holy Spirit,
one God, now and for ever.

Amen.

Dedication

    Gracious God,
    when your kindness and generosity
    dawned upon the world,
    and you lavished your love upon us
    in Jesus Christ our Saviour,
    you called us to believe in you
    and to devote ourselves to good works.
    Now we bring our gifts to you,
    and offer them, and our whole life,
    with joy for your service;
    through Jesus Christ our Lord.   ***Amen.***

Intercessions

    God of all kindness,
    you gave your only Son,
    because you loved the world so much.

    We pray for the peace of the world.
    Move among us by your Spirit,
    break down barriers
    of fear, suspicion, and hatred.
    Heal the human family of its divisions
    and unite it in the bonds of justice and peace.

    We pray for our country.
    Enrich our common life;
    strengthen the forces of truth and goodness;
    teach us to share prosperity,
    that those whose lives are impoverished
    may pass from need and despair
    to dignity and joy.

    We pray for those who suffer.
    Surround them with your love,
    support them with your strength,

console them with your comfort,
and give them hope
and courage beyond themselves.

We pray for our families,
for those whom we love.
Protect them at home;
support them in times of difficulty and anxiety,
that they may grow together
in mutual love and understanding,
and rest content in one another.

We pray for the Church.
Keep her true to the Gospel
and responsive to the gifts and needs of all.
Make known your saving power in Jesus Christ,
by the witness of her faith,
her worship,
and her life.

Commemoration of the Faithful Departed
Eternal God,
we remember with thanksgiving
those who have gone before us
in the way of Christ.
Keep us united with all your people
on earth and in heaven.
Grant that, as we journey through the years,
we may know joys that are without end,
and at the last come to that abiding city
where you reign in glory everlasting;
through Jesus Christ our Lord.   ***Amen.***

     Our Father . . .

16   HYMN

17 Dismissal and Blessing

The minister says:

Go in the peace of God,
in whom there is no darkness,
but the night shines as the day.
May he renew your hearts with quietness,
your bodies with untroubled sleep;
and may he waken you to use his gift of life
with faith and joy.

Amen.

The minister blesses the people from God:

The blessing of God almighty,
Father, Son, and Holy Spirit,
be with you all.

Amen.

Second Evening Service

1 SCRIPTURE SENTENCE

> There are many who say,
> 'If only we might see good times!
> Let the light of your face shine on us, Lord.'
>
> *Psalm 4: 6*

2 PRAYERS

Let us pray.

Approach
> Look upon us, Lord:
> may the darkness of our souls
> vanish before the beams of your brightness.
>
> Fill us with holy love:
> open to us treasures of your wisdom;
> encourage what you have begun in us,
> and prompt us to ask in prayer
> what your spirit already desires for us.
>
> Turn your face to us and show us your glory:
> then shall our longing be satisfied,
> and our life complete.

Confession
Gracious God,
in the company of your people,
we confess our sins to you.

We have been angry and impatient,
complaining about the faults of others,
and failing to see our own.

We have been lazy and selfish,
neglecting the interests of others,
and pursuing our own.

We have been faithless and unworthy,
ignoring the strength you offer
and relying upon our own.

silence

God of mercy,
you have promised to forgive those
who truly repent.
Help us to accept your forgiveness,
and dwell in us by your Spirit;
through Jesus Christ our Lord.

Amen.

Supplication
Father,
care for us.

Give us
knowledge of your will,
strength of spirit to follow Christ's teaching,
and courage to face the complexities of life.

Grant that at all times
we may stand firm for the faith
and truly serve your Son, Christ Jesus our Lord,
who lives and reigns
with you and the Holy Spirit,
one God, now and forever.   *Amen.*

3   PRAYERS

Let us pray.

Adoration
Praise the Lord!
Praise the Lord, you that are his servants.
Praise the name of the Lord.
Blessed be the name of the Lord
now and evermore.

From the rising of the sun to its setting
may the Lord's name be praised.
High is the Lord above all nations,
his glory above the heavens.

There is none like the Lord our God
in heaven or on earth.

Glory to the Father, and to the Son,
and to the Holy Spirit:
*as it was in the beginning, is now,
and will be for ever.*   *Amen.*

Thanksgiving
Generous God,
we give thanks
for the richness of life;
for the beauty and wonder of the world;

for the care of those who love us;
for strength and hope
in the trials and difficulties of life;
for the gospel of the risen Lord,
and for his presence with us
through the Holy Spirit.

Intercessions
Loving God,
we pray for all who are ill:
ease their pain, calm their restlessness;
give them such trust in you
that they may know
they are always in your keeping.
Bless all who care for them:
give them such trust in you
that they may win new strength;
and may their love and tireless patience
bring your grace and comfort
to those who suffer.

silence

Shepherd of our souls,
be with us in the dark valley,
and give your gentle companionship
to all who are about to die.
Be with us at our partings,
and comfort with your presence
all who grieve in loneliness or tears.

Remember your Church on earth.
Enable Christian people
to walk with Christ in their daily lives
and to work for the coming of his kingdom.
Strengthen the witness of the Church

in this parish and in every place,
that the world may learn to live your truth
and seek your peace.

Remember the nations of the world.
Bring to an end all war and strife;
break down the barriers of race and creed,
that all may live
as members of one family of God.

Remember our country.
Bless the Queen and her family;
and guide us in the influence we have
on our community and nation.
Preserve us as a people
from all that is degrading,
and raise us to the righteousness
of serving your will.

silence

We remember with thanksgiving
those who have died in the faith,
especially those known and dear to us.
Grant us a living hope,
and bring us, when our days on earth are over,
to share the joys of everlasting life;
through Jesus Christ our Lord.

We commend ourselves to your keeping.
Grant that our hearts may find
their peace and rest in you;
through Jesus Christ our Lord,
to whom with you and the Holy Spirit,
be glory, for ever and ever.

Amen.

Our Father ...

4   DEDICATION OF THE OFFERING

Let us pray.

God of all goodness,
accept the gifts we bring.
Use them and us for your glory
and the work of your Church;
through Jesus Christ our Lord.

Amen.

5   DISMISSAL AND BLESSING

Go in peace.

And may God himself, the God of peace,
make you holy through and through,
and keep you sound in spirit, soul, and body,
free of any fault
when our Lord Jesus Christ comes.

And the blessing of God almighty,
the Father, the Son, and the Holy Spirit,
be with you all.

Amen.

Third
Evening Service

1 INTRODUCTION

The minister says:

> In preparation for our prayers, here is a poem
> by .... (or a passage from ....)

(the reading is not necessarily given by the minister)

> silence

2 PRAYERS

The minister says:

> Let us pray.
>
> Let us acknowledge the company
> in which we meet:
> the church on earth and in heaven;
> the faithful who worshipped here before us;
> the hundreds of thousands
> of every place and language
> who, on the Lord's Day, seek to set their lives
> within the atmosphere of renewing grace.
> As we think of them,
> let us take deliberate encouragement
> from our unity with them all.

silence

Let us acknowledge
that all round the world people pray for us:
and, without embarrassment,
let us take heart from the knowledge
that we pray for one another here,
seeking not only our own peace,
but the peace of our brothers and sisters.

silence

Let us cast our minds
over the week that has gone,
with its ups and downs,
its kindnesses and faithful goodness,
its mixture of the regular and the surprising;
if there were moments of great happiness
or great sadness or both,
let us seek to bring them all
to the strengthening comfort
and healing mercy of the Lord,
and ask him to confirm
whatever is good and useful in our experience,
and to transform or purge
the things that are harmful and wrong.

silence

As we are assured
of God's renewing mercy and liberating grace,
and know that we are accepted in his love,
let us live the lives of forgiven people,
transmitting the grace which comes to us
and extending to others
the love which is shown to us.

As the Creator of all things deals with us
with the patience and good humour
of a loving mother,
let us seek to be given
the imagination and opportunity
to deal similarly with our fellows.

As by his generosity we are made confident
that we belong in our Father's house
and our Father's world,
let us serve as channels of that hospitality,
ministers of that acceptance,
angels and agents of that deep sense
of liberated belonging.

silence

These thoughts and desires we offer
in the name and Spirit of Jesus Christ,
in whom the holiest in the height
touched our hearts
and shared our joys and sorrows,
our circumstances, and our hope.

silence

3   HYMN

4   OLD TESTAMENT

A period of silence

5   MAGNIFICAT *said together*

> **My soul proclaims
> the greatness of the Lord,**

my Spirit rejoices in God my Saviour,
who has looked with favour
on his lowly servant.
From this day all generations
will call me blessed:
the Almighty has done great things for me
and holy is his name.
God has mercy on those who fear him,
from generation to generation.
The Lord has showed strength with his arm
and scattered the proud in their conceit,
casting down the mighty from their thrones
and lifting up the lowly.
God has filled the hungry with good things
and sent the rich away empty.
He has come to the aid of his servant Israel,
to remember the promise of mercy,
the promise made to our forebears,
to Abraham and his children for ever.

6 NEW TESTAMENT

A period of silence

7 NUNC DIMITTIS *said together*

Now, Lord,
you let your servant go in peace:
your word has been fulfilled.
My own eyes have seen the salvation
which you have prepared
in the sight of every people:
a light to reveal you to the nations
and the glory of your people Israel.

8 PRAYERS

The minister says:

Let us pray.

Let us call to mind
our concerns and commitments,
and let us join our prayers
for peace and well-being
to the prayers of the whole Church
as they are offered this day for the whole world.

silence

Let us remember those people we know
who are in trouble,
and pray for healing and happiness for all.

silence

Let us seek divine encouragement
for honest trade and decent commerce,
for useful and courteous service in daily life,
for medicine and education,
and for those gifts and aptitudes in every person
which make for happier
and fairer community living.

silence

Let us pray
for peace on earth,
for the generous sharing of the earth's resources
and the responsible sharing
of the earth's problems;
for tolerance across divisions

and willingness to regard
the diversity of human culture
as more stimulating than threatening;
for the turning of swords into ploughshares
and spears into pruning hooks.

silence

Let us pray for the Church,
by all its names and in all its places;
for its continuing usefulness
as a channel of grace and hope;
for its rescue
from pretentiousness and pomposity
and from taking some things
more seriously than is healthy.

silence

Let us commend to the Lord
our families and friends;
and let us ask him to help us
in the days of this coming week.

silence

Our Father . . .

9 HYMN

10 *Here may be given a short sermon, address,
meditation, or visual presentation.*

11 HYMN *(during which the Offering may be taken up)*

12 BENEDICTION

Fourth
Evening Service

1   *Before the service, the church is partially lit.*
    When the people have gathered and the service
    is about to begin, the lights are switched off.

2   *After a moment's silence, a voice in the darkness says:*

> The Lord is my light and salvation,
> the Lord is the stronghold of my life.
>
> *Psalm 27: 1*

> My God will lighten my darkness.
>
> *Psalm 18: 28*

> His word is a lamp to my feet,
> a light on my path.
>
> *Psalm 119: 105*

3   *A light is switched on, or a candle is lit.*

4   *The minister says:*

> The light of conscience flashes within us,
> discovering the dark places of sin
> and confirming the goodness within us.

> The light of the word of God
> shines through history,
> displacing darkness and awakening life.

The light of the presence of Jesus Christ
gleams with judgement and joy,
for he is the light of life.
Let us come into the light.

All the lights and candles are lit.

5 HYMN (*such as 'Hail, gladdening Light'*)

6 *The minister says:*

Jesus Christ is the light of the world.
The light shines in the darkness,
and the darkness has never mastered it.

Let us pray.

God of power and might,
as the day departs and shadows lengthen,
we hear your promise
that out of darkness light will shine.
Shine now in our hearts
with the light which is knowledge
of the glory of God in the face of Jesus Christ.
Disperse the gloomy clouds of night,
and enlighten us
with the radiance of your truth and love.

Merciful God and eternal Judge,
your Son came to bring to light
things hidden in darkness,
and to reveal the secret thoughts of many.

Forgive the wrong desires of our hearts,
the sinful devisings of our minds,
the calculating envy of our eyes.

silence

If we live in the light,
as God himself is in the light,
then we share a common life,
and the blood of Jesus his Son
cleanses us from all sin.

silence

Arise, shine, for your light has come,
and over you the glory of God has dawned.

As Christians, you are light.
Prove yourselves at home in the light,
for where light is,
there is goodness, righteousness, and truth.

silence

> **With the flame**
> **of your eternal light, O God,**
> **kindle in us the fire of love;**
> **and renew us with your Holy Spirit,**
> **that we may shine like stars**
> **in a dark world;**
> **through Jesus Christ our Lord.**
>
> **Amen.**

7 HYMN *(such as 'O Light that knew no dawn')*

8 OLD TESTAMENT

9 PSALM *sung or said*

10 EPISTLE

11 GOSPEL

12 ALLELUIA *or* GLORIA

13 APOSTLES' CREED

14 HYMN (*such as 'Be thou my vision'*)

15 INVOCATION OF THE HOLY TRINITY

16 SERMON

17 ASCRIPTION OF PRAISE

18 OFFERING

19 *The minister says:*

Let us pray.

Father of lights,
every good and perfect gift comes from you.
Keep us in the light of Christ,
to shine in your world,
that all may believe in you;
through Jesus Christ our Lord.

To you, O God, be glory and praise for ever!
You dwell in light unapproachable
but make visible the mystery of your presence.
In the changing year,
your light never fails.
You light the day with the sun's light,
the midnight with shining stars.
You sent forth your Sun of Righteousness
to call us out of darkness

into his marvellous light.
Through your kindness
healing dawns upon the world,
your grace gives joy
to those who walk in shadow,
your light fills our life with song.
To you, O God, be glory and praise for ever!

Fill your church with truth and love,
that she may lead all people
to a knowledge of your salvation,
and be found without fault
on the day of Christ's coming.

Give your light to all nations and peoples,
that respect and forbearance
may grow among them,
and peace enfold the world.

Refresh and strengthen those for whom
the dark brings neither rest nor sleep:
who guard our shores,
defend our homes,
and keep the peace;
who carry on the unresting business of the world;
who through the night,
at home, in hospice, or in hospital,
watch over others.
Make darkness light around them,
and grant them peace.

Protect those who are in danger;
care for those who suffer;
and when the shadow of death is falling,
make bright with your presence the path of those
who walk in the valley of darkness.

Set free our friends and families
from anxiety and fear,
that they may live in joy, in peace, in health.

God of life and glory,
you have given us a share
in the inheritance of the saints in light.
They surround our steps as we journey on
towards the splendour of the eternal city.
Open our eyes to see the radiance of your glory;
and bring us to rejoice with them
in your everlasting kingdom,
where there is no dark nor dazzling
but one equal light;
and where in light undimmed, unending,
you are worshipped and adored,
Father, Son, and Holy Spirit,
one God, now and ever.   ***Amen.***

Our Father . . .

20   Hymn (*such as 'Thou, whose almighty Word'*)

21   Dismissal and Blessing

The minister says:

Go forth in the peace of God.

The Lord bless you and guard you;
the Lord make his face shine on you
and be gracious to you;
the Lord look kindly on you
and give you peace.   ***Amen.***

Fifth
Evening Service

1   CALL TO WORSHIP

    Let us worship God.

2   SCRIPTURE SENTENCES *said responsively*

    From the rising of the sun to its setting,
    may the Lord's name be praised:
        Blessed be the name of the Lord
        now and evermore.   *Psalm 113: 3, 2*

    Give thanks to the Lord, invoke him by name;
    make known his deeds among the peoples.
        Pay him honour with song and psalm,
        and tell of all his marvellous deeds.
                          Psalm 105: 1 - 2

    Exult in his hallowed name;
    let those who seek the Lord be joyful in heart.
        Look to the Lord and be strong;
        at all times seek his presence.
                          Psalm 105: 3 - 4

3   HYMN

4   PRAYER OF CONFESSION
    AND ASSURANCE OF PARDON

    Let us pray.

Let us in quietness
each offer our own prayers to God,
laying before him the burden of our sinfulness,
asking him to forgive what we have been,
to change what we are,
and to direct what we shall be.

silence

> **Lord, in your mercy,**
> **forgive us and restore us**
> **to your fellowship.**

'Christ Jesus came into the world to save sinners.'
Hear the word of grace,
and receive the assurance of pardon:
Your sins are forgiven,
for the sake of Jesus Christ our Saviour.

> **Saviour Christ,**
> **you take upon yourself all our burdens.**
> **You free us from all that weighs us down,**
> **so that we constantly begin anew.**
> **You lead us on, with lightened step,**
> **from worry towards trusting,**
> **from weariness towards well-being,**
> **from our own will towards the vision**
> **of your coming kingdom.**
> **Make us servants of your gospel,**
> **that we may know your peace**
> **and the world be bright with hope.**
> **Amen.**

5   SCRIPTURE READINGS

6   ALLELUIA *or* SONG OF GLORY

7   MEDITATION

This may be in the form of brief comment on the
Bible passages as an introduction to a theme for
reflection, followed by silence; or by quiet music,
perhaps with projected images as a visual focus.

8   CONFESSION OF FAITH

> **We believe in God;**
> **who has created and is creating,**
> **who has come in the true man, Jesus,**
> **to reconcile and make new,**
> **who works in us and others by his Spirit.**
>
> **We trust him.**
> **He calls us to be his Church,**
> **to celebrate his presence,**
> **to love and serve others,**
> **to seek justice and resist evil,**
> **to proclaim Jesus, crucified and risen,**
> **our judge and our hope.**
>
> **In life, in death, in life beyond death,**
> **God is with us.**
> **We are not alone.**
> **Thanks be to God**
>
> **Amen.**

or The Apostles' Creed may be said

9   HYMN

10   PRAYERS

Let us pray.

Thanksgiving

Lord of all being and source of every blessing,
we thank you for all good things:
for life and love,
for health and food,
for work and home,
for nature's beauty and comfort,
for human skills and laughter,
for memory and hope,
and for everything in this past week
which has given us pleasure,
nourishment, and strength.

Dedication of the Offering

In the name and in the spirit of Jesus,
we bring our gifts to you;
and seek the grace to give with them
a ready mind, a willing spirit, and a joyful heart,
and to dedicate our lives
to the truth of your gospel;
for the sake of Jesus Christ our Lord,
in whom we see your everlasting goodness
and receive your kindly care.

Prayers for Others

Loving God,
remember this night the whole human family,
especially those who hunger for food or justice,
those who lack homes or human dignity;
so many are unknown to us,
yet each known to you
and each a child of your love.

Remember your people
in every part of the world,
redeemed by Christ,

dedicated to service,
called to love.

Remember your Church in this place,
set in this community
to light the way to your grace and truth.

Remember those who are ill or sorrowing,
those who are concerned for dear ones,
those who have difficult choices to make,
especially any known to us
whom we commend to you now . . .
May they know that nothing is able
to separate them from your love in Christ Jesus.

By your mercy,
bring us at the last, with all your faithful people,
to the peace and joy of your nearer presence;
through Jesus Christ our Lord.

> *God our Creator,*
> *by your mercy and might*
> *the world turns safely into darkness*
> *and returns again to light.*
>
> *We give into your hands*
> *our unfinished tasks,*
> *our unsolved problems,*
> *and our unfulfilled hopes,*
> *knowing that only those things*
> *which you bless will prosper.*
>
> *To your love and protection*
> *we commit one another*
> *and all for whom we have prayed;*
> *through Jesus Christ our Lord.*   *Amen.*

11 HYMN

12 BENEDICTION

III
The
SACRAMENTS
and
ORDINANCES
of the
CHURCH

Order for the Sacrament of Holy Baptism

For a Child

This order provides for the baptism of children. They may be accompanied by members of their families, and by their district elders.

Normally, the Sacrament is administered during Sunday worship, usually after the sermon.

1 INSTITUTION

The minister says:

> The Gospel tells us that
> 'Jesus was baptized in the Jordan by John.
> As he was coming up out of the water,
> he saw the heavens break open
> and the Spirit descend on him, like a dove.
> And a voice came from heaven;
> "You are my beloved Son;
> in you I take delight."'
>
> *St Mark 1: 9 - 11*

> Jesus himself said:
> Full authority in heaven and on earth
> has been committed to me.
> Go therefore to all nations
> and make them my disciples;
> baptize them in the name of the Father
> and the Son and the Holy Spirit,

and teach them to observe
all that I have commanded you.
I will be with you always, to the end of time.

St Matthew 28: 18 - 20

On the Day of Pentecost, the Apostle Peter said:
Repent and be baptized, every one of you,
in the name of Jesus the Messiah;
then your sins will be forgiven
and you will receive the gift of the Holy Spirit.
The promise is to you and to your children
and to all who are far away,
to everyone whom the Lord our God may call.

Acts 2: 38 - 39

*In addition, one or more of the following
may be read:*

But now, Jacob, this is the word of the Lord,
the word of your Creator,
of him who fashioned you, Israel:
Have no fear, for I have redeemed you;
I call you by name; you are mine.
When you pass through water
I shall be with you;
when you pass through rivers
they will not overwhelm you.   *Isaiah 43: 1 - 2a*

I shall sprinkle pure water over you.
I shall give you a new heart
and put a new spirit within you.

Ezekiel 36: 25a, 26a

Jesus called for the children, and said,
'Let the children come to me;
do not try to stop them;

for the kingdom of God belongs to such as these.
Truly I tell you:
whoever does not accept the kingdom of God
like a child will never enter it.'

St Luke 18: 16 - 17

No one can enter the kingdom of God
without being born from water and spirit.
Flesh can give birth only to flesh;
it is spirit that gives birth to spirit.
You ought not to be astonished when I say
'You must all be born again.'

St John 3: 5 - 7

Have you forgotten
that when we were baptized
into union with Christ Jesus
we were baptized into his death.
By that baptism into his death
we were buried with him,
in order that, as Christ was raised from the dead
by the glorious power of the Father,
so also we might set out on a new life.

Romans 6: 3 - 4

There is one body and one Spirit,
just as there is one hope
held out in God's call to you;
one Lord, one faith, one baptism;
one God and Father of all,
who is over all and through all and in all.

Ephesians 4: 4 - 6

When the kindness and generosity
of God our Saviour dawned upon the world,
then, not for any good deeds of our own,

but because he was merciful,
he saved us through the water of rebirth
and the renewing power of the Holy Spirit,
which he lavished upon us
through Jesus Christ our Saviour,
so that, justified by his grace,
we might in hope become heirs to eternal life.

Titus 3: 4 - 7

You are a chosen race, a royal priesthood,
a dedicated nation,
a people claimed by God for his own,
to proclaim the glorious deeds of him
who has called you out of darkness
into his marvellous light.

1 Peter 2: 9

2   STATEMENT

The minister says:

When Jesus was baptized
in the waters of the Jordan,
the Spirit of God came upon him.
His baptism was completed
through his dying and rising again.

Our baptism is the sign of dying to sin
and rising to new life in Christ.

It is Christ himself who baptizes us.
By the Spirit of Pentecost,
he makes us members of his body, the Church,
and calls us to share his ministry in the world.

By water and the Holy Spirit,
God claims us as his own,
washes us from sin,
and sets us free from the power of death.

In this sacrament,
the love of God is offered to each one of us.
Though we cannot understand or explain it,
we are called to accept that love
with the openness and trust of a child.
In baptism,
N . . . is assured
of the love that God has for *her*,
and the sign and seal of the Holy Spirit
is placed upon *her*.

3   CONFESSION

The minister says to the parents:

In presenting your child for baptism,
desiring that *she* may be grafted into Christ
as a member of his body, the Church,
do you receive the teaching of the Christian faith
which we confess in the Apostles' Creed?

The parents answer:

I do.

The minister says:

Will the congregation please stand.

Let us affirm the faith.

I believe in God, the Father almighty,
    creator of heaven and earth.

I believe in Jesus Christ,
    God's only Son, our Lord,
    who was conceived by the Holy Spirit,
    born of the Virgin Mary,
    suffered under Pontius Pilate,
    was crucified, died, and was buried;
    he descended to the dead.
    On the third day he rose again;
    he ascended into heaven,
    he is seated
    at the right hand of the Father,
    and he will come to judge
    the living and the dead.

I believe in the Holy Spirit,
    the holy catholic Church,
    the communion of saints,
    the forgiveness of sins,
    the resurrection of the body,
    and the life everlasting.   *Amen.*

4   PRAYER

The minister says:

Let us pray.

We thank you, gracious God,
for your gifts of water and the Holy Spirit.
[In the beginning, you moved over the waters
and brought light and life to a formless waste.
By the waters of the flood,
you cleansed the world,

and made with Noah and his family
a new beginning for all people.
In the time of Moses, you led your people
out of slavery through the waters of the sea,
making covenant with them in a new land.
At the appointed time,
in the waters of the Jordan
when Jesus was baptized by John,
you sent your Spirit upon him.
And now, by the baptism
of his death and resurrection,
Christ sets us free from sin and death
and opens the way to eternal life.]

The minister may pour water into the font.

Send your Holy Spirit
upon us and upon this water,
that *N* . . . ,
being buried with Christ in baptism,
may rise with him to newness of life;
and being born anew of water and the Holy Spirit
may remain for ever
in the number of your faithful children;
through Jesus Christ our Lord,
to whom with you and the Holy Spirit
be all honour and glory, now and for ever.

Amen.

5   DECLARATION

For each child, the minister says such words as:

N . . . ,
for you Jesus Christ came into the world:
for you he lived and showed God's love;

for you he suffered the darkness of Calvary
and cried at the last, 'It is accomplished';
for you he triumphed over death
and rose in newness of life;
for you he ascended to reign at God's right hand.
All this he did for you, *N . . . ,*
though you do not know it yet.
And so the word of Scripture is fulfilled:
'We love because God loved us first.'

6   BAPTISM

*The minister pours or sprinkles water on each
child's head, saying:*

N . . . , I baptize you
in (*or* into) the name of the Father,
and of the Son,
and of the Holy Spirit.   ***Amen.***

7   BLESSING

The minister says:

The blessing of God Almighty,
Father, Son, and Holy Spirit,
descend upon you,
and dwell in your heart for ever.   ***Amen.***

This blessing may be said or sung:

The Lord bless you and keep you;
the Lord make his face to shine upon you,
and be gracious unto you;
the Lord lift up his countenance upon you,
and give you peace.   ***Amen.***

The minister says:

> *N* . . . is now baptized into Jesus Christ.
> We receive and welcome *her* as a member
> of the one holy catholic and apostolic Church.

8 PROMISE

The minister says to the parents:

> Your child belongs to God in Christ.
> From this day *she* will be at home
> in the Christian community,
> and there will always be a place for *her*.
> Tell *her* of *her* baptism,
> and unfold to *her* the treasure
> *she* has been given today,
> so that *she* may know *she* is baptized,
> and, as *she* grows,
> make *her* own response in faith and love,
> and come in due time
> to share in the communion
> of the body and blood of Christ.

> Do you promise,
> depending on the grace of God,
> to teach your child
> the truths and duties of the Christian faith;
> and by prayer and example
> to bring *her* up in the life
> and worship of the Church?

> **I do.**

9   COMMITMENT OF CONGREGATION

The minister says to the congregation:

> You who are gathered here
> represent the whole Church,
> the Church catholic.
> Word and Sacrament bring you
> the joy of Christ's presence in your midst.
> They also bring you responsibilities
> as Christ's people in this place.
> Do you welcome *N* . . . ;
> and do you renew your commitment,
> with God's help,
> to live before all God's children
> in a kindly and Christian way,
> and to share with them
> the knowledge and love of Christ?

The congregation says:

> **We do.**

The minister and congregation say together:

> **We will nurture one another in faith,**
> **uphold one another in prayer,**
> **encourage one another in service.**

10   PRAYERS

The minister says:

> Let us pray.

God of love, we rejoice again
to receive your grace in Word and Sacrament.
We have heard your call
and are made new by your Spirit.

Guide and guard *N . . .* all *her* days.
May your love hold *her*,
your truth guide *her*,
your joy delight *her*.
Bless *her* parents,
that *she* may grow up
in a secure and happy home.
Give to *her* family,
wisdom and courage,
laughter and peace,
and the love that endures all things.

God of grace,
in whose church there is one Lord,
one Faith, one Baptism,
help us to acknowledge
that Jesus Christ is Lord,
to profess with our whole lives
the one true faith,
and to live in love and unity
with all who are baptized in his name,
through Jesus Christ our Lord,
who lives and reigns,
and is worshipped and glorified,
with you, Father, and the Holy Spirit,
one God for ever.

Amen.

Our Father . . .

In addition, the following may be used:

> Gracious God,
> touch us all again this day
> with the grace of our baptism.
> Give us new lives for old,
> new spirits, new faith, new commitment,
> in place of all that has grown tired and stale
> and dead in our lives.
> So may we rise and go from here,
> to whatever awaits us, in joy and trust.

> Eternal God,
> we rejoice in the communion of all the saints,
> and remember with thanksgiving
> those who have already passed through
> the waters of death into life eternal.
> May we follow them,
> faithfully and expectantly,
> in the strength of our baptism
> in Christ Jesus our Lord,
> who lives and reigns,
> and is worshipped and glorified
> with you, Father, and the Holy Spirit,
> one God for ever.   **Amen.**

11   *The rest of the service follows.*

Order for the Sacrament of Holy Baptism

For an Adult, with Confirmation

This order provides for the baptism of adults. They may be accompanied by members of their families, and by their district elders.

Normally, the Sacrament is administered during Sunday worship, usually after the sermon.

Before candidates proceed to confirmation, the kirk session is required to satisfy itself as to their profession of faith in Christ Jesus, their knowledge of the doctrine and practice of the Church, and their Christian character; and, being satisfied, to resolve to admit them to full Communion.

1 INSTITUTION

The minister says:

> The Gospel tells us that
> 'Jesus was baptized in the Jordan by John.
> As he was coming up out of the water,
> he saw the heavens break open
> and the Spirit descend on him, like a dove.
> And a voice came from heaven;
> "You are my beloved Son;
> in you I take delight."'

St Mark 1: 9 - 11

Jesus himself said:
Full authority in heaven and on earth
has been committed to me.
Go therefore to all nations
and make them my disciples;
baptize them in the name of the Father
and the Son and the Holy Spirit,
and teach them to observe
all that I have commanded you.
I will be with you always, to the end of time.

St Matthew 28: 18 - 20

On the Day of Pentecost, the Apostle Peter said:
Repent and be baptized, every one of you,
in the name of Jesus the Messiah;
then your sins will be forgiven
and you will receive the gift of the Holy Spirit.
The promise is to you and to your children
and to all who are far away,
to everyone whom the Lord our God may call.

Acts 2: 38 - 39

*In addition, one or more of the following
may be read:*

But now, Jacob, this is the word of the Lord,
the word of your Creator,
of him who fashioned you, Israel:
Have no fear, for I have redeemed you;
I call you by name; you are mine.
When you pass through water
I shall be with you;
when you pass through rivers
they will not overwhelm you.

Isaiah 43: 1 - 2a

I shall sprinkle pure water over you.
I shall give you a new heart
and put a new spirit within you.

Ezekiel 36: 25a, 26a

Jesus called for the children, and said,
'Let the children come to me;
do not try to stop them;
for the kingdom of God belongs to such as these.
Truly I tell you:
whoever does not accept the kingdom of God
like a child will never enter it.'

St Luke 18: 16 - 17

No one can enter the kingdom of God
without being born from water and spirit.
Flesh can give birth only to flesh;
it is spirit that gives birth to spirit.
You ought not to be astonished when I say
'You must all be born again.'

St John 3: 5 - 7

Have you forgotten
that when we were baptized
into union with Christ Jesus
we were baptized into his death.
By that baptism into his death
we were buried with him,
in order that, as Christ was raised from the dead
by the glorious power of the Father,
so also we might set out on a new life.

Romans 6: 3 - 4

There is one body and one Spirit,
just as there is one hope
held out in God's call to you;

one Lord, one faith, one baptism;
one God and Father of all,
who is over all and through all and in all.

Ephesians 4: 4 - 6

When the kindness and generosity
of God our Saviour dawned upon the world,
then, not for any good deeds of our own,
but because he was merciful,
he saved us through the water of rebirth
and the renewing power of the Holy Spirit,
which he lavished upon us
through Jesus Christ our Saviour,
so that, justified by his grace,
we might in hope become heirs to eternal life.

Titus 3: 4 - 7

You are a chosen race, a royal priesthood,
a dedicated nation,
a people claimed by God for his own,
to proclaim the glorious deeds of him
who has called you out of darkness
into his marvellous light.

1 Peter 2: 9

2 STATEMENT

The minister says:

When Jesus was baptized
in the waters of the Jordan,
the Spirit of God came upon him.
His baptism was completed
through his dying and rising again.

Our baptism is the sign of dying to sin
and rising to new life in Christ.

It is Christ himself who baptizes us.
By the Spirit of Pentecost,
he makes us members of his body, the Church,
and calls us to share his ministry in the world.

By water and the Holy Spirit,
God claims us as his own,
washes us from sin,
and sets us free from the power of death.

In this sacrament,
the love of God
is offered to each one of us.
Though we cannot understand or explain it,
we are called to accept that love
with the openness and trust of a child.
In baptism,
N . . . is assured
of the love that God has for *her*,
and the sign and seal of the Holy Spirit
is placed upon *her*.

3   PROFESSION OF FAITH

The minister says:

In seeking baptism,
do you reject sin
and confess your need of God's forgiving grace;
and, believing the Christian faith,
do you pledge yourself to glorify God
and to love your neighbour?

Each candidate answers:

I do.

The minister says:

Will the congregation please stand.

Let us affirm the faith
in the words of the Apostles' Creed.

> **I believe in God, the Father almighty,**
> **creator of heaven and earth.**
>
> **I believe in Jesus Christ,**
> **God's only Son, our Lord,**
> **who was conceived by the Holy Spirit,**
> **born of the Virgin Mary,**
> **suffered under Pontius Pilate,**
> **was crucified, died, and was buried;**
> **he descended to the dead.**
> **On the third day he rose again;**
> **he ascended into heaven,**
> **he is seated**
> **at the right hand of the Father,**
> **and he will come to judge**
> **the living and the dead.**
>
> **I believe in the Holy Spirit,**
> **the holy catholic Church,**
> **the communion of saints,**
> **the forgiveness of sins,**
> **the resurrection of the body,**
> **and the life everlasting.**   **Amen.**

4   PRAYER

The minister says:

Let us pray.

We thank you, gracious God,
for your gifts of water and the Holy Spirit.
In the beginning, you moved over the waters
and brought light and life to a formless waste.
By the waters of the flood,
you cleansed the world,
and made with Noah and his family
a new beginning for all people.
In the time of Moses, you led your people
out of slavery through the waters of the sea,
making covenant with them in a new land.
At the appointed time,
in the waters of the Jordan
when Jesus was baptized by John,
you sent your Spirit upon him.
And now, by the baptism
of his death and resurrection,
Christ sets us free from sin and death
and opens the way to eternal life.

The minister may pour water into the font.

Send your Holy Spirit
upon us and upon this water,
that *N* . . . ,
being buried with Christ in baptism,
may rise with him to newness of life;
and being born anew of water and the Holy Spirit
may remain for ever
in the number of your faithful children;
through Jesus Christ our Lord,
to whom with you and the Holy Spirit
be all honour and glory, now and for ever.

                                        Amen.

5 DECLARATION

For each candidate,
the minister says such words as:

> N . . . ,
> for you Jesus Christ came into the world:
> for you he lived and showed God's love;
> for you he suffered the darkness of Calvary
> and cried at the last, 'It is accomplished';
> for you he triumphed over death
> and rose in newness of life;
> for you he ascended to reign at God's right hand.
> All this he did for you, N . . . ,
> before you knew anything of it.
> And so the word of Scripture is fulfilled:
> 'We love because God loved us first.'

6 BAPTISM

The minister pours or sprinkles water on each
candidate's head, saying:

> N . . . , I baptize you
> in (*or* into) the name of the Father,
> and of the Son,
> and of the Holy Spirit.   *Amen.*

7 BLESSING

The minister says:

> The blessing of God Almighty,
> Father, Son, and Holy Spirit,
> descend upon you,
> and dwell in your heart for ever.   *Amen.*

This blessing may be said or sung:

> The Lord bless you and keep you;
> the Lord make his face to shine upon you,
> and be gracious unto you;
> the Lord lift up his countenance upon you,
> and give you peace. **Amen.**

The minister says:

> *N* . . . is now baptized into Jesus Christ.
> We receive and welcome *her* as a member
> of the one holy catholic and apostolic Church.

[8 PROMISE

*For a candidate not proceeding to Confirmation,
the minister says:*

> *N* . . . ,
> Your baptism makes you a member in Christ,
> and brings you into the family of God.
> Now your home is in the Christian community,
> and you will always have a place in it.
>
> Do you promise, depending on the grace of God,
> to serve the Lord
> and to continue in the fellowship of the Church
> all the days of your life?

Each candidate answers:

> *I do.*]

9 CONFIRMATION

The minister says:

> N . . . ,
> your baptism makes you a member of Christ,
> and brings you into the family of God.
> Now your home is in the Christian community,
> and you will always have a place in it.
>
> Believing in one God,
> Father, Son, and Holy Spirit,
> and confessing Jesus Christ
> as your Saviour and Lord,
> do you promise to join regularly
> with your fellow Christians
> in worship on the Lord's day?

> **I do.**

> Do you promise
> to be faithful in reading the Bible,
> and in prayer?

> **I do.**

> Do you promise
> to give a fitting proportion
> of your time, talents, and money
> for the Church's work in the world?

> **I do.**

> Do you promise,
> depending on the grace of God,
> to profess publicly your loyalty to Jesus Christ,

to serve him in your daily work,
and to walk in his ways all the days of your life?

I do.

The new member kneels and the minister lays hands on her *head and says:*

Defend, O Lord, your servant *N* . . . ,
with your heavenly grace,
that *she* may continue yours for ever,
and daily increase in your Holy Spirit
until *she* comes into your everlasting kingdom.

The new member stands.
The minister says:

In the name of the Lord Jesus Christ,
the King and Head of the Church,
and by the authority of this kirk session,
I welcome and receive you
within the fellowship of the Lord's Table,
and admit you
to the full privileges of the children of God
and to the responsibilities of membership
within this congregation
of the one holy catholic and apostolic Church.
May your sharing in our life together
bring blessing to you and to us all.

The peace of the Lord Jesus be always with you.
And also with you.

The minister and kirk session greet her
and offer the right hand of fellowship.
The district elder may give her *a Bible.*

10 COMMITMENT OF CONGREGATION

The minister says to the congregation:

You who are gathered here
represent the whole Church,
the Church catholic.
Word and Sacrament bring you
the joy of Christ's presence in your midst.
They also bring you responsibilities
as Christ's people in this place.
Do you welcome *N* . . . ;
and do you renew your commitment,
with God's help,
to live before all God's children
in a kindly and Christian way,
and to share with them
the knowledge and love of Christ?

The congregation says:

We do.

The minister and congregation say together:

**We will nurture one another in faith,
uphold one another in prayer,
encourage one another in service.**

11 PRAYERS

The minister says:

Let us pray.

God of love, we rejoice again
to receive your grace in Word and Sacrament.
We have heard your call
and are made new by your Spirit.

Guide and guard *N . . .* all *her* days.
May your love hold *her*,
your truth guide *her*,
your joy delight *her*.
Since you have called *her,*
and you keep faith and will do it,
make *her* holy through and through,
free of any fault,
when our Lord Jesus Christ comes
with all those who are his own.

God of grace,
in whose church there is one Lord,
one Faith, one Baptism,
help us to acknowledge
that Jesus Christ is Lord,
to profess with our whole lives
the one true faith,
and to live in love and unity
with all who are baptized in his name,
through Jesus Christ our Lord,
who lives and reigns,
and is worshipped and glorified,
with you, Father, and the Holy Spirit,
one God for ever.

Amen.

Our Father . . .

In addition, the following may be used:

Gracious God,
touch us all again this day
with the grace of our baptism.
Give us new lives for old,
new spirits, new faith, new commitment,
in place of all that has grown tired and stale
and dead in our lives.
So may we rise and go from here,
to whatever awaits us, in joy and trust.

Eternal God,
we rejoice in the communion of all the saints,
and remember with thanksgiving
those who have already passed through
the waters of death into life eternal.
May we follow them,
faithfully and expectantly,
in the strength of our baptism
in Christ Jesus our Lord,
who lives and reigns,
and is worshipped and glorified
with you, Father, and the Holy Spirit,
one God for ever.   ***Amen.***

12   *The rest of the service, which may include Holy*
     Communion, follows.

Order for the Public Profession of Faith, Confirmation, and Admission to the Lord's Supper

With the Sacrament of Holy Baptism

Before the service, the kirk session meets to hear of the preparation of the candidates and resolves to proceed.

Normally, public profession of faith takes place during Sunday worship, usually after the sermon.

Where candidates have not yet been baptized, use section 5 and omit section 6.

Where candidates have already been baptized, omit section 5 and use section 6.

Where, on the same occasion, there are candidates in each category, use section 5 and then section 6.

1   HYMN

A hymn is sung, during which the candidates for confirmation [and for baptism] come from their places in the congregation to stand at the front of the church.

2   PROLOGUE

The minister says:

If the confession 'Jesus is Lord'
is on your lips,
and the faith that God raised him from the dead
is in your heart,
you will find salvation.
> **Everyone who calls on the name
> of the Lord shall be saved.**

In the one Spirit we were all brought
into one body by baptism;
we were all given that one Spirit to drink.
> **When we were baptized into union
> with Christ Jesus
> we were baptized into his death.**

By that baptism into his death
we were buried with him.
> **So that as Christ was raised from the dead
> by the glorious power of the Father,
> we also might set out on a new life.**

3 PROFESSION OF FAITH

The minister says to the candidates:

In baptism we become heirs
of the covenant of grace
which God has made with us in Jesus Christ.
We are brought into God's family,
made members of the Church of Christ,
and promised the gift of the Holy Spirit.

A . . . , B . . . , C . . . , D . . . ,
you now come of your own choice
to acknowledge this covenant of grace,
to profess publicly your own faith

in the Lord Jesus,
and to receive the strengthening
of the Holy Spirit.

Do you reject sin,
confess your need of God's forgiving grace,
and pledge yourself to glorify God
and to love your neighbour?

The candidates say together:

I do.

The minister says:

Do you believe the Christian faith
into which we are baptized?

The candidates say together:

I do.

The minister says:

Will the congregation please stand.

Let us affirm the faith.

Do you believe in God
who made you and loves you?

**I believe in God, the Father almighty,
creator of heaven and earth.**

Do you believe in Jesus Christ,
your Saviour and Lord?

I believe in Jesus Christ,
God's only Son, our Lord,
who was conceived by the Holy Spirit,
born of the Virgin Mary,
suffered under Pontius Pilate,
was crucified, died, and was buried;
he descended to the dead.
On the third day he rose again;
he ascended into heaven,
he is seated
at the right hand of the Father,
and he will come to judge
the living and the dead.

Do you believe in the Holy Spirit,
and the continuing work of our salvation?

I believe in the Holy Spirit,
the holy catholic Church,
the communion of saints,
the forgiveness of sins,
the resurrection of the body,
and the life everlasting.   ***Amen.***

4   PRAYERS

The minister says (the congregation still standing):

Please remain standing.

Let us pray.

Loving Father,
we praise you
for our confidence and hope in Jesus Christ.
We thank you

for our shared life in one Church,
our one baptism into Jesus Christ,
and our experience of your Holy Spirit
in fellowship and service.
Anoint and cheer us
with the abundance of your grace,
that we may always be ready
to respond to your call
to commit ourselves further
in Christian discipleship;
through Jesus Christ our Lord.   ***Amen.***

God of love and faithfulness,
through water and the Holy Spirit
you claim these your servants as your own.
Confirm in them the covenant sealed in baptism,
and send them forth
in the power of the Holy Spirit,
that they may fulfil their calling
as disciples of Jesus Christ,
and be found blameless in him
when he comes with all those who are his own;
through the same Jesus Christ our Lord.
                                        Amen.

Where no baptism follows, the service continues at no. 6.

[5 BAPTISM AND CONFIRMATION

The minister says:

Let us pray.

We thank you, gracious God,
for the gifts of water and your Spirit.
In the beginning, you moved over the waters
and brought light and life to a formless waste.
By the waters of the flood,
you cleansed the world,
and made with Noah and his family
a new beginning for all people.
In the time of Moses, you led your people
out of slavery through the waters of the sea,
making covenant with them in a new land.
At the appointed time,
in the waters of the Jordan
when Jesus was baptized by John,
you sent your Spirit upon him.
And now, by the baptism
of his death and resurrection,
Christ sets us free from sin and death
and opens the way to eternal life.

The minister may pour water into the font.

Send your Holy Spirit
upon us and upon this water,
that *A* . . . ,
being buried with Christ in baptism
may rise with him to newness of life;
and being born anew of water
and the Holy Spirit
may remain for ever
in the number of your faithful children;
through Jesus Christ our Lord,
to whom with you and the Holy Spirit
be all honour and glory, now and for ever.

Amen.

The candidates kneel.

The minister baptizes those to be baptized, pouring or sprinkling water on each head and saying:

> *A* . . . , I baptize you
> in (*or* into) the name of the Father,
> and of the Son,
> and of the Holy Spirit.
>
> **Amen.**

After each baptism, the minister lays hands on the head of the candidate, and says:

> Defend, O Lord, your servant *A* . . .
> with your heavenly grace,
> that *he* may continue yours for ever,
> and daily increase in your Holy Spirit
> until *he* comes to your everlasting kingdom.
>
> **Amen.**]

The newly-baptized and confirmed stand.

Where no confirmation follows, the service continues at no. 7.

6   CONFIRMATION

The candidates kneel.

The minister lays hands on each of the candidates in turn, and says:

Defend, O Lord, your servant *A* . . .
with your heavenly grace,
that *he* may continue yours for ever,
and daily increase in your Holy Spirit
until *he* comes to your everlasting kingdom.

Amen.

The newly-confirmed stand.

7   WELCOME

The minister says to them:

In the name of the Lord Jesus Christ,
the King and Head of the Church,
and by the authority of this kirk session,
I welcome and receive you
within the fellowship of the Lord's Table
and admit you
to the full privileges of the children of God
and to the responsibilities of membership
within this congregation
of the one holy catholic and apostolic Church.
May your sharing in our life together
bring blessing to you and to us all.

The peace of the Lord Jesus be always with you.
And also with you.

The minister and elders greet the newly-confirmed.

*Individual elders may hand each of them a gift,
such as a Bible.*

8   QUESTIONS

The minister says:

Will the congregation please sit.

The newly-confirmed remain standing.

The minister says:

Jesus said,
'Whoever will acknowledge me before others,
I will acknowledge before my Father in heaven.

St Matthew 10: 32

The harvest of the Spirit is love, joy, peace,
patience, kindness, goodness,
fidelity, gentleness and self-control.

If the Spirit is the source of life,
let the Spirit also direct its course.

Galatians 5: 22, 23, 25

A . . . , *B* . . . , *C* . . . , *D* . . . ,
believing in one God,
Father, Son and Holy Spirit,
and confessing Jesus Christ,
as your Saviour and Lord,
do you promise to join regularly
with your fellow Christians
in worship on the Lord's Day?

I do.

Do you promise
to be faithful in reading the Bible,
and in prayer?

I do.

Do you promise
to give a fitting proportion
of your time, talents, and money
for the Church's work in the world?

I do.

Do you promise,
depending on the grace of God,
to profess publicly your loyalty to Jesus Christ,
to serve him in your daily work,
and to walk in his ways all the days of your life?

I do.

The minister may say one or more of the following:

May God who is the ground of hope,
fill you with all the joy and peace
as you lead the life of faith
until, by the power of the Holy Spirit,
you overflow with hope.

Romans 15: 13

Out of the treasures of his glory
may God grant you inward strength
and power through his Spirit,
that through faith
Christ may dwell in your hearts in love.

And may you be filled
with the very fullness of God.

Ephesians 3: 16 - 17, 19

May God himself, the God of peace,
make you holy through and through,
and keep you sound in spirit, soul, and body,
free of any fault
when our Lord Jesus Christ comes.
He who calls you keeps faith; he will do it.

1 Thessalonians 5: 23 - 24

Stand firm and immovable,
and work for the Lord always,
work without limit,
since you know that in the Lord
your labour cannot be lost.

1 Corinthians 15: 58

Be on the alert; stand firm in the faith;
be valiant, be strong.
Let everything you do be done in love.

1 Corinthians 16: 14 - 15

Let every word and action, everything you do,
be in the name of the Lord Jesus,
and give thanks through him to God the Father.

Colossians 3: 17

Be expert in goodness, but innocent of evil,
and the God of peace will soon crush Satan
beneath your feet.
The grace of our Lord Jesus Christ be with you!

Romans 16: 19 - 20

Make your most sacred faith
the foundation of your lives.
Continue to pray in the power of the Holy Spirit.
Keep yourselves in the love of God.

Jude 20

9 PRAYER

The minister says:

Let us pray.

God of all grace,
guard these your servants
whom you have called
to your eternal glory in Christ.
Confirm them by your Spirit,
sustain them by your Word and Sacrament,
fill them with all joy in your service,
and help them to live by faith,
walk in hope,
and be renewed in love,
until the world reflects your glory,
and you are all in all;
through Jesus Christ our Lord.

Amen.

10 *The rest of the service, which may include Holy
Communion, follows.*

First Order for the Sacrament of the Lord's Supper or Holy Communion

1   *The Bible is brought into the church.*
     The congregation stands.

2   CALL TO WORSHIP

     The minister says:

       Let us worship God.

3   HYMN

4   SCRIPTURE SENTENCES
     (*or* SEASONAL SENTENCES *pp 645 to 692*)

     The minister says:

       God so loved the world
       that he gave his only Son,
       that everyone who has faith in him
       may not perish but have eternal life.

                              St John 3: 16

       It is good to give thanks to the Lord,
       for his love endures for ever.

                              Psalm 106: 1

     or

How can I repay the Lord
for all his benefits to me?
I will lift up the cup of salvation
and call on the Lord by name.
I will pay my vows to the Lord
in the presence of all his people.

Psalm 116: 12 - 14

5   PRAYERS

The minister says:

Let us pray.

Almighty God,
to whom all hearts are open,
all desires known,
and from whom no secrets are hidden;
cleanse the thoughts of our hearts
by the inspiration of your Holy Spirit,
that we may perfectly love you
and worthily magnify your holy name;
through Christ our Lord.

Most merciful God,
we confess that we have sinned,
in thought, word, and deed,
through our own fault
and in common with others.
We are truly sorry
and turn humbly from our sins.

Lord, have mercy.
   Christ, have mercy.
Lord, have mercy.

Almighty God
have mercy upon you,
pardon and deliver you from all your sins,
confirm and strengthen you in all goodness,
and keep you in life eternal,
through Jesus Christ our Lord.   ***Amen.***

or

In the name of Jesus Christ,
I declare to you
who have confessed your sin to God
that he of his love
freely forgives you
and absolves you of all your sin.
He offers you now
the grace and strength of his Holy Spirit.

Amen.

Merciful God,
you have prepared for those who love you
such good things as pass human understanding.
Pour into our hearts such love towards you
that we, loving you above all things,
may obtain your promises,
which exceed all that we can desire;
through Jesus Christ our Lord.

Amen.

Collect of the day

6   GLORIA IN EXCELSIS *said or sung*

> ***Glory to God in the highest,***
> ***and peace to God's people on earth.***

Lord God, heavenly King,
almighty God and Father,
we worship you, we give you thanks,
we praise you for your glory.
Lord Jesus Christ, only Son of the Father,
Lord God, Lamb of God,
you take away the sin of the world:
have mercy on us;
you are seated
at the right hand of the Father:
receive our prayer.

For you alone are the Holy One,
you alone are the Lord,
you alone are the Most High,
Jesus Christ,
with the Holy Spirit,
in the glory of God the Father.   *Amen.*

7   OLD TESTAMENT

8   PSALM *sung or read*

9   EPISTLE

10   GOSPEL *(the congregation may stand)*

11   ALLELUIA *or* HYMN

12   SERMON

Before the Sermon this or other prayer is offered.

The minister says:

Let us pray.

God of life and truth,
you have taught us
that we cannot live on bread alone,
but on every word
that comes from the mouth of the Lord.
Feed us with the word of life,
and by your Spirit
lead us into truth;
through Jesus Christ our Lord.   *Amen.*

This or other Ascription follows the Sermon.

Glory to the Father, and to the Son,
and to the Holy Spirit:
as it was in the beginning, is now,
and will be for ever.   *Amen.*

13   NICENE CREED

We believe in one God,
the Father, the Almighty,
maker of heaven and earth,
of all that is, seen and unseen.

We believe in one Lord, Jesus Christ,
the only Son of God,
eternally begotten of the Father,
God from God, Light from Light,
true God from true God,
begotten, not made,
of one Being with the Father;
through him all things were made.
For us and for our salvation
he came down from heaven,
was incarnate of the Holy Spirit
and the Virgin Mary

and became truly human.
For our sake he was crucified
under Pontius Pilate;
he suffered death and was buried.
On the third day he rose again
in accordance with the Scriptures;
he ascended into heaven
and is seated at the right hand of the Father.
He will come again in glory
to judge the living and the dead,
and his kingdom will have no end.

We believe in the Holy Spirit,
the Lord, the giver of life,
who proceeds from the Father [and the Son],
who with the Father and the Son
is worshipped and glorified,
who has spoken through the prophets.
We believe in one holy catholic
and apostolic Church.
We acknowledge one baptism
for the forgiveness of sins.
We look for the resurrection of the dead,
and the life of the world to come.   *Amen.*

14   HYMN

15   INTIMATIONS

16   PRAYERS

The minister says:

Let us pray.

God of faith and love,

by your grace alone
we are called to be your people.
As members of the Christian family in this place,
we pray for the whole Church of Jesus Christ.
Take from her all that disrupts her unity,
and make her faithful in your service.
May your people so live in Christ
and he in them,
that they may be his body in the world today.

We pray for the world which you love,
and for which Christ gave his life.
Guide the leaders of the nations
and all who strive for peace and justice.
Look in mercy on all who are powerless,
and shelter those who are homeless,
hungry, or oppressed.
Help us to care for our neighbours
and to cherish the life of your creation,
that your will may be done on earth.

We pray for our nation.
Bless the Queen and the Royal Family.
Direct the Government, members of Parliament,
and all who in various ways
serve the community.
Grant that none in our land
may be despised or rejected,
and that your kingdom of love may prevail.

We pray for those in need,
for ill or distressed people,
and for those who draw near to death.
In the name of him who bears our griefs
and carries our sorrows,
bring them your comfort and peace.

We give you thanks
for all who have departed this life in faith.
Keep us with them in communion
with Christ our risen Lord,
and bring us at the last with all your saints
to eat and drink
in the glory of your eternal kingdom;
through Jesus Christ,
to whom with you, Father, and the Holy Spirit,
be praise and honour for ever.

Amen.

17   INVITATION

The minister says:

This is the Lord's table.

The Lord Jesus invites us
to share this joyful feast.

From east and west, from north and south,
people will come and take their places
at the banquet in the kingdom of God.

St Luke 13: 29

either

Jesus said,
'Come to me, all who are weary
and whose load is heavy;
I will give you rest.
Take my yoke upon you, and learn from me,
for I am gentle and humble-hearted;
and you will find rest for your souls.'

St Matthew 11: 28 - 29

or

Jesus said,
'I am the bread of life.
Whoever comes to me will never be hungry,
and whoever believes in me will never be thirsty.'

St John 6: 35

or

Jesus said,
'Blessed are those who hunger and thirst
to see right prevail;
they shall be satisfied.'   *St Matthew 5: 6*

18   OFFERING

19   THE GREAT ENTRANCE

*During the singing of a psalm or hymn, the offerings
of money, along with the gifts of bread and wine, are
brought to the Communion Table.*

20   THE GRACE

The minister says:

The grace of the Lord Jesus Christ be with you.
Amen.

21   UNVEILING OF THE ELEMENTS

*The minister unveils the elements,
and while doing so may say:*

Let us pray.

O God,
by the blood of your dear Son,
you have consecrated for us a new and living way
into the holiest of all.
Assure us of your mercy,
and sanctify us by your heavenly grace;
that we, approaching you with pure heart
and cleansed conscience,
may offer you a sacrifice in righteousness;
through Jesus Christ our Lord.   **Amen.**

Out of the fullness of your gifts, O God,
we make our offerings to you,
and present this bread and this wine at your table;
for all things come from you,
and of your own do we give you.
Blessed be your holy name for ever;
through Jesus Christ our Lord.   **Amen.**

22   NARRATIVE OF THE INSTITUTION
     (see Note A., p 143)

The minister says:

Hear the words of the institution
of the Lord's Supper,
according to St Paul:

The tradition which I handed on to you
came to me from the Lord himself:
that on the night of his arrest
the Lord Jesus took bread,
and after giving thanks to God
broke it and said:
'This is my body, which is for you;
do this in memory of me.'

In the same way, he took the cup after supper,
and said:
'This cup is the new covenant
sealed by my blood.
Whenever you drink it, do this in memory of me.'
For every time you eat this bread
and drink the cup,
you proclaim the death of the Lord,
until he comes.   *1 Corinthians 11: 23 - 26*

23   TAKING OF THE BREAD AND WINE

The minister says:

As the Lord Jesus,
the same night in which he was betrayed,
took bread,
I take these elements of bread and wine,
to be set apart from all common uses
to this holy use and mystery;
and as he gave thanks and blessed,
let us draw near to God
and offer him our prayers and thanksgiving.

24   THANKSGIVING

The minister says:

The Lord be with you.
   And also with you.

Lift up your hearts.
   We lift them to the Lord.

Let us give thanks to the Lord our God.
   It is right to give our thanks and praise.

Use either a., b., or c.

a. It is indeed right, it is our duty and our joy,
at all times and in all places,
to give you thanks and praise,
holy Father, heavenly King,
almighty and eternal God.

We give thanks
that in the creation of the world,
when you laid the earth's foundation
and set its corner-stone in place,
the morning stars sang in chorus
and the angels of God all shouted for joy.
By the power of your Spirit,
you made the universe;
by the might of your Word,
you gave us life.

We give thanks
that in the new creation,
when you gave your Son to raise us up again,
since we and all our human race had fallen,
you claimed us for your own people;
that we might proclaim the glorious deeds
of him who has called us out of darkness
into his marvellous light.
By the life of your Spirit,
you fill the hearts of the faithful;
by the light of your Word,
you give us strength and love.

Here may be added the Proper Preface (pp 185 to 189)

Therefore, with your people
of all places and times,

and with the whole company of heaven,
we proclaim your greatness
and sing your praise in the angels' song:

> ***Holy, holy, holy Lord,***
> ***God of power and might,***
> ***heaven and earth are full of your glory.***
> ***Hosanna in the highest.***

> ***Blessed is he who comes***
> ***in the name of the Lord.***
> ***Hosanna in the highest.***

In tune with all the heavenly hosts,
we here on earth acknowledge your glory,
and give you thanks that in the fullness of time
you sent your Son to be our Saviour.

We bless you
for his incarnation among us,
his holy birth,
his perfect life on earth,
his suffering for us, and his triumph over death;
for his ascension to your right hand
and his gift of the Holy Spirit;
and for the promise of his coming again.

Remembering his work and passion,
and pleading his eternal sacrifice,
we follow his example and obey his command.

Send down your Holy Spirit
to bless us
and these your gifts of bread and wine,
that the bread which we break
may be for us the communion

of the body of Christ,
and the cup of blessing which we bless
the communion of the blood of Christ;
that we, receiving them,
by faith may be made partakers
of his body and blood,
with all his benefits,
to nourish us
and help us grow in grace,
to the glory of your most holy name.

And here we offer and present to you
our very selves,
to be a living sacrifice,
dedicated and fit for your acceptance;
through Jesus Christ our Lord.

*[Brief remembrance may be made here of matters and
people that lie close to the worshippers' hearts, each
petition beginning, 'Remember, O Lord, ...' (see p
163).]*

> **Through him, with him, in him,
> in the unity of the Holy Spirit,
> all honour and glory are yours,
> almighty Father, now and for ever.**
>
> **Amen.**

Continue with the Lord's Prayer at no. 25.

b. Father of mercy and God of all comfort,
    we acknowledge you to be the Lord,
    and at all times we honour
    your greatness and glory.
    First, because you created us
    in your own image and likeness;

but chiefly, because you freed us
from the enslavement of sin,
through your only Son.

You gave him in love to be made man,
like us in all things except sin,
that by his death and resurrection,
he might bring again life to the world.

Lord, we are not able, in our dullness,
to understand the breadth and length
and height and depth of your love;
but true to the commandment
of Jesus Christ, our Lord,
we come to this table,
which he has left to us,
to be used in remembrance of his death,
until he comes again.

Here, we declare
and witness before the world that,
by him alone we have received liberty and life,
by him alone you claim us as children and heirs,
by him alone we have access to your favour,
freely shown,
by him alone we are raised
into your spiritual kingdom,
there to eat and drink with you and the Son
at that most joyful table of eternal life.

In this present time,
we on earth have communion with you in heaven.
But in the time to come,
we shall be raised to that endless joy,
prepared for us before the foundation
of the world was laid.

We acknowledge that we have received
these inestimable gifts,
by your free mercy and grace,
through your only Son Jesus Christ.
Moved by your Holy Spirit,
we, your congregation,
give you all thanks, praise, and glory,
for ever and ever.   ***Amen.***

Continue with the Lord's Prayer at no. 25.

c. It is right to give you thanks and praise,
    O Lord, our God, sustainer of the universe.
    At your command all things came to be.
    By your will, the vast expanse of space,
    galaxies, suns, the planets in their courses,
    and this fragile earth, our island home,
    were all created and have their being.

    You brought forth the human race,
    and blessed us with memory, reason, and skill.
    You made us the stewards of creation,
    but we turned against you,
    and betrayed your trust.

    Yet your mercy is like a spring that never fails.
    You yourself, in Christ your Son,
    come to deliver us:
    you redeem us in your love and pity;
    you create new heavens and a new earth
    where the cry of distress is heard no more.

Here may be added the Proper Preface (pp 185 to 189)

Therefore we praise you,
joining with the heavenly chorus,

and with those in every generation
who have looked to you in hope,
to proclaim with them your glory
in their unending hymn:

> *Holy, holy, holy Lord,*
> *God of power and might,*
> *heaven and earth are full of your glory.*
> *Hosanna in the highest.*
>
> *Blessed is he who comes*
> *in the name of the Lord.*
> *Hosanna in the highest.*

Gracious God,
we recall the death of your Son, Jesus Christ,
we proclaim his resurrection and ascension,
and we look with expectation
for his coming as Lord of all the nations.

We who have been redeemed by him,
and made a new people by water and the Spirit,
now bring you these gifts.
Send your Holy Spirit upon us
and upon this bread and wine
that we who eat and drink at this holy table
may share the life of Christ our Lord.

Pour out your Spirit upon the whole earth
and bring in your new creation.
Gather your Church together
from the ends of the earth into your kingdom,
where peace and justice are revealed,
that we, with all your people,
of every language, race, and nation,
may share the banquet you have promised.

> ***Through Christ, with Christ, in Christ,***
> ***all honour and glory are yours for ever.***
> ***Amen.***

25   LORD'S PRAYER

> ***Our Father in heaven,***
> ***hallowed be your name,***
> ***your kingdom come,***
> ***your will be done,***
> ***on earth as in heaven.***
> ***Give us today our daily bread.***
> ***Forgive us our sins***
> ***as we forgive those who sin against us.***
> ***Save us from the time of trial***
> ***and deliver us from evil.***
> ***For the kingdom, the power,***
> ***and the glory are yours***
> ***now and forever.***   ***Amen.***

26   BREAKING OF BREAD

The minister may hold up the bread and wine,
and say:

> Holy things of God for the holy people of God.
> ***Only Jesus Christ is holy;***
> ***we are made holy in him.***

The minister [returns the elements to the table,
and] says:

> According to the holy institution, example,
> and command of our Lord Jesus Christ,
> and as a memorial of him,
> we do this:

who, on the night when he was betrayed,
took bread
(*the minister takes the bread*),
and when he had given thanks he broke it
(*the minister breaks the bread*),
and said, 'This is my body
which is (broken) for you;
do this in remembrance of me.'
In the same way he took the cup
(*the minister [pours wine into the cup and]
raises the cup*)
saying, 'This cup is the new covenant
sealed by my blood.
Whenever you drink it, do it in memory of me.'

27   *The minister says:*

Jesus, Lamb of God,
have mercy on us.
Jesus, bearer of our sins,
have mercy on us.
Jesus, redeemer of the world,
grant us peace.

Silence may be kept for a time.

28   COMMUNION

The minister partakes of the bread and wine.

The minister says:

Draw near with faith:
receive the body of our Lord Jesus Christ
which was given for you,
and his blood which was shed for you,

and feed on him in your hearts by faith,
with thanksgiving.

Taste and see that the Lord is good.
Happy are those who find refuge in him!

In giving the bread, the minister says:

Take, eat. This is the body of Christ
which is (broken) for you.
Do this, remembering him.

In giving the cup, the minister says:

This cup is the new covenant
sealed by Christ's blood
which was shed that the sins of many
might be forgiven.
Drink from it, all of you.

*The elements may be taken to the people in their
seats, or the people may gather round the Holy
Table.*

*When all have received, the vessels are returned to
the Holy Table and covered.*

29   THE PEACE

The minister says:

The peace of the Lord Jesus Christ be with you.
                                                         Amen.

The minister may say:

On the evening of the first Easter Day,
'when the disciples were together
behind locked doors for fear,
Jesus came and stood among them.
"Peace be with you!" he said;
thei he showed them his hands and his side.
On seeing the Lord,
the disciples were overjoyed.
Jesus said again, "Peace be with you!"'

In the joyful presence of our risen Lord,
let us give one another a sign of peace.

The people may greet one another with a hand-
shake or an embrace, and say:

The peace of Christ.

30   PRAYERS

The minister says:

Let us pray.

Gracious God,
we thank you for the love
which brings us, as food from heaven,
the life of your dear Son,
and assures us that we belong
to the company of all his faithful people
in heaven and on earth.

Grant that, strengthened by this fellowship
and by the power of his Holy Spirit,
we may continue his work in the world,
until we come

to the glory of your eternal kingdom;
through the same Jesus Christ,
your Son, our Lord.

Amen.

Glory to God the Father,
who brought back from the dead
our Lord Jesus Christ
and crowned him with glory and honour.

Glory to God the Son,
who lives to plead our cause
at the right hand of God,
and who will come again
to make all things new.

Glory to God the Holy Spirit,
who brings us the taste
of the good Word of God
and the power of the age to come.

Amen! Praise and glory and wisdom,
thanksgiving and honour,
power and might be to our Lord for ever!

Amen.

31   HYMN

32   DISMISSAL AND BLESSING

The minister says:

Your eyes have seen God's love;
open them to look for the glorious hope.
Your ears have heard his songs;
close them to clamour and dispute.

Your tongues have uttered his praise;
guard them to speak the truth in love.
Your hands have been raised in worship;
stretch them out
to bring forth fruit for God's glory.
Your feet have walked in his courts;
direct them into light.
Your souls and bodies have been fed
by the Word of life;
serve the Lord with joy and gladness.   ***Amen.***

The minister blesses the people from God.

The blessing of God almighty,
the Father, the Son, and the Holy Spirit,
be with you.   ***Amen.***

33 *The bread and wine are taken from the Church, the
people standing.*

Note A. The narrative of the Institution (no. 22) may be incorporated within the
Thanksgiving (no. 24, p 131) thus: ' ... we follow his example and obey his
command, who on the night of his arrest, took bread, and after giving thanks to
God broke it and said: "This is my body, which is for you; do this in memory of
me." In the same way, he took the cup after supper, and said: "This cup is the new
covenant sealed by my blood. Whenever you drink it, do this in memory of me."
Send down your Holy Spirit .... '

Note B. 26 and 28. Although the word *broken* does not appear in *The Revised
English Bible*, its optional use here, at 26 and 28, and at corresponding places in
the following services, reflects its occurrence in many ancient texts, and its use in
many ancient liturgies.

Second Order for the Sacrament of the Lord's Supper or Holy Communion

1   CALL TO WORSHIP

The minister says:

> This is the day of Resurrection.
>
> Today the Son is risen,
> Jesus the Son of Mary,
> Jesus the King of Glory.
>
> Let us worship God.

2   HYMN

3   PRAYERS

The minister says:

> In the name of the Father,
> in the name of the Son,
> in the name of the Spirit holy,
> Three in One:
>
> > ***God make us holy,***
> > ***Christ make us holy,***
> > ***Spirit make us holy,***
> > ***Three all-holy.***

Count us not as nothing, O God,
count us not as nothing, O Christ,
count us not as nothing, O kind Spirit,
nor abandon us to eternal loss.

We confess our sins to you,
Father, Son, and Spirit holy.
Compassionate God of life,
your kindly pardon give:
for our careless talk,
our broken oath,
our empty speech;
for all that we have left undone;
for all that we have done amiss.

Jesus, only-begotten Son
and Lamb of God the Father,
you gave the blood of your body
to save us from the grave.

As we receive the word and knowledge
of your forgiveness,
enshield, encircle us,
each day, each night,
each dark, each light.
Uphold us,
be our treasure,
our triumph everlasting;
strong Son of God most high.

Amen.

[4 Hymn]

5   Old Testament

6   Psalm *sung or read*

7   EPISTLE

8   GOSPEL *the people may stand*

Before and after the reading of the Gospel,
the following may be said:

> The Gospel of the God of life:
> **to shelter us, to aid us;**
> The Gospel of beloved Christ:
> **the holy Gospel of the Lord.**

9   SERMON

10 THE BELIEF *the following, or the Apostles' Creed,*
    is said by all, standing.

> **Father, bless to us our belief.**
>
> **We believe, O God of all gods,**
> **that you are the eternal Father of life.**
> **We believe, O God of all gods,**
> **that you are the eternal Father of love.**
>
> **You are the eternal Father of the saints;**
> **you are the eternal Father of us all.**
>
> **We believe, O Lord and God of the peoples,**
> **that you are the creator**
> **of the ends of the earth,**
> **the creator of the skies above,**
> **the creator of the oceans below.**
>
> **You made our bodies from dust;**
> **you gave to our bodies breath,**
> **and to our souls their life.**

We believe, O God of all gods,
that you gave your beloved Son
in covenant for us.
He lived as we must live;
he died as we must die.
You raised him from death's dark domain,
and set us free to live for ever.
He speaks for us before your throne,
and brings us grace to help
in time of need.
We believe that he will return
to give new life to all the world.

We believe, O Lord and God of the peoples,
that you gave your Spirit of healing
to redeem our souls.
We believe, Father eternal and Lord of life,
that at the gift of baptism
you poured on us the Spirit of grace,
the Spirit of life and truth and love.

Praise to the Father,
praise to the Son,
praise to the Spirit:
Three in One.   *Amen.*

11   INVITATION

The minister says:

This is the table of the risen Lord Christ.

either

This is the table of the morning meal,
benefit to the body and the frame of the soul.

This is the table of the bread that shall last,
and the wine that shall never hurt.

or

In this feast comes the root of our joy,
in this feast gleams
the glory of the heavens high,
in this feast Christ comes, the King of greatness.

12 OFFERING

*A hymn or anthem is sung, during which the Offer-
ings are received; and after which the gifts of money,
bread and wine are brought to the Holy Table, the
congregation standing.*

All say:

> **Each thing we have received
> came from you.
> Each thing for which we hope
> will come from you.
> Each thing we enjoy
> is of your giving.
> Each thing for which we ask
> comes from your disposing.   Amen.**

13 NARRATIVE OF THE INSTITUTION

The minister says:

On the night of his arrest
the Lord Jesus took bread,
and after giving thanks to God broke it and said:
'This is my body, which is for you;

do this in memory of me.'
In the same way,
he took the cup after supper, and said,
'This cup is the new covenant
sealed by my blood.
Whenever you drink it, do this in memory of me.'

1 Corinthians 11: 23a - 25

14   TAKING OF THE BREAD AND THE WINE

The minister says:

As the Lord Jesus, the same night
in which he was betrayed, took bread,
I take these elements of bread and wine,
to be set apart to this holy use and mystery;
and as he gave thanks and blessed,
let us draw near to God and offer him
our prayers and thanksgiving.

15   THANKSGIVING

The minister says:

The Lord be with you.
     And also with you.

Lift up your hearts.
     We lift them to the Lord.

Let us give thanks to the Lord our God.
     It is right to give our thanks and praise.

Living God, we acclaim you,
majestic in holiness, worthy of praise,
worker of wonders.

In the beginning you created the universe.
You made the sun and stars above our heads,
the earth beneath our feet.
Your word brought forth
the rocks and streams,
the surging seas,
the wild winds and the mild.

You fashioned life in all its myriad forms,
and shaped from clay
the wonder of the human frame.

You spoke your word
to those whom you had chosen;
in disobedience they turned
from your commands.

You came yourself
in Christ the Word made flesh;
but he was shunned, despised by all,
forsaken in the darkness of the Cross.

You made the tree of death the tree of life,
the empty grave a sign of glorious hope.
You raised your Son
and brought him to your side again,
where now he lives to pray on our behalf.

Therefore with all your people,
and with the whole company of heaven,
we praise you in the angels' hymn:

> *Holy, holy, holy Lord,*
> *God of power and might,*
> *Heaven and earth are full of your glory.*
> *Hosanna in the highest.*

Blessed is he who comes
in the name of the Lord.
Hosanna in the highest.

Now we celebrate the feast of our redemption,
and proclaim the death of Jesus
and announce his resurrection and ascension
until he comes in glory.

Send down your Holy Spirit on us
and on these gifts of bread and wine;
that they may become for us
the body and blood of your most dear Son,
and that we may become for you his living body,
loving and caring for the world
until the dawning of the perfect day.

Most gracious God,
accept this our sacrifice
of praise and thanksgiving,
and receive the offering of ourselves
which now we make,
our thoughts and words, desires and deeds.
Gather into one in your kingdom
all who share this one bread and this one cup,
that with the faithful of all ages
we may with one voice and one heart
glorify your name;
through Jesus Christ your Son our Lord,
who lives and reigns
and is worshipped and glorified
with you and the Holy Spirit,
one God for ever.   *Amen.*

Our Father . . .

16 BREAKING OF BREAD

The minister says:

> We do this in obedience
> to Christ's example and appointment.
> On the night of his betrayal,
> he took bread
> (*the minister takes the bread*),
> and after giving thanks to God,
> he broke it
> (*the minister breaks the bread*),
> and said, 'This is my body
> which is (broken) for you;
> do this in memory of me.'
>
> In the same way he took the cup
> (*the minister raises the cup*)
> saying, 'This cup is the new covenant
> sealed by my blood.
> Whenever you drink it, do this in memory of me.'

17 *The minister says:*

> Jesus, Lamb of God,
> **have mercy on us.**
> Jesus, bearer of our sins,
> **have mercy on us.**
> Jesus, redeemer of the world,
> **grant us peace.**

18 COMMUNION

The minister partakes of the bread and wine.

In giving the bread, the minister says:

Eat this, the bread of heaven.

In giving the cup, the minister says:

Drink this, the cup of salvation.

19   THE PEACE

The minister says:

The peace of Christ above all peace
be with you.   **Amen.**

20   PRAYERS

The minister says:

Let us pray.

Thanks be to you, Jesus Christ,
for winning everlasting life for our souls.

Send your Holy Spirit upon your Church,
that in all her words and works
she may serve you better and love you more.

Encircle with your care the world
and all the people;
support and shield the Queen
and those who seek the good of our own land.
Relieve each one in suffering on land or sea,
each one in grief, wounded or weeping,
and lead them with us to the house of your peace,
this day and for ever.

Keep us in fellowship with all who rest in you;
bring us at last
into the paradise of your presence,
into the communion of the everlasting love
of Father, Son, and Holy Spirit,
one God, blessed for ever.   ***Amen.***

21   HYMN

22   BLESSING

The minister says:

The blessing of God be yours,
the blessing of the beloved Son be yours,
the blessing of the perfect Spirit be yours,
the blessing of the Three
be poured out upon you,
serenely and generously,
today and for ever.   ***Amen.***

Third (Shorter) Order for the Sacrament of the Lord's Supper or Holy Communion

For use at a Second Service or other suitable time

1   CALL TO WORSHIP

The minister says:

Let us worship God.

2   HYMN

3   SCRIPTURE SENTENCE (*or* SEASONAL SENTENCE)

The minister says one or more of the following:

Blessed are those who hunger and thirst
to see right prevail;
they shall be satisfied.

St Matthew 5: 6

I shall lift up the cup of salvation
and call on the Lord by name.

Psalm 116: 13

Taste and see that the Lord is good.
Happy are they who find refuge in him!

Psalm 34: 8

4   PRAYERS

The minister says:

Let us pray.

Almighty God,
to whom all hearts are open,
all desires known,
and from whom no secrets are hidden;
cleanse the thoughts of our hearts
by the inspiration of your Holy Spirit
that we may perfectly love you
and worthily magnify your holy name;
through Christ our Lord.   ***Amen.***

Lord God, Holy and Immortal,
we confess
that we have broken your commandments;
we have sinned by selfishness,
unbelief, and pride;
we have not acted justly, loved mercy
nor walked humbly with you.

In the fullness of your mercy,
blot out our misdeeds;
in your loving-kindness,
wash away our sin.
Give us a willing spirit
and the chastened heart you do not despise;
and help us to forgive others
as you forgive us;
through Jesus Christ our Lord.   ***Amen.***

Almighty God
have mercy upon you,

pardon and deliver you from all your sins,
confirm and strengthen you in all goodness,
and keep you in life eternal;
through Jesus Christ our Lord.

Amen.

Merciful God,
you have prepared for those who love you
such good things as pass human understanding.
Pour into our hearts such love towards you
that we, loving you above all things,
may obtain your promises,
which exceed all that we can desire;
through Jesus Christ our Lord.   *Amen.*

5 SCRIPTURE LESSONS *short passages may be read
from the Old and New Testaments.*

6 SERMON

7 APOSTLES' CREED *may be said*

8 OFFERING

9 HYMN

*During the singing of the hymn, the offerings of money,
along with the gifts of bread and wine, are brought to
the Communion Table.*

10 THE GRACE

The minister says:

The grace of the Lord Jesus Christ be with you.
Amen.

11 NARRATIVE OF THE INSTITUTION

Invitation: This is the LORD's Table ..... all who love Him and want to obey Him commands to keep FELLOWSHIP with Him.

The minister says:

Welcome new members < *By profession of faith*
by transfer from another church.

Hear the words of the institution
of the Lord's Supper,
according to St Paul:

The tradition which I handed on to you
came to me from the Lord himself:
that on the night of his arrest
the Lord Jesus took bread,
and after giving thanks to God broke it, and said:
'This is my body, which is for you;
do this in memory of me.'
In the same way, he took the cup after supper,
and said:
'This cup is the new covenant
sealed by my blood.
Whenever you drink it,
do this in memory of me.'
For every time you eat this bread
and drink the cup,
you proclaim the death of the Lord,
until he comes.

1 Corinthians 11: 23 - 26

12 TAKING OF THE BREAD AND WINE

The minister says:

As the Lord Jesus,
the same night in which he was betrayed,
took bread,
I take these elements of bread and wine,
to be set apart from all common uses

to this holy use and mystery;
and as he gave thanks and blessed,
let us draw near to God
and offer him our prayers and thanksgiving.

13   THANKSGIVING

The minister says:

The Lord be with you.
And also with you.

Lift up your hearts.
We lift them to the Lord.

Let us give thanks to the Lord our God.
It is right to give our thanks and praise.

It is indeed right, it is our duty and our joy,
at all times and in all places,
to give you thanks and praise,
holy Father, heavenly King,
almighty and eternal God,
for the majesty of your glory,
the wonder of your works,
the riches of your grace.

Here may be added the Proper Preface (pp 185 to 189).

Therefore, with your people
of all places and times,
and with the whole company of heaven,
we proclaim your greatness
and sing your praise in the angels' song:

Holy, holy, holy Lord,
God of power and might,
heaven and earth are full of your glory.
Hosanna in the highest.

Blessed is he who comes
in the name of the Lord.
Hosanna in the highest.

We bless you
for his holy birth,
his perfect life on earth,
his suffering for us
and his triumph over death;
for his ascension to your right hand
and his gift of the Holy Spirit;
and for the promise of his coming again.

Remembering his work and passion,
and pleading his eternal sacrifice,
we follow his example and obey his command.

Send down your Holy Spirit
to bless us
and these your gifts of bread and wine,
that the bread which we break
may be for us
the communion of the body of Christ,
and the cup of blessing which we bless
the communion of the blood of Christ;
that we, receiving them,
by faith may be made partakers
of his body and blood,
with all his benefits,
to nourish us
and help us grow in grace,

to the glory of your most holy name.

And here we offer and present to you
our very selves,
to be a living sacrifice,
dedicated and fit for your acceptance;
through Jesus Christ our Lord.

> *Through him, with him, in him,*
> *in the unity of the Holy Spirit,*
> *all honour and glory are yours,*
> *almighty Father, now and forever.*

Lamb of God, who takes away ......   ***Amen.***   ← p. 14.

Remember, O Lord,
your holy Church throughout the world
and reveal your glory among the nations.
Save your people
and bless those who belong to you,
shepherd them and carry them for ever.

Remember, O Lord,
our families and friends,
and surround them with your steadfast love.

Remember, O Lord,
those who are sick,
those who suffer pain or loneliness or grief,
those who draw near to death,
and those whom we name
in our hearts before you . . .
Comfort them with your presence,
sustain them by your promises,
grant them your peace.

And now, rejoicing
in the communion of the saints,
we remember with thanksgiving
all your faithful servants
and those dear to us
who serve you in the glory of heaven.
Keep us in unbroken fellowship
with your whole Church in heaven and on earth,
and bring us at the last
to the joy of your eternal kingdom;
through Jesus Christ our Lord.

who taught us to pray together saying...... **Amen.**

Our Father . . .

14 BREAKING OF BREAD

The minister says:

According to the holy institution, example,
and command of our Lord Jesus Christ,
and as a memorial of him,
we do this:

who, on the night when he was betrayed,
took bread
(*the minister takes the bread*),
and when he had given thanks he broke it
(*the minister breaks the bread*),
and said, 'This is my body
which is (broken) for you;
do this in remembrance of me.'

In the same way he took the cup
(*the minister raises the cup*)
saying, 'This cup is the new covenant

sealed by my blood.
Whenever you drink it, do it in memory of me.'

15   COMMUNION

The minister partakes of the bread and wine.

In giving the bread, the minister says:

Take, eat. This is the body of Christ
which is (broken) for you.
Do this, remembering him.

In giving the cup, the minister says:

This cup is the new covenant
sealed by Christ's blood
which was shed that the sins of many
might be forgiven.
Drink from it, all of you.

*When all have received, the vessels are returned to the
Holy Table and covered.*

16   THE PEACE

The minister says:

The peace of the Lord Jesus Christ be with you.
Amen.

17   PRAYERS

The minister says:

Let us pray.

Gracious God
we give you glory, thanks, and praise
for the dying and undying love
of our Saviour Jesus Christ.
In your great goodness
you have brought us into communion with him
and with all who love him,
and made us heirs of your everlasting kingdom.
By your grace,
may we continue in this holy fellowship,
and live to the glory of your name;
through Jesus Christ our Lord. ---- --- **Amen.**

18 HYMN

19 DISMISSAL AND BLESSING

The minister says:

Go in peace.

The peace of God,
which is beyond all understanding,
will guard your hearts and your thoughts
in Christ Jesus.

And the blessing of God almighty,
the Father, the Son, and the Holy Spirit,
be with you. **Amen.**

Fourth Order for the Sacrament of the Lord's Supper or Holy Communion

For use at a service when children communicate

It is assumed that the earlier part of the service will have been conducted, and that the presence and participation of children will have been taken into account.

1 INVITATION

The minister says:

The grace of the Lord Jesus Christ
be with you all.

This is the table of the Lord.
He invites all who love him
to sit with him
and share in this joyful feast.

2 THE GREAT ENTRANCE

During the singing of an appropriate song or hymn members of the congregation, including children and their families, may bring the bread and wine and the offerings to the Holy Table and join the minister in the distribution of the elements.

3 INSTITUTION

The minister says:

We are here
because Jesus has invited us.

When Jesus was on earth,
he often enjoyed
meals with his friends.

On the night before he died,
when darkness was beginning to fall,
he sat at table with the disciples
in an upper room in Jerusalem.

At this Last Supper,
he broke bread and took wine,
and told his disciples
to remember him
by following his example.

Today, we are his disciples,
and we are glad to do what he has told us.

4   TAKING OF THE BREAD AND WINE

*The minister uncovers the elements
(and pours the wine), and says:*

As the Lord Jesus took bread,
I take this bread and wine
to be set apart for this holy use.
And as he gave thanks,
let us give our thanks and praise.

5   THANKSGIVING

The minister says: Let us pray.

The Lord be with you.
And also with you.

Lift up your hearts.
We lift them to the Lord.

Let us give thanks to the Lord our God.
It is right to give our thanks and praise.

Loving God,
you made this world marvellous
for us to enjoy.

You gave Jesus
to be our friend
and to bring us to you.

You send your Spirit,
to make us one family in Christ.

For these gifts of your love we thank you,
and join with angels and saints
in this joyful hymn of praise:

Holy, holy, holy Lord,
God of power and might,
heaven and earth are full of your glory.
Hosanna in the highest.

Blessed is he
who comes in the name of the Lord.
Hosanna in the highest.

For your kindness to us
and your goodness to all,
we give you thanks.

We thank you that you showed your love
by sending your Son,
who gave his life for us,
and rose again from death,
and lives to pray for us for ever.

We thank you that he has taken away ~~our sins and~~
all that separates us from you,
and has made us friends with you
and with one another.

We thank you that   ~~to~~
he has brought us together at this table,
to strengthen us by his love.

Send your Holy Spirit
on us and these your gifts of bread and wine,
that we may know Christ's presence,
real and true,
and be his faithful followers,
showing your love for the world.

> ***Through Christ, with Christ, in Christ,***
> ***in the unity of the Holy Spirit,***
> ***all glory and honour is yours,***
> ***almighty Father, for ever.***
>
>   ***Amen.***

         Our Father . . .   Lamb of God, who takes away...

6   BREAKING OF BREAD

The minister says:

The Lord Jesus took bread
(*the minister takes the bread*),

and when he had given thanks,
he broke it
(*the minister breaks the bread*),
and said, 'This is my body,
which is (broken) for you.
Do this to remember me.'

Now taste & see that the Lord is Good! Eat ye All of it with Thanksgiving in your hearts.

In the same way he took the cup
(*the minister raises the cup*)
saying, 'This cup is the new covenant
sealed by my blood.
Drink from it, all of you.' *... with Thanksgiving in your heart.*

CUP

7 COMMUNION

The minister partakes of the bread and wine.

In giving the bread and wine, the minister says:

Taste and see the Lord is good.
Happy are they who find refuge in him!

Those assisting the minister may take the bread and wine to the congregation to share with one another; or the people may come forward and gather round the Communion Table.

During this time, a song or hymn may be sung.

When all have received, the vessels are returned to the Communion Table and covered.

8 THE PEACE

The minister says:

When Jesus rose from the dead,
he came and stood among his friends;
and showing them his hands and his side,
he said, 'Peace be with you!'

In his name and in his risen presence, I say:
The peace of the Lord Jesus be with you.

The minister may say:

Let us give one another a sign of peace.

*People may greet one another with a handshake or
an embrace, saying:*

The peace of Christ.

9 PRAYERS

*Prayers follow, which may include intercessions in
this form, if not offered earlier in the service.*

The minister says:

Let us pray.

Gracious God,
we thank you for your goodness to us
at the table of our Lord,
where we have remembered him
and offered ourselves to his service
till he comes again in glory.
In the name of our risen Lord
we pray for all the children of your love,

Lord, in your mercy
hear our prayer.

We pray for our homes and families:
that parents may be faithful
to the promises of baptism;
that children may grow
in love and happiness;
that young people may discover
the joy of obedience to Jesus Christ;
and that those who are old
may be honoured and loved.

We pray in silence for our friends, who need the
touch of God's hand. . . . .

Lord, in your mercy
hear our prayer.

We pray for the family of the Church:
that your people may be attentive
to the things of Christ,
and that your love may be reflected in our lives.

For the families of persecuted Xians murdered in Pakistan

Lord, in your mercy
hear our prayer.

We pray for the whole human family:
that the peoples of the world,
from east and west, from north and south,
may share in the good things you have given.

Lord, in your mercy
hear our prayer.

Bring nearer the day
when all people will live in peace
and praise your name for ever.

Lord, in your mercy
hear our prayer.

Glory to the Father, and to the Son,
and to the Holy Spirit:
**As it was in the beginning, is now,
and will be for ever.**   **Amen.**

10   HYMN

11   BLESSING

The minister says:

Go in peace and serve the Lord.

And the blessing of God almighty,
Father, Son, and Holy Spirit,
be with you always.   **Amen.**

Fifth Order for the
Sacrament of the Lord's Supper
or Holy Communion

For use at home or in hospital

The elements are prepared and placed upon a table.

1   SCRIPTURE SENTENCES

   The minister says:

> Our help is in the name of the Lord,
> maker of heaven and earth.   *Psalm 124: 8*

> God so loved the world
> that he gave his only Son,
> that everyone who has faith in him
> may not perish,
> but have eternal life.   *St John 3: 16*

2   PRAYERS

   The minister says:

> Let us pray.

> Almighty God,
> to whom all hearts are open,
> all desires known,
> and from whom no secrets are hidden:
> cleanse the thoughts of our hearts
> by the inspiration of your Holy Spirit,
> that we may perfectly love you

and worthily magnify your holy name;
through Christ our Lord.

Amen.

God, be gracious to us in your faithful love;
in the fullness of your mercy
blot out our misdeeds.
Wash away our iniquity
and cleanse us from our sin.
In your great tenderness
create a pure heart in us,
and give us a new and steadfast spirit.
Be our Saviour again,
renew our joy,
and give us peace;
for the sake of Jesus Christ our Lord.

Amen.

God forgives you your sins,
strengthens you by his Spirit,
and keeps you in life eternal;
through Jesus Christ our Lord.   **Amen.**

Gracious God,
you have assured us of your continuing love,
and by your mercy
you bring us to the table of your Son our Lord.
Help us to feed on him by faith,
that nourished by this sacrament
we may live to your honour and glory,
through Jesus Christ our Lord.

Amen.

3   OLD TESTAMENT

The following or other passage(s) may be read:

God, you are my God; I seek you eagerly
with a heart that thirsts for you
and a body wasted with longing for you,
like a dry land, parched and devoid of water.
With such longing I see you in the sanctuary
and behold your power and glory.
Your unfailing love is better than life;
therefore I shall sing your praises.
Thus all my life I bless you;
in your name I lift my hands in prayer.
I am satisfied as with a rich feast
and there is a shout of praise on my lips.
I call you to mind on my bed
and meditate on you in the night watches,
for you have been my help
and I am safe in the shadow of your wings.

Psalm 63: 1 - 7

4 NEW TESTAMENT

The following or other passage(s) may be read:

The tradition which I handed on to you
came to me from the Lord himself:
that on the night of his arrest
the Lord Jesus took bread,
and after giving thanks to God broke it and said:
'This is my body which is for you;
do this in memory of me.'
In the same way,
he took the cup after supper, and said:
'This cup is the new covenant
sealed by my blood.
Whenever you drink it, do this in memory of me.'
For every time you eat this bread
and drink the cup,

you proclaim the death of the Lord,
until he comes.   *1 Corinthians 11: 23 - 26*

Jesus said,
'I am the vine; you are the branches.
Anyone who dwells in me,
as I dwell in him,
bears much fruit;
apart from me you can do nothing.
As the Father has loved me,
so have I loved you.
Dwell in my love.
If you heed my commands,
you will dwell in my love,
as I have heeded my Father's commands
and dwell in his love.
I have spoken this to you,
so that my joy may be in you,
and your joy complete.
This is my commandment:
love one another as I have loved you.'
                           St John 15: 5, 9 - 12

After the reading the minister may say:

Thanks be to God for his Holy Word.

5   INVITATION

The minister says:

This is the Lord's Table.
Our Saviour invites us
to share the feast he has prepared.

The grace of the Lord Jesus Christ be with you.

(The minister unveils the bread and wine.)

6 THANKSGIVING

The minister says:

> The Lord be with you.
> **And also with you.**

> Lift up your hearts.
> **We lift them to the Lord.**

> Let us give thanks to the Lord our God.
> **It is right to give him thanks and praise.**

> Great and wonderful are your works,
> God the Creator of all.

> We thank you for your Son Jesus Christ,
> who lived our human life
> and knew our joys and sorrows.
> He showed your love;
> he healed the sick;
> he was a friend to sinners.
> In obedience to you,
> he took up his cross
> and died in love for us and all the world.
> You raised him from the dead
> to live and reign for ever,
> the friend of sinners still.

Here may be added the Proper Preface (pp 185 to 189)

> Therefore, with all the angels,
> and with people of faith of all times and places,
> we lift up our hearts in joyful praise, saying:

Holy, holy, holy Lord,
God of power and might,
heaven and earth are full of your glory.
Hosanna in the highest.

Blessed is he who comes
in the name of the Lord.
Hosanna in the highest.

Heavenly Father,
send your Holy Spirit
to bless us and these your gifts
of bread and wine,
that in communion with Christ our Lord
we may receive his life
and remain his glad and faithful people
until we feast with him in glory.

As we share in the body and blood of Christ,
may we become a living sacrifice,
dedicated and fit for your acceptance;
through Jesus Christ our Lord.

Amen.

Our Father . . .

7   BREAKING OF BREAD

The minister says:

We do this in obedience
to Christ's example and command.

On the night when he was betrayed,
Jesus took bread

(the minister takes the bread),
and after giving thanks to God he broke it
(the minister breaks the bread),
and said: 'This is my body
which is (broken) for you;
do this in memory of me.'

In the same way he took the cup
(the minister raises the cup),
and said: 'This cup is the new covenant
sealed by my blood.
Whenever you drink it,
do this in memory of me.'

Jesus Lamb of God:
> ***have mercy on us.***
Jesus bearer of our sins:
> ***have mercy on us.***
Jesus redeemer of the world:
> ***grant us peace.***

8   COMMUNION

The minister partakes of the bread and wine.

In giving the bread, the minister says:

Take, eat.
This is the body of Christ,
which is (broken) for you.
Do this, remembering him.

In giving the cup, the minister says:

This cup is the new covenant
sealed by Christ's blood

which was shed that the sins of many
might be forgiven.
Drink it, remembering him.

*When all have received, and the vessels are
covered, the minister says:*

Christ has died.
Christ has risen.
Christ will come again.

The peace of the Lord Jesus Christ be with you.
Amen.

9 PRAYERS

The minister says.

Let us pray.

Loving God,
we praise you for your goodness to us
at our Lord's Table.
You have fed us with the bread of life,
made us one with all your people
in heaven and on earth,
and assured us of your everlasting love.

We pray for the Church of Jesus Christ,
especially for our congregation and parish,
that many may believe in your love,
and live to give you glory.

We pray for those who are in trouble,
whether in body, mind, or spirit,
that they may know the comfort

and healing of your presence day by day.

We pray for our families and friends,
that they may be sure that there is
nothing in death or life,
nothing in the world as it is or as it shall be,
nothing in all creation,
that can separate them from your love
in Christ Jesus our Lord.

Eternal God,
we praise you for those
who have made known your love and joy,
and who now rejoice with you in heaven.
Bring us with them at the last
to eat and drink
in the glory of your eternal kingdom;
through Jesus Christ our Lord.   *Amen.*

10   BLESSING

The minister says:

The peace of God,
which is beyond all understanding,
guard your hearts and thoughts in Christ Jesus.

And the blessing of God almighty,
the Father, the Son, and the Holy Spirit,
be with you.   *Amen.*

Proper
Prefaces

ADVENT

And now we give thanks
that in the coming of Christ
the day of our deliverance is dawning.
For he comes to judge the world with justice,
and the people by his faithfulness.

We wait for the Lord with longing,
like those who watch for morning.
For the Lord is love unfailing,
and great is his power to save.

Therefore, . . .

CHRISTMAS (AND THE SUNDAY AFTER)

And today especially we give thanks
that at the appointed time
you sent your Son,
born as a child, the child of Mary:
that through him
we might become the children of God,
one with you for ever
as you in Christ became one with us.

Therefore, . . .

EPIPHANY (AND SUNDAYS AFTER)
> And now we give thanks
> that the shining of a star
> led wise men to worship him,
> the light of the world,
> the hope of the nations,
> the bright radiance of the Father's glory.
>
> Therefore, . . .

TRANSFIGURATION
> And now we give thanks
> for the glory of Christ
> revealed on the mountain,
> when he spoke of his death,
> confronted his cross,
> and was transfigured before his disciples;
> that, by the same cross,
> we may be changed into his likeness
> from glory to glory.
>
> Therefore, . . .

LENT
> And now we give thanks
> that, Son though he was,
> Jesus learned obedience through suffering;
> and is able to help those
> who are in the midst of their trial
> to overcome evil and grow in grace.
>
> Therefore, . . .

PASSIONTIDE

And now we give thanks
that, out of love for you, his Father,
and for all the world,
he humbled himself and was obedient,
even to the point of death,
death on a cross;
where, lifted up from the earth
he draws everyone to himself,
and makes the cross of shame a cross of glory.

Therefore, . . .

PALM SUNDAY

And now we give thanks
for the majesty of Christ
who rode into Jerusalem as a King;
but entered not into glory before he suffered pain,
nor went up to joy before he was crucified;
and made the way of the cross
the way of life and peace.

Therefore, . . .

EASTER

And today especially we give thanks
for the glorious resurrection of your Son.
He who was dead is alive again
and lives for evermore.
By his death he has destroyed the power of death.
By his rising again
he has opened the way to your kingdom
and brought us the gift of eternal life.
By his victory over the grave,

the long reign of sin is ended,
the world is being renewed,
and we are once again made whole.

Therefore, . . .

ASCENSION
And now we give thanks
that Christ is crowned with glory and honour,
exalted a Prince and a Saviour at your right hand
where he has gone to prepare a place for us,
that we may ascend to where he is
and reign with him in glory.

Therefore, . . .

PENTECOST (AND THE SUNDAYS AFTER)
And now we give thanks
that you sent your life-giving Holy Spirit
upon the Church,
that by his glorious power
the joy of the everlasting Gospel
might captivate the world;
and a new birth of holiness,
new understandings of truth,
and a new unity and love
possess all nations.

Therefore, . . .

TRINITY SUNDAY
And now we give thanks
that you have revealed

that the infinite glory of the Father
is the infinite glory of the Son
and of the Holy Spirit,
three persons,
equal in majesty,
undivided in splendour,
yet one Lord, one God,
ever to be worshipped and adored.

Therefore, . . .

ALL SAINTS

And now we give thanks,
for the glorious pledge of the hope of our calling
in the blessedness of the saints.
Following their example
and strengthened by their fellowship,
we run with resolution
the race which lies ahead of us,
that with them we may receive the crown of glory.

Therefore, . . .

DEDICATION (ANNIVERSARY) OF A CHURCH

And now we give thanks
that we are built up by your Holy Spirit
into a living temple made without hands,
even the body of your Son Jesus Christ;
and are granted the privilege of proclaiming
the good news of the unfathomable riches of Christ,
in this place where you cause your name
to be invoked
and where you come to bless your people.

Therefore, . . .

Prayers
for Use
at Holy Communion

AT THE OFFERING OF THE BREAD AND WINE

1 Blessed are you, Lord, God of all creation.
   Through your goodness we have this bread to offer,
   which earth has given and human hands have made.
   It will become for us the bread of life.
   Blessed be God for ever.

   Blessed are you, Lord, God of all creation.
   Through your goodness we have this wine to offer,
   fruit of the vine and work of human hands.
   It will become for us the cup of salvation.
   Blessed be God for ever.

   Blessed are you Lord, God, of all creation
   Through your goodness we have ourselves to offer,
   fruit of the womb, and formed by your love.
   We will become your people for the world.
   Blessed be God for ever.

AFTER THE CONSECRATION OR AFTER COMMUNION

2 Lord, in your mercy, hear our prayer.
   Receive this offering
   of our praise and thanksgiving.
   And as the corn once scattered on the fields
   and the grapes once spread on the hillsides

are brought together on this table in bread and wine,
so may your Church be gathered into your kingdom
from the ends of the earth;
through Jesus Christ our Lord.

Amen.

AFTER COMMUNION

3   Most gracious God,
we praise you for what you have given
and for what you have promised us here.
You have made us one
with all your people
in heaven and on earth.
You have fed us with the bread of life,
and renewed us for your service.
Now we give ourselves to you;
and we ask that our daily living
may be part of the life of your kingdom,
and that our love may be your love
reaching out into the life of the world;
through Jesus Christ our Lord.

Amen.

4   Accomplished and concluded, Christ our Lord,
is the mystery you have ordained.
We have tasted your death,
shared your resurrection,
and been filled with your unending life.
We have enjoyed your inexhaustible love,
through the grace of your eternal Father,
and the Holy Spirit,
now and for ever.

Amen.

5   Father of all,
     we give you thanks and praise,
     that when we were still far off
     you met us in your Son and brought us home.
     Dying and living, he declared your love,
     gave us grace, and opened the gate of glory.
     May we who share Christ's body live his risen life;
     we who drink his cup bring life to others;
     we whom the Spirit lights give light to the world.
     Keep us firm in the hope you have set before us,
     so we and all your children may be free,
     and the whole earth live to praise your name;
     through Christ our Lord.   ***Amen.***

6   God our Father,
     continue with us your family,
     and guard with watchful tenderness
     the hearts which have been hallowed
     by your sacred mysteries.

     By your mercy we have received
     the healing gift of your salvation;
     by your protection may we retain it
     until we come to the glory of your eternal kingdom;
     through Jesus Christ our Lord.

                          Amen.

7   Lord,
     you have put gladness in our hearts,
     you have satisfied our hunger with good things.
     In giving all, you have not withheld from us
     your own dear Son, your very self:
     how can we withhold anything from you,
     our Lord and our God?

Renew us day by day with the gift of your Spirit,
that we may give ourselves completely
to your service,
and walk with joy in the footsteps
of Jesus Christ our Lord.

Amen.

8 Lord Jesus Christ,
you have opened to us the scriptures
and made yourself know to us
in the breaking of the bread.
Stay with us,
that in the strength of your presence and truth
we may go all our journey through
and at its end see you face to face
in the glory of the eternal Trinity,
with the Father and the Holy Spirit
one God, now and for ever.

Amen.

9 God of unfailing love,
in your holy mysteries
you have graciously fed us
with the flesh and blood of your dear Son.
We pray that we,
and all who faithfully receive him,
may grow together in the communion
of the body of Christ,
and finally attain to the glory of the resurrection;
through Christ our Lord.

Amen.

First Order
for Marriage

On the arrival of the bride at the church, the bridegroom and best man take their places at the front of the church.

The minister greets the bride at the door of the church, and during the singing of a processional hymn, or the playing of appropriate music, leads her to the front of the church where she takes her place beside the bridegroom.

or

The bride and bridegroom may walk together to their places at the front of the church.

1 CALL TO WORSHIP

    The minister says:

        God is love;
        and those who dwell in love are dwelling in God,
        and God in them.

        or

        Grace and peace to you from God our Father
        and the Lord Jesus Christ.

        Let us worship God.

2 HYMN

3 STATEMENT

The minister says:

We have come together in the presence of God,
for the marriage of *A* . . . , and *B* . . . ;
to share their joy,
and to promise them our support and love.

Marriage is a gift of God
and a means of grace.
In the life-long union of marriage
we can know the joy of God,
who made us in his own image, male and female.

Marriage is founded in God's loving nature,
and in his covenant of love with us in Christ.
Husband and wife,
in giving themselves to each other in love,
reflect the love of Christ for his Church.

In Christian marriage,
wife and husband are called
to live faithfully together,
to love each other with respect,
tenderness, and delight.
The companionship and comfort of marriage
enable the full expression
of physical love between husband and wife.

They share the life of a home
[and may be trusted
with the gift and care of children].
They help to shape a society
in which human dignity and happiness
may flourish and abound.

Our Lord Jesus Christ was himself
a guest at a wedding in Cana of Galilee.
Through his Spirit he is with us now,
to enrich our love
and to give us his peace and joy.

4   PRAYERS

The minister says:

Let us pray.

Gracious God,
we thank you for all the gifts of your love,
and especially for the gift of marriage.

We praise you for your guidance
in the lives of *A* . . . and *B* . . . ,
for the joy they find in each other,
and for the love and trust they bring
to the happiness of this day.

And since we know that without you
nothing is strong, nothing is holy,
we pray that you will enrich them
with your grace
as they make their marriage covenant together.
Grant that your joy may be in them,
and that their joy may be full;
through Jesus Christ our Lord.

Amen.

5   EXCHANGE OF VOWS

*The congregation standing, the minister says to the
man and woman:*

As a seal to the vows you are about to make,
will you join hands.

*The man and woman turn and face each other,
and each takes the other by the right hand, or by
both hands.*

*The vows may be made by the man first, or by the
woman first. They may be made by reading them or
by repeating them after the minister, or by responding to a question put by the minister.*

The man says:

> **In the presence of God**
> **and before these witnesses,**
> **I, A . . . ,**
> **give myself to you, B . . . ,**
> **to be your husband,**
> **and take you now**
> **to be my wife.**
> **I promise to love you,**
> **to be faithful and loyal to you,**
> **for as long as we live.**

The woman says:

> **In the presence of God**
> **and before these witnesses,**
> **I, B . . . ,**
> **give myself to you, A . . . ,**
> **to be your wife,**
> **and take you now**
> **to be my husband.**
> **I promise to love you,**

to be faithful and loyal to you,
for as long as we live.

Alternatively, the vows may be put in the form of a
question.

The minister says:

> In the presence of God
> and before these witnesses,
> do you, *A* . . . , give yourself to *B* . . .
> to be her husband,
> and take her now to be your wife?
> Do you promise to love her,
> to be faithful and loyal to her,
> for as long as you both shall live?

> **I do.**

> In the presence of God
> and before these witnesses,
> do you, *B* . . . , give yourself to *A* . . .
> to be his wife,
> and take him now to be your husband?
> Do do you promise to love him,
> to be faithful and loyal to him,
> for as long as you both shall live?

> **I do.**

6   GIVING AND RECEIVING OF THE RING(S)

The minister receives the ring(s) and says:

> As a token of the covenant
> into which you have entered
> this ring (*these rings*)
> is (*are*) given and received.

May it (*they*) be a sign of the unending love
you have pledged to each other this day.

(*Where there are two rings, the exchange may be
begun by the man or the woman.*)

*The man places a ring on the fourth finger of the
woman's left hand, and may say:*

**B . . . , I give you this ring in God's name,
as a symbol of all that we have promised,
and all that we shall share.**

*The woman places a ring on the fourth finger of the
man's left hand, and may say:*

**A . . . , I give you this ring in God's name,
as a symbol of all that we have promised,
and all that we shall share.**

or, if there be only one ring, the recipient says:

**A . . . , I receive this ring in God's name,
as a symbol of all that we have promised,
and all that we shall share.**

The minister says:

By this sign you take each other,
to have and to hold from this day forward;
for better, for worse,
for richer, for poorer,
in sickness and in health,
to love and to cherish,
for as long as you live.

7 DECLARATION OF MARRIAGE

The man and woman join hands,
and the minister places his hand over their joined
hands and says:

Since you have covenanted together in marriage,
and have declared your love for each other
before God and these witnesses,
I proclaim you to be husband and wife,
in the name of the Father, and of the Son,
and of the Holy Spirit.   ***Amen.***

Those whom God has joined together,
no one must separate.

8 MARRIAGE BLESSING

The husband and wife kneel.

The minister says:

Blessed be God the Father,
who gives joy to bridegroom and bride.
Blessed be the Lord Jesus Christ,
who brings new life to the world.
Blessed be the Holy Spirit of God,
who brings us together in love.
Blessed be the Father, Son, and Holy Spirit,
one God to be praised for ever.

Amen.

May the Lord bless you
and guard you;
may the Lord make his face shine on you
and be gracious to you;

may the Lord look kindly on you
and give you peace.   ***Amen.***

*The Marriage Schedule may be signed here, in front
of the congregation, or at the end of the service.*

[9 HYMN]

10   SCRIPTURE LESSONS, *including a* GOSPEL READING

11   ADDRESS

12   PRAYERS

The minister says:

Let us pray.

Almighty God,
we thank you for all the ways
love comes into our lives,
and for the opportunities of joy and fulfilment
that marriage brings.

Bless *A* . . . and *B* . . .
who have been joined together in your name.
Confirm them in their happiness;
keep them faithful and true to each other,
ready to forgive and be forgiven.
As they grow together in love,
may each be to the other
a companion in joy,
a comfort in sorrow,
and a strength in need.

May your presence in their home,
make it a place of welcome and sharing,
of security and peace.
[Bless them with the gift and care of children,
that together they may grow
to know and love you in your Son.]

Bless their families and friends,
who have given them love and friendship
through the years.

We pray for your whole human family,
and for those who suffer while we rejoice.
Bring near the day when all people
will live in peace
and in the knowledge of your love.

Eternal God,
we remember those who were close to us,
who have passed through death
into life everlasting.
Bring us with them at the last
to the Father's house,
the family of God complete
in the glory of your presence;
through Jesus Christ our Lord.

Amen.

Our Father ...

13   HYMN

14   BLESSING

The minister says:

Go in peace, and in the joy of the Lord.

And the blessing of God almighty,
the Father, the Son, and the Holy Spirit,
be with you all.

Amen.

Second Order
for Marriage

On the arrival of the bride at the church, the bridegroom and the best man take their places at the front of the church.

The minister greets the bride at the door of the church.

or

The minister greets the bride and bridegroom at the door of the church.

1   CALL TO WORSHIP

   From the entrance to the church, the minister says:

   The grace of the Lord Jesus Christ
   be with you all.

   Let us worship God.

2   HYMN

   During the singing, the minister leads the procession to the front of the church, and each takes the appropriate place.

3   STATEMENT

The congregation still standing, the minister says:

Unless the Lord builds the house,
its builders labour in vain.   *Psalm 127: 1*

We are gathered as a congregation
of God's people,
to witness the joining together
of *A* . . . and *B* . . . in marriage.

Marriage reveals the loving nature
and wise purpose of God.
He made man and woman
in his own image,
so that the love and community of his nature
are reflected in the human family.
He brings a man and a woman together
in such a way that for ever after
each is incomplete without the other.

Christian marriage is an image
of the union of Christ and his Church.
Through his cross,
our broken relationships
with God and with one another
are forgiven and healed,
and we are reconciled.

In Christian marriage, the Holy Spirit
seals the covenant between a man and a woman,
and lifts them up into the love, joy,
and peace of God.

4   INTENTION

The minister asks the bride and bridegroom:

A . . . and *B* . . . , have you come here
freely to give yourselves
to each other in marriage?

We have.

5   PRAYERS

The minister says:

Let us pray.

Holy Father,
we boldly approach your throne of grace
through our Lord Jesus Christ.
Look upon his merits
and not on our unworthiness;
and grant that our prayers in his name
may be accepted for his sake,
who with you and the Holy Spirit
is worshipped and glorified,
one God, now and for ever.   **Amen.**

Let us confess our sins.

Righteous God,
we confess the sins
which separate us from you
and divide us from one another:
the pride that puts self at the centre of life,
the resentment that corrodes our love.
We acknowledge that we are powerless to change,
and we turn to you,
longing to know the perfection of human life
shown by our Saviour Jesus Christ.

Lord, have mercy.
Christ, have mercy.
Lord, have mercy.

The almighty and merciful God
grant you pardon and absolution of all your sins
and the power of a new life in Christ.

Amen.

Merciful God,
in Jesus Christ you have brought us once again
into communion with yourself.
Grant that this service of covenant and union
may witness to that reconciliation
by which we now live as a people
healed and forgiven,
one with you and with one another,
to your honour and praise;
through Jesus Christ our Lord.

Amen.

6 SCRIPTURE LESSONS, *including a* GOSPEL READING

7 ADDRESS

8 APOSTLES' CREED *the congregation standing.*

9 HYMN

10 PRAYERS

The minister says:

The Lord be with you!
The Lord bless you!

Lift up your hearts.
We lift them to the Lord.

Let us give thanks to the Lord our God.
It is right to give our thanks and praise.

God of love, ever faithful, ever sure:
we do well always and everywhere
to give you thanks and praise
through Jesus Christ our Lord.

Through him, you have entered
into a new covenant
with your people.
You have restored humankind to grace
in the saving mystery of redemption.
You grant us to share in your divine life
through our union with Christ.
You have made us heirs with him
of your eternal glory.

We praise you for the outpouring of your love
in the new covenant of grace,
and for this symbol of it
in the marriage covenant
which seals the love of husband and wife
and reflects your plan of love for the world.

With heart and voice, we join with all creation
and your whole family in heaven and on earth
to worship you and proclaim your praise:

> *Holy, holy, holy Lord,*
> *God of power and might,*
> *heaven and earth are full of your glory.*
> *Hosanna in the highest.*

We thank you, our Father,
for our friends *A* . . . and *B* . . .
We thank you for their homes and families,
and for the love, support, and encouragement
they have been given.
We thank you for the place
they have won in our affections
and for the honour in which they are held.
We thank you for leading them to each other,
and for the friendship and love,
commitment and trust
in which they have grown together.
We thank you for bringing them here,
and for the fulfilment of this holy hour
when they come with praise
to be united by your Spirit.

Living God,
by the presence and power of your Holy Spirit,
may they know the risen Christ
to be with them now
as they make their covenant in your sight
and before all the company of heaven.

Now to him who is able
through the power which is at work among us
to do immeasurably more than all
we can ask or think,
to him be glory in the church and in Christ Jesus
from generation to generation
for evermore!

                                            Amen.

11   EXCHANGE OF VOWS

   The congregation stands.

The minister says to the man and the woman:

As a seal to the vows you are about to make,
will you join hands.

The man and the woman turn and face each other,
and each takes the other by the right hand or by both
hands.

(either partner may make the vows first)

The man says:

> **I, A . . . ,**
> **take you, B . . . ,**
> **to be my wife.**
> **In the presence of God**
> **and before this congregation,**
> **I promise and covenant**
> **to be a loving,**
> **faithful, and loyal husband to you**
> **so long as we both shall live.**

The woman says:

> **I, B . . . ,**
> **take you, A . . . ,**
> **to be my husband.**
> **In the presence of God**
> **and before this congregation,**
> **I promise and covenant**
> **to be a loving,**
> **faithful, and loyal wife to you**
> **so long as we both shall live.**

12   GIVING AND RECEIVING OF THE RING(S)

The minister says:

As a token of the covenant
into which you have entered,
this ring (*these rings*)
is (*are*) given and received.

The minister takes the ring(s) and says:

God of steadfast love,
by your blessing
may this ring (*these rings*)
be to *A* . . . and *B* . . . a symbol (*symbols*)
of the vow they have made this day
and the covenant into which they have entered.
May they ever remain faithful
the one to the other
in unbroken love.

                                        Amen.

*(where there are two rings, either partner may give
a ring first)*

*As the ring(s) is (are) given and received,
the minister says:*

By this sign you take each other,
to have and to hold from this day forward;
for better, for worse,
for richer, for poorer,
in sickness and in health,
to love and to cherish,
so long as you both shall live.

13   DECLARATION OF MARRIAGE

The man and woman join hands.

The minister, taking their joined hands, says:

A . . . and B . . . ,
before God and this congregation,
you have covenanted in holy marriage.

In the name of God,
Father, Son, and Holy Spirit,
I therefore declare you to be husband and wife.

Those whom God has joined together,
no one must separate.

14   MARRIAGE BLESSING

The husband and wife kneel.

The minister says:

God the Father,
God the Son,
God the Holy Spirit,
bless, preserve, and keep you;
the Lord mercifully grant you
the riches of his grace,
that you may please him both in body and soul,
and, living together in faith and love,
may receive the blessings of eternal life.
                                            Amen.

[15 *The Aaronic Blessing may be sung or said.*]

The Lord bless you and keep you:
the Lord make his face to shine upon you,
and be gracious unto you:
the Lord lift up his countenance upon you,
and give you peace.

or

May the Lord bless you and guard you;
may the Lord make his face shine on you
and be gracious to you;
may the Lord look kindly on you
and give you peace.

16   PRAYERS

The minister says:

Let us pray.

Most holy God,
we give you thanks
for the joy and privilege
of sharing with *A* . . . and *B* . . .
in their happiness today.

We pray that the blessing you have given them
may so inspire them
throughout their life together,
that their love for each other
may grow with the passing years.
Keep guard over the covenant they have made,
and make them strong within your holy love.

Loving Father,
bless their home and defend it from evil.

May it be a home
where Christ is known and loved,
where his perfect love casts out fear,
and where his cross
brings reconciliation and peace.
May it be a place of happy welcome
and loving, joyful service.
In blessing them with the gift
and heritage of children,
make them loving and wise parents.
Grant *A . . .* and *B . . .* all that they need,
and give them a generous heart
and a kindly spirit.

Faithful God,
remember in your love
each family represented here.
May those who made vows
to each other in the past
renew their vows today
and find them strengthened.

Lead us through this life, O God.
And when we have fully served you
in our generation,
bring us into the presence of your glory,
to be numbered with all those
who are called
to the marriage supper of the Lamb,
even Jesus Christ our Lord.   ***Amen.***

   Our Father . . .

17   HYMN

18   BLESSING

The minister says:

The peace of God,
which is beyond all understanding,
will guard your hearts and your thoughts
in Christ Jesus.

The blessing of God almighty,
the Father, the Son, and the Holy Spirit,
be upon you and remain with you always.

Amen.

Third Order
for Marriage

On the arrival of the bride outside the church, the bride-groom and best man take their places in front of the congregation.

The minister greets the bride at the door of the church, and during the singing of a processional hymn, or the playing of music, leads her to the front of the church.

When the bride has taken her place beside the bride-groom, the bride's father takes his place in the congregation.

or

The bride and bridegroom may walk together to their places at the front of the church.

1   CALL TO WORSHIP

The minister says:

Let us worship God.

2   HYMN

3   STATEMENT

The minister says:

We are here in the presence of God
to witness the vows of *A* . . . and *B* . . .
as they give themselves to each other
in Christian marriage.
We offer them our continuing support and love
in their covenant with each other.
We rejoice in the uniqueness of their marriage,
and seek with them God's blessing.

Marriage is to be entered upon
thoughtfully and reverently,
and with a deep awareness
of its sacred and enduring nature.

Marriage is honourable and holy.
It is founded in the loving nature of God.
It is part of God's purpose for humanity,
and was provided by him
for the comfort and happiness
of man and woman
and for the welfare of human society.

It was hallowed by our Lord's gracious presence
at the marriage in Cana of Galilee;
and is consecrated as the symbol
of the union between Christ and his Church.

Today as *A* . . . and *B* . . .
become husband and wife,
we are confident that this deepening
of their commitment to each other
will lead to enrichment and joy in their lives.

4 PRAYERS

The minister says:

Let us pray.

Gracious God,
we give you thanks and praise
for all your gifts of goodness and grace.
We praise you for your gift of love,
uniting our families,
blessing our lives,
enfolding us all our days.

Especially we thank you
for the love which dwells and grows
in the hearts of *A* . . . and *B* . . . ,
and for the happiness and trust
that has led them here.

As they seek now in marriage
to confirm that happiness and deepen that trust,
may your Spirit of love
sanctify their joy and enrich their love.

Guide them by your grace,
surround them with your presence,
and keep them in your love;
through Christ Jesus our Lord.   ***Amen.***

5   EXCHANGE OF VOWS

The minister says:

Will the congregation please stand.

The minister says to the bridegroom and bride:

As a seal to the vows you are about to make,
will you join hands.

*The man and woman turn and face each other,
and each takes the other by the right hand or by
both hands.*

*They make their vows, either by reading them, or by
repeating them after the minister, or by responding
to a question put by the minister.*

The minister says:

> Jesus said,
> 'This is my commandment:
> love one another as I have loved you.'

(either partner may make the vow first)

The man says:

> **Before God
> and in the presence
> of our families
> and friends,
> I, A . . . ,
> declare my love
> for you, B . . .
> and I give myself to you
> as your husband.
> I promise you my love,
> my loyalty, and my trust
> for as long as we both shall live.**

The woman says:

> **Before God
> and in the presence of our families
> and friends,**

I, B . . . ,
declare my love
for you, A . . .
and I give myself to you
as your wife.
I promise you my love,
my loyalty, and my trust
for as long as we both shall live.

6 GIVING AND RECEIVING OF THE RING(S)

The minister says:

As a token of these promises
and as a symbol of your marriage,
this ring (*these rings*)
is (*are*) given and received.

May this ring (*these rings*) be to you
a sign of the endless love
you have pledged to each other this day.

(*either partner may give the ring first*)

*The man places a ring on the fourth finger of the
woman's left hand.*

*The woman places a ring on the fourth finger of the
man's left hand.*

7 DECLARATION OF MARRIAGE

*The bride and bridegroom join hands,
and the minister places his right hand upon their
joined hands.*

The minister says:

A . . . and B . . . ,
you have declared your love for each other
before God and this congregation.
You have pledged that you will live together
in Christian marriage,
in the words of your promises
and in the symbolism
of the joining of hands and the giving of rings.
I therefore declare you to be husband and wife.
In the name of God,
Father, Son, and Holy Spirit.   **Amen.**

Those whom God has joined together,
no one must separate.

8   MARRIAGE BLESSING

The husband and wife kneel.

The minister says:

A . . . and B . . . ,
may the blessing of God rest upon you
in the keeping of the promises you have made.
May his holy presence sanctify your love
and dwell richly in your lives.

Amen.

God guard you on every side.
God guide you in truth and peace.
God gird you with faith and love.   **Amen.**

9   SCRIPTURE LESSONS, *including a* GOSPEL READING

10   ADDRESS

11   PRAYERS

The minister says:

Let us pray.

Gracious God,
for the promise,
for the hope,
for the love of this day,
we praise you.

Bless your children now
with the strength of your Spirit,
that they may build a life of joy and fulfilment
on the foundations of commitment and love.

May they be sustained by the love and support
that now surrounds them.
May they always remain open-hearted,
courageous, and strong.
Give to them generosity of spirit,
understanding of each other,
warm and loyal friendship.

Grant that they may go forward from this day
delighting in their love.
May their love grow,
and in time to come may it prove able
to heal and to help,
to overcome difficulties,
and to bring reconciliation.

So may all see in them
a symbol of your love
from which nothing can separate us
and which nothing can overcome.

Be with them now
and remain with them for ever.   ***Amen.***

> ***Our Father . . .***

12   HYMN

13   BLESSING

The minister blesses the people from God:

I wish you joy in the Lord always.

And the blessing of God almighty,
the Father, the Son, and the Holy Spirit,
be with you all.   ***Amen.***

Scripture
Readings
for Marriage Services

OLD TESTAMENT

The Lord God took the man
and put him in the garden of Eden
to till it and look after it.

Then the Lord God said,
'It is not good for the man to be alone;
I shall make a partner suited to him.'
So from the earth
he formed all the wild animals
and all the birds of the air,
and brought them to the man
to see what he would call them;
whatever the man called each living creature,
that would be its name.
The man gave names to all cattle,
to the birds of the air,
and to every wild animal;
but for the man himself
no suitable partner was found.
The Lord God then put the man into a deep sleep
and, while he slept, he took one of the man's ribs
and closed up the flesh over the place.
The rib he had taken out of the man
the Lord God built up into a woman,
and he brought her to the man.
The man said:

'This one at last
is bone from my bones,
flesh from my flesh!
She shall be called woman,
for from man was she taken.'
That is why a man leaves his father and mother
and attaches himself to his wife,
and the two become one.
Both were naked,
the man and his wife,
but they had no feeling of shame.

Genesis 2: 15, 18 - 25

Wear me as a seal over your heart,
as a seal upon your arm;
for love is strong as death,
passion cruel as the grave;
it blazes up like a blazing fire,
fiercer than any flame.
Many waters cannot quench love,
no flood can sweep it away;
if someone were to offer for love
all the wealth in his house,
it would be laughed to scorn.

Song of Songs 8: 6 - 7

The days are coming, says the Lord,
when I shall establish a new covenant
with the people of Israel and Judah.
It will not be like the covenant
I made with their forefathers
when I took them by the hand
to lead them out of Egypt,
a covenant they broke,

though I was patient with them, says the Lord.
For this is the covenant
I shall establish with the Israelites
after those days, says the Lord:
I shall set my law within them,
writing it on their hearts;
I shall be their God, and they will be my people.
No longer need they teach one another,
neighbour or brother,
to know the Lord;
all of them, high and low alike,
will know me, says the Lord,
for I shall forgive their wrongdoing,
and their sin I shall call to mind no more.

Jeremiah 31: 31 - 34

also

Genesis	1: 26 - 28, 31a
	24: 34 - 38, 42 - 49, 56 - 57
Song of Songs	2

May God be gracious to us and bless us,
may he cause his face to shine on us,
that your purpose may be known on earth,
your saving power among all nations.
Let the peoples praise you, God;
let all peoples praise you.

Let nations rejoice and shout in triumph;
for you judge the peoples with equity
and guide the nations of the earth.
Let the peoples praise you, God;
let all peoples praise you.

The earth has yielded its harvest.
May God, our God, bless us.
God grant us his blessing,
that all the ends of the earth may fear him.

Psalm 67

Happy are all who fear the Lord,
who conform to his ways.
You will enjoy the fruit of your labours,
you will be happy and prosperous.

Within your house
your wife will be like a fruitful vine;
your sons round your table
will be like olive saplings.
Such is the blessing in store
for him who fears the Lord.

May the Lord bless you from Zion;
may you rejoice in the prosperity of Jerusalem
all the days of your life.
And may you live
to see your children's children!

Peace be on Israel!   *Psalm 128*

also

Psalm   33: 2 - 9
                 118: 1 - 4
                 144: 9 - 15

*The following passages may be read from the
Old Testament Apocrypha*

After they were left alone
and the door was shut,
Tobias got up from the bed, saying to Sarah,
'Rise, my love; let us pray
and beseech our Lord to show us mercy
and keep us in safety.'
She got up, and they began to pray
that they might be kept safe.
Tobias said: 'We praise you, God of our fathers,
we praise your name for ever and ever.
Let the heavens and all your creation
praise you for ever.
You made Adam and also Eve his wife,
who was to be his partner and support;
and those two
were the parents of the human race.
This was your word:
"It is not good for the man to be alone;
let us provide a partner suited to him."
So now I take this my beloved to wife,
not out of lust but in true marriage.
Grant that she and I may find mercy
and grow old together.'
They both said 'Amen, Amen',
and they slept through the night.   *Tobit 8: 4 - 9*

A good wife makes a happy husband;
she doubles the length of his life.
A staunch wife is her husband's joy;
he will live out his days in peace.
A good wife is a blessing;
she is one of the Lord's gifts
to those who fear him.
Rich or poor, they are in good heart,
with always a smile on their faces.
                    Ecclesiasticus 26: 1 - 4

NEW TESTAMENT

Epistle

Therefore, my friends,
I implore you by God's mercy
to offer your very selves to him:
a living sacrifice,
dedicated and fit for his acceptance,
the worship offered by mind and heart.
Conform no longer
to the pattern of this present world,
but be transformed
by the renewal of your minds.
Then you will be able to discern
the will of God,
and to know what is good,
acceptable, and perfect.

Love in all sincerity,
loathing evil and holding fast to the good.
Let love of the Christian community
show itself in mutual affection.
Esteem others more highly than yourself.
With unflagging zeal, aglow with the Spirit,
serve the Lord.
Let hope keep you joyful;
in trouble stand firm;
persist in prayer;
contribute to the needs of God's people,
and practise hospitality.

Romans 12: 1 - 2, 9 - 13

Love is patient and kind.
Love envies no one, is never boastful,

never conceited, never rude;
love is never selfish,
never quick to take offence.
Love keeps no score of wrongs,
takes no pleasure in the sins of others,
but delights in the truth.
There is nothing love cannot face;
there is no limit to its faith,
its hope, its endurance.
Love will never come to an end.

There are three things that last for ever:
faith, hope, and love;
and the greatest of the three is love.

1 Corinthians 13: 4 - 8a, 13

With this in mind, then,
I kneel in prayer to the Father,
from whom every family in heaven and on earth
takes its name,
that out of the treasures of his glory
he may grant you inward strength and power
through his Spirit,
that through faith
Christ may dwell in your hearts in love.
With deep roots and firm foundations
may you, in company with all God's people,
be strong to grasp
what is the breadth and length
and height and depth
of Christ's love,
and to know it, though it is beyond knowledge.
So may you be filled
with the very fullness of God.
Now to him who is able

through the power which is at work among us
to do immeasurably more
than all we can ask or conceive,
to him be glory in the church
and in Christ Jesus
from generation to generation
for evermore! Amen.

Ephesians 3: 14 - 21

In a word, as God's dear children,
you must be like him.
Live in love as Christ loved you
and gave himself up on your behalf,
an offering and sacrifice
whose fragrance is pleasing to God.

Be subject to one another
out of reverence for Christ.
Wives, be subject to your husbands
as though to the Lord;
for the man is the head of the woman,
just as Christ is the head of the church.
Christ is, indeed, the saviour of that body;
but just as the church is subject to Christ,
so must women be subject to their husbands
in everything.
Husbands, love your wives,
as Christ loved the church
and gave himself up for it,
to consecrate and cleanse it by water and word,
so that he might present the church to himself
all glorious, with no stain or wrinkle
or anything of the sort,
but holy and without blemish.
In the same way men ought to love their wives,

as they love their own bodies.
In loving his wife a man loves himself.
For no one ever hated his own body;
on the contrary, he keeps it nourished and warm,
and that is how Christ treats the church,
because it is his body,
of which we are living parts.
'This is why' (in the words of scripture)
'a man shall leave his father and mother
and be united to his wife,
and the two shall become one flesh.'
There is hidden here a great truth,
which I take to refer to Christ and to the church.
But it applies also to each one of you:
the husband must love his wife
as his very self,
and the wife must show reverence
for her husband.

Ephesians 5: 1 - 2, 21 - 33

And this is my prayer,
that your love may grow ever richer
in knowledge and insight of every kind,
enabling you to learn by experience
what things really matter.
Then on the day of Christ
you will be flawless and without blame,
yielding the full harvest of righteousness
that comes through Jesus Christ,
to the glory and praise of God.

Philippians 1: 9 - 11

also

Colossians	3: 12 - 17
1 Peter	3: 1 - 12
1 John	3: 18 - 24
1 John	4: 7 - 13
Revelation	19: 1, 5 - 9a

Gospel

'Not everyone who says to me, "Lord, Lord"
will enter the kingdom of Heaven,
but only those who do the will
of my heavenly Father.'

'So whoever hears these words of mine
and acts on them
is like a man who had the sense to build
his house on rock.
The rain came down, the floods rose,
the winds blew and beat upon that house;
but it did not fall,
because its foundations were on rock.
And whoever hears these words of mine
and does not act on them
is like a man who was foolish enough
to build his house on sand.
The rain came down, the floods rose,
the winds blew
and battered against that house;
and it fell with a great crash.'

St Matthew 7: 21, 24 - 27

But in the beginning, at the creation,
'God made them male and female.'

'That is why a man leaves his father and mother,
and is united to his wife,
and the two become one flesh.'
It follows that
they are no longer two individuals:
they are one flesh.
Therefore what God has joined together,
man must not separate.

St Mark 10: 6 - 9

Two days later
there was a wedding at Cana-in-Galilee.
The mother of Jesus was there,
and Jesus and his disciples
were also among the guests.
The wine gave out, so Jesus's mother said to him,
'They have no wine left.'
He answered, 'That is no concern of mine.
My hour has not yet come.'
His mother said to the servants,
'Do whatever he tells you.'
There were six stone water-jars standing near,
of the kind used for Jewish rites of purification;
each held from twenty to thirty gallons.
Jesus said to the servants,
'Fill the jars with water,'
and they filled them to the brim.
'Now draw some off,' he ordered,
'and take it to the master of the feast';
and they did so.
The master tasted the water
now turned into wine,
not knowing its source,
though the servants
who had drawn the water knew.

He hailed the bridegroom and said,
'Everyone else serves the best wine first,
and the poorer
only when the guests have drunk freely;
but you have kept the best wine till now.'

So Jesus performed at Cana-in-Galilee
the first of the signs which revealed his glory
and led his disciples to believe in him.

St John 2: 1 - 11

As the Father has loved me,
so I have loved you.
Dwell in my love.
If you heed my commands,
you will dwell in my love,
as I have heeded my Father's commands
and dwell in his love.

I have spoken thus to you,
so that my joy may be in you,
and your joy complete.
This is my commandment:
'love one another, as I have loved you.'

St John 15: 9 - 12

also

St Matthew	5: 3 - 10
St Matthew	5: 13 - 16
St John	15: 1 - 8

Order for the Blessing of a Civil Marriage

Sections 1 to 12 (i.e. the whole service) are used at any time other than at public worship on the Lord's Day.
The couple seeking a blessing on their marriage stand together at the front of the church, and may be attended by friends.

Sections 6 to 12 are used on the Lord's Day at public worship, immediately after the sermon.
The couple and their friends come forward, perhaps during the singing of a hymn, and stand before the minister.

1 CALL TO WORSHIP

The minister says:

> The grace of the Lord Jesus Christ
> be with you all.

> Let us worship God.

2 HYMN

3 SCRIPTURE SENTENCE

The minister says:

> Jesus said,
> 'This is my commandment:

love one another, as I have loved you.'

St John 15: 12

4 PRAYERS

The minister says:

Let us pray.

God of wonder and of joy:
grace comes from you,
and you alone are the source of life and love.
Without you, we cannot please you;
without your love, our deeds are worth nothing.

Send your Holy Spirit,
and pour into our hearts
that most excellent gift of love,
that we may worship you now
with thankful hearts
and serve you always with willing minds;
through Jesus Christ our Lord.   ***Amen.***

5 SCRIPTURE READINGS

*The minister, or some other person appointed to
read, says:*

Hear the Word of God.

St John 15: 9 - 12 is read

6 STATEMENT

The minister says:

God is love:

those who dwell in love dwell in God,
and God in them.   *1 John 4: 16*

We rejoice in the marriage
of *A* . . . and *B* . . .
and are happy to ask God to bless it.

A . . . and *B* . . . have been married
according to the law of the land.
They have pledged their love and loyalty
to each other.
Now, in faith, they come before God
and his Church
to acknowledge their covenant of marriage.

In Christian marriage,
a man and a woman
bind themselves to each other in love,
and become one,
even as Christ is one with the Church.
They are committed to love each other
as Christ loved the Church
and gave himself for it.

7   PRAYERS

The minister says:

Let us pray.

Loving God,
without your grace no promise is sure.
Strengthen *A* . . . and *B* . . .
by the gift of your Holy Spirit
as they seek your blessing upon their marriage.
May they keep the vows they have already made,

and be faithful to each other and to you.
Fill them with your joy,
and guide them by your word
to follow you all the days of their life together;
through Jesus Christ our Lord.   **Amen.**

8   PROMISES

The couple join hands and face each other.

The husband says to his wife:

> **B . . . , you are my wife.**
> **With God's help,**
> **I promise to be your faithful husband,**
> **to love you as Christ commands,**
> **to comfort you and protect you,**
> **to honour you**
> **as long as we both shall live.**

The wife says to her husband:

> **A . . . , you are my husband.**
> **With God's help,**
> **I promise to be your faithful wife,**
> **to love you as Christ commands,**
> **to comfort you and protect you,**
> **to honour you**
> **as long as we both shall live.**

The minister says:

> May the ring(s) you wear
> be a symbol of unending love and faithfulness,
> to remind you of the covenant
> into which you have entered.

9   MARRIAGE BLESSING

The couple kneel.

The minister says:

> Blessed be God the Father,
> who gives joy to bridegroom and bride.
> Blessed be the Lord Jesus Christ,
> who brings new life to the world.
> Blessed be the Holy Spirit of God,
> who brings us together in love.
> Blessed be the Father, Son, and Holy Spirit,
> one God to be praised for ever.   ***Amen.***

> May the Lord bless you
> and guard you;
> may the Lord make his face shine on you
> and be gracious to you;
> may the Lord look kindly on you
> and give you peace.   ***Amen.***

10   DECLARATION

The couple stand.

The minister says:

> *A* . . . and *B* . . . , you are husband and wife
> according to the witness
> of the one holy catholic and apostolic Church.

> Those whom God has joined together,
> no one must separate.

11   THE PEACE

The minister says:

The peace of the Lord be with you.

The husband and wife and all present may offer to each other some sign of peace and love.

12   *If the Order of Blessing is used on a Sunday at Public Worship, the service proceeds in the normal way, either to Holy Communion or to the prayers and the closing hymn and Benediction.*

If the Order of Blessing is used on a week-day, it concludes with the Benediction.

BENEDICTION

The couple kneel.

The minister says:

May God the Father give you joy;
may God the Son give you grace;
may God the Holy Spirit
fill your hearts with love.

And the blessing of God almighty,
Father, Son, and Holy Spirit,
descend upon you and abide in you,
now and always.

Amen.

Order
for Thanksgiving
for Marriage

With the Renewal of the Marriage Vows

This order may be used at an anniversary; or after a time of separation; or when a couple has experienced difficulty in their marriage; or when several couples request, or are invited to make, a public reaffirmation of marriage.

It may be used at home or in church.

When used in church, it may form part of a public service of worship, and could be included within the service of Holy Communion, at an appropriate place between the sermon and the prayers of intercession.

The order is prepared for use with one couple only. If there is more than one couple on the same occasion, the rubrics and text will need to be varied.

The minister may give a suitable introduction by explaining the circumstances that lead to the occasion.

1 HYMN

   During the singing of a hymn, the couple stand before the minister.

2 SCRIPTURE SENTENCES

   The minister says:

God created human beings in his own image;
male and female he created them;
and God blessed them. *Genesis 1: 27, 28*

God is love;
and those who dwell in love are dwelling in God,
and God in them. *1 John 4: 16b*

Unless the Lord builds the house,
its builders labour in vain. *Psalm 127: 1*

3   STATEMENT

The minister says:

Marriage is a way of life founded in God.

It is his gift to us,
to help man and woman find
companionship, help, and comfort.
It is also a means of grace
in which husband and wife,
living faithfully together,
may find the fulfilment of human love
in tenderness and respect.
In Christian marriage,
God makes his servants one.
Their life together is a witness to his love
in this troubled world,
a love by which unity overcomes division,
forgiveness heals injury,
and joy triumphs over sorrow.

By marriage God enriches society
and strengthens the sanctity of family life.

A . . . and *B* . . . are here today
to celebrate their marriage
(*on its . . . th anniversary*)
and to reaffirm their commitment
to this way of life
which God provided and Christ has blessed.
We rejoice with them,
and support them with our prayers.

4   PRAYERS

The minister says:

Let us pray.

Living God,
we thank you for all the ways
by which your love reaches us:
through family and relations
whose care and trust have helped us;
through friends and companions
whose patience and concern
have brought us strength and hope.

We thank you for the love of *A* . . . and *B* . . . .
Fill their hearts with the presence of Christ
as they re-commit themselves to each other.
May they find that the new joy he brings
will make their lives new;
through the same Jesus Christ our Lord.   ***Amen.***

When the dominant note is thanksgiving,
Section 5 is used, followed by Section 7.

When the dominant note is recommitment,
Section 6 is used, and Section 5 omitted.

5 THANKSGIVING

The minister says:

Will the congregation please stand.

*The husband and wife face each other
and join hands.*

The husband says:

**I, A . . . ,
in the presence of God,
renew my commitment
to you, B . . . ,
as your husband.
I give thanks
that you have shared my life.
All that I am
and all that I have
I continue to share with you.
Whatever the future holds,
I will love you
and stand by you,
as long as we both shall live.**

The wife says:

**I, B . . . ,
in the presence of God,
renew my commitment
to you, A . . . ,
as your wife.
I give thanks
that you have shared my life.
All that I am**

> *and all that I have*
> *I continue to share with you.*
> *Whatever the future holds,*
> *I will love you*
> *and stand by you,*
> *as long as we both shall live.*

6 RECOMMITMENT

The minister says:

Will the congregation please stand.

The husband and wife face each other
and join hands.

The husband says:

> *I, A . . . ,*
> *in the presence of God,*
> *renew my commitment*
> *to you, B . . . ,*
> *as your husband.*
> *All that I am*
> *I give to you,*
> *and all that I have*
> *I share with you.*
> *Whatever the future holds,*
> *I will love you*
> *and stand by you,*
> *as long as we both shall live.*

The wife says:

> *I, B . . . ,*
> *in the presence of God,*

> *renew my commitment*
> *to you, B . . . ,*
> *as your wife.*
> *All that I am*
> *I give to you,*
> *and all that I have*
> *I share with you.*
> *Whatever the future holds,*
> *I will love you*
> *and stand by you,*
> *as long as we both shall live.*

7   AFFIRMATION BY THE PEOPLE

The minister says:
> Will you, the family and friends
> of *A . . .* and *B . . . ,*
> who have gathered here today,
> continue to uphold them in their marriage?

> **We will.**

8   PRAYERS

The minister says:

> Let us pray.

> Generous God,
> your Son has shown us how to love
> and invites us to love one another as he loves us.

> We pray for *A . . .* and *B . . . ,*
> with their shared memories of the past;
> of joy and laughter,
> sadness and disappointment,

forgiving and being forgiven.
Grant that they may put their trust in you
to guide and guard them in the future.

Loving God,
we thank you that in our earthly life
you speak to us of eternal life.
May we know you more clearly,
love you more dearly,
and follow you more nearly,
day by day;
through Jesus Christ our Lord.

Amen.

Our Father . . .

9   BLESSING

The couple kneel while the minister blesses them:

The riches of God's grace be upon you,
that you may continue together in faith and love
and receive the blessing of eternal life.

May the Lord bless you
and guard you;
may the Lord make his face shine on you
and be gracious to you;
may the Lord look kindly on you
and give you peace.   **Amen.**

*A hymn may be sung before the people disperse; or, if
this order is used at a service of public worship, the people
may return to their places during the singing of the hymn,
and the service then proceeds in the normal way.*

First Order
for a
Funeral Service

The address at no. 5, which may include reference by way of tribute to the deceased, should proclaim the Gospel of the Resurrection. Any separate tribute may be added before the Prayers at no. 6.

1 CALL TO WORSHIP

The minister says:

The grace of our Lord Jesus Christ,
and the love of God,
and the fellowship of the Holy Spirit
be with you all. **Amen.**

2 Corinthians 13: 14

*One or more of the following sentences
may be used:*

I shall not fail you or forsake you,
says the Lord. *Joshua 1: 5*

Jesus said, I will be with you always,
to the end of time.

St Matthew 28: 20

In the tender compassion of our God
the dawn from heaven will break upon us,
to shine on those who live in darkness,

under the shadow of death,
and to guide our feet into the way of peace.

St Luke 1: 78 - 79

Blessed are the sorrowful;
they shall find consolation.   *St Matthew 5: 4*

The eternal God is our refuge,
and underneath are the everlasting arms.

Deuteronomy 33: 27 (AV)

Praised be the God and Father
of our Lord Jesus Christ!
In his great mercy by the resurrection
of Jesus Christ from the dead,
he gave us a new birth into a living hope.

1 Peter 1: 3

One thing I ask of the Lord,
it is the one thing that I seek;
that I may dwell in the house of the Lord
all the days of my life,
to gaze on the beauty of the Lord
and to seek him in his temple.   *Psalm 27: 4*

Things beyond our seeing,
things beyond our hearing,
things beyond our imagining,
have all been prepared by God
for those who love him.   *1 Corinthians 2: 9*

In his favour there is life.
Tears may linger at nightfall,
but rejoicing comes in the morning.

Psalm 30: 5

We all know that God's judgement is just;
and do you imagine
that you will escape the judgement of God?

Romans 2: 2, 3

Our help is in the name of the Lord,
maker of heaven and earth.

Psalm 124: 8

The souls of the righteous are in God's hands;
no torment will touch them.
They are at peace.

Wisdom 3: 1, 3

Let us worship God.

2 HYMN

3 PRAYERS

The minister says:

Let us pray.

Lord of life and conqueror of death,
you are our help in every time of trouble.
In the presence of death,
you comfort those who mourn.
We bow before you,
believing you bear our grief
and share our sense of loss.
Give us grace to worship you,
and to trust in your goodness and mercy.
Assure us that because Christ lives,
we shall live also;
through the same Jesus Christ our Lord.

Loving God,
in our pain,
we remember with sorrow
how we have failed one another
and grieved your heart.
In your kindness,
forgive our past sins,
set us free from guilt,
and make us strong to live our lives in love;
through Jesus Christ your Son our Saviour.

God of grace and power,
send your Holy Spirit among us,
that we may hear your promises
and know them to be true,
and so receive the comfort and peace they bring;
through Jesus Christ our Lord.

Amen.

4   SCRIPTURE READINGS

The minister says:

Lord, to whom shall we go?
Your words are words of eternal life.

St John 6: 68

Hear the Word of God.

OLD TESTAMENT

A PSALM   *sung or read*

NEW TESTAMENT   *ending with a Gospel*

5   ADDRESS

6 PRAYERS

The minister says:

Let us pray.

God·of all grace,
we thank you that you sent your Son, Jesus,
to break the power of death
and bring life and immortality to light
through the gospel.
He shared our life,
took upon himself our death,
and opened the kingdom of heaven
to all believers.
Look not on us:
but look on us as found in him,
and bring us safely through the judgement
to the joy and peace of your presence.

Eternal God,
you hold all souls in life.
We praise you for those
who have shared this earthly life with us,
and have entered into eternal life with you.
Especially, we thank you for *N . . .* ,
for all that made *him* special,
all that you gave *him* and accomplished in *him*,
all that *he* meant
to those who knew and loved *him*.

We remember with gratitude . . .
(*particular qualities and gifts may be mentioned*)

(*Thanks may also be given for care and kindness
shown to N . . .*)

And now we thank you that for *N* . . .
all pain and suffering are ended,
and that death itself is conquered.
Help us to release *him* into your care and keeping,
in the confidence that all life
finds its fulfilment with you
in the joy of your everlasting kingdom.

We commend to you
those who will miss *N* . . . most
in the days to come
because they loved *him* best,
especially *X* . . . , and *Y* . . . , and *Z* . . . ,
and all the members of *his* family.
Grant that, casting every care on you,
they may know the consolation of your love.

God of all comfort,
in the midst of pain
heal us with your love;
in the darkness of sorrow
shine upon us as the morning star.
Awaken in us the spirit of mercy,
that, as we feel the pain of others,
we may share with them
the comfort we receive from you.
Bring us, at the last, with all your people
into the kingdom of your glory,
where death itself is ended,
and every tear is wiped from every eye.

To you, Father, Son, and Holy Spirit,
be glory both now and for all eternity.

Amen.

Our Father . . .

7 HYMN

8 COMMENDATION

The minister says:

Let us commend our *brother N* . . .
to the mercy of God our Maker and Redeemer.

Let us pray.

Gracious God,
by your power you gave us life,
and in your love you are giving us new life
in Jesus Christ.
We entrust *N* . . . to your safe keeping,
in the faith of Jesus Christ your Son our Lord,
who died and rose again to save us,
and to bring us all
to a joyful resurrection
and the glory of your eternal kingdom.

Amen.

Rest eternal grant unto *him*, O Lord.
And let light perpetual shine upon *him*. **Amen.**

9 *If the Committal is to take place elsewhere, this part
of the service may end with an Ascription of Glory,
followed by a Blessing.*

ASCRIPTION OF GLORY

**Glory to the Father, to the Son,
and to the Holy Spirit;
as it was in the beginning, is now,
and shall be for ever.** **Amen.**

or

The minister may say:

> Now to the One who can keep you from falling,
> and set you in the presence of his glory,
> jubilant and above reproach,
> to the only God our Saviour,
> be glory and majesty, power and authority,
> through Jesus Christ our Lord.
>
> **Amen.**

BLESSING

> The peace of God,
> which is beyond all understanding,
> guard your hearts and your thoughts
> in Christ Jesus.
> And the blessing of God,
> Father, Son, and Holy Spirit,
> be with you, now and for ever more.
>
> **Amen.**

THE COMMITTAL

10   SCRIPTURE SENTENCES

One or more of the following sentences may be said:

> We exult in the hope of the divine glory
> which is to be ours.
> Such hope is no fantasy:
> through the Holy Spirit,
> God's love has flooded our hearts.
>
> *Romans 5: 2, 5*

We brought nothing into this world,
and we can take nothing out.

1 Timothy 6: 7

The Lord gives, and the Lord takes away;
blessed be the name of the Lord.

Job 1: 21

As in Adam all die,
so in Christ all will be brought to life.

1 Corinthians 15: 22

Do not be afraid.
I am the first and the last, says the Lord,
and I am the living One;
I was dead and now I am alive for evermore.

Revelation 1: 8, 17 - 18

You were buried with Christ in baptism,
and in that baptism you were raised with him.
And although you were dead because of your sins,
God has brought you to life with Christ.

Colossians 2: 12, 13

If we died with Christ, we shall live with him;
if we endure, we shall reign with him.
If we are faithless, he remains faithful.

2 Timothy 2: 11, 12, 13

There is nothing in death or life,
in the world as it is, or the world as it shall be,
nothing in all creation that can separate us
from the love of God in Christ Jesus our Lord.

Romans 8: 38, 39

Jesus said,
For the moment you are sad;
but I shall see you again,
and then you will be joyful,
and no one shall rob you of your joy.

St John 16: 22

Jesus said,
Because I live, you too will live.

St John 14: 19

Jesus said,
I am the resurrection and the life.
Whoever has faith in me shall live,
even though he dies;
and no one who lives and has faith in me
shall ever die.

St John 11: 25 - 26

11   COMMITTAL

The minister says:

at the grave
We have entrusted our *brother, N . . . ,*
to God's merciful keeping.
We now commit *his* body to the ground,
earth to earth, ashes to ashes, dust to dust,
in the sure and certain hope
of the resurrection to eternal life,
through our Lord Jesus Christ,
who died, was buried,
and rose again for us,
and is alive and reigns for evermore.

Amen.

in the crematorium

> We have entrusted our *brother, N . . . ,*
> to God's merciful keeping.
> We now commit *his* body to be cremated,
> ashes to ashes, dust to dust,
> in the sure and certain hope
> of the resurrection to eternal life,
> through our Lord Jesus Christ,
> who died, was buried,
> and rose again for us,
> and is alive and reigns for evermore.

Amen.

after a brief silence, the minister may say:

> Now, Lord, let your servant go in peace:
> your word has been fulfilled.
> My own eyes have seen the salvation
> which you have prepared
> in the sight of every people:
> a light to reveal you to the nations
> and the glory of your people Israel.

Let us pray.

> God of grace and peace,
> in your Son, Jesus Christ,
> you have given us new birth into a living hope.
> Strengthen us now to live
> in the power of the resurrection,
> and keep us united with our loved one
> and with all your people in heaven and on earth,
> from whom in death we are not divided.
> For you live and reign for ever and ever.

Amen.

12 BLESSING

The minister says:

> The peace of God,
> which is beyond all understanding,
> guard your hearts and your thoughts
> in Christ Jesus.

> And the blessing of God,
> Father, Son, and Holy Spirit,
> be with you, now and for evermore.
>
> *Amen.*

Second Order for a Funeral Service

1 INTRODUCTION

The minister says:

We meet to give thanks for *N* . . . ,
who has gone on before us
into the world of God's eternal light.

While we are glad for *her,*
we feel the sadness of the parting;
and our loving sympathy goes out
to *X* . . . and *Y* . . . and all the family.

Death is always a mystery
[more so when it comes
unexpectedly and suddenly].
Whenever it comes,
it is never the end, but is always a beginning.
We know this because Jesus went down
into the darkness of death,
and came back from it
like the sun in full strength.

The death and resurrection of Jesus
lead to the glory of the morning.
We follow him through the door of death
into a life of perfection and peace,
the life of God himself.

Let us worship God.

2   HYMN

3   PRAYERS

The minister says:

Let us pray.

Living God,
you have lit the day with the sun's light
and the midnight with shining stars.
Lighten our hearts with the bright beams
of the Sun of Righteousness
risen with healing in his wings,
Jesus Christ our Lord.
And so preserve us in the doing of your will,
that at the last we may shine
as the stars for ever;
through the same Jesus Christ our Lord.

Amen.

Heavenly Father,
you have not made us for darkness and death,
but for life with you for ever.
Without you, we have nothing to hope for;
with you, we have nothing to fear.
Speak to us now your words of eternal life.
Lift us from anxiety and guilt
to the light and peace of your presence,
and set the glory of your love before us;
through Jesus Christ our Lord.

Amen.

4   SCRIPTURE READINGS

5   ADDRESS

6   PRAYERS

The minister says:

Let us pray.

Almighty God,
you are the author of life and the giver of victory.
You deliver our eyes from tears,
our feet from falling,
and our souls from death.

In your love for the world
you gave your Son to be our Saviour,
to live our life,
to bear our griefs,
to die our death upon the cross.
You brought him back from death
with power and glory,
and gave him full authority
in heaven and on earth.

We thank you that he conquered
sin and death for us
and opened to us the gate of everlasting life.
We praise you for the great company
of the faithful
whom he has brought through death
to behold your face in glory,
and for those among them
whom we have known and loved,
especially your servant *N* . . .
We praise you
for all the tender and precious memories

she leaves behind.
Now that you have called *her* to yourself,
help us to learn to be content
to release *her* to you,
her Father and our Father.

We trust in your unending mercy
and commend *her* to your care.
Rest eternal grant unto *her*, O Lord.
And let light perpetual shine upon *her*.

God and Father of us all,
by all your dealings with us,
whether of joy or sorrow,
bring us closer to one another and to you.
Help us to walk amid the things of this world
with our eyes wide open to your glory.

Make us sure in every sorrow
that you are still loving us,
sure in every darkness
that you are still guiding us,
sure in death
that you are giving us life for evermore.

To your loving care
we commend those who mourn,
especially *X* . . . and *Y* . . . , and all the family.
Sustain them in the days to come
with treasured memories of the past
and radiant hopes for the future.
And bring us all at the last to fullness of life
with your saints in the kingdom of heaven;
through Jesus Christ our Lord.   ***Amen.***

Our Father . . .

7 HYMN

8 COMMITTAL

The minister says:

Our Lord Jesus Christ said,

'I am the resurrection and the life.
Whoever has faith in me shall live,
even though he dies;
and no one who lives and has faith in me
shall ever die.'   *St John 11: 25 - 26*

at the grave
We have entrusted our *sister*, *N* . . . ,
into the hands of God.
We therefore commit *her* body to the ground,
earth to earth, ashes to ashes, dust to dust,
in the sure and certain hope
of the resurrection to eternal life,
through our Lord Jesus Christ,
who died, was buried,
and rose again for us,
and is alive and reigns for evermore.

at the crematorium
We have entrusted our *sister*, *N* . . . ,
into the hands of God.
We therefore commit *her* body to be cremated,
ashes to ashes, dust to dust,
in the sure and certain hope
of the resurrection to eternal life,
through our Lord Jesus Christ,
who died, was buried,
and rose again for us,

and is alive and reigns for evermore.

God will show us the path of life;
in his presence is fullness of joy,
at his right hand
there are pleasures for evermore.   *Psalm 16: 11*

Let us pray.

Eternal God,
in Jesus Christ
you have given to us a true faith and a sure hope.
Help us to live
as those who believe and trust in
the communion of saints,
the forgiveness of sins,
and the resurrection to eternal life.
Strengthen this faith and hope in us
all the days of our life;
then bring us at our last awakening
to the house and gate of heaven,
to enter into that gate
and to dwell in that house,
where we shall be one with you
and with all your saints for ever;
through Jesus Christ our Lord.   **Amen.**

9   BLESSING

The minister says:

Go forth in the peace of God.

And the blessing of God almighty,
Father, Son, and Holy Spirit,
be with you all.   **Amen.**

Scripture Readings
for
Funeral Services

OLD TESTAMENT

Every being born of woman
is short-lived and full of trouble.
He blossoms like a flower and withers away;
fleeting as a shadow, he does not endure.
Truly the days of such a one's life
are determined
and the number of his months is known to you;
you have laid down a limit
which cannot be exceeded.

Job 14: 1 - 2, 5

For everything its season,
and for every activity under heaven its time:

a time to be born and a time to die;
a time to plant and a time to uproot;
a time to kill and a time to heal;
a time to break down and a time to build up;
a time to weep and a time to laugh;
a time for mourning and a time for dancing;
a time to scatter stones
and a time to gather them;
a time to embrace
and a time to abstain from embracing;
a time to seek and a time to lose;

a time to keep and a time to discard;
a time to tear and a time to mend;
a time for silence and a time for speech;
a time to love and a time to hate;
a time for war and a time for peace.
God has made everything to suit its time.
I know that whatever God does lasts for ever;
there is no adding to it, no taking away.
And he has done it all in such a way
that everyone must feel awe in his presence.

Ecclesiastes 3: 1 - 8, 11, 14

The Lord God will destroy death for ever.
He will wipe away the tears from every face,
and throughout the world
remove the indignities from his people.
The Lord has spoken.

On that day, the people will say:
'See, this is our God;
we have waited for him and he will deliver us.
This is the Lord for whom we have waited;
let us rejoice and exult in his deliverance.'

Lord, you keep those of firm purpose
untroubled because of their trust in you.
Trust in the Lord for ever,
for he is an eternal rock.

Isaiah 25: 8 - 9; 26: 3 - 4

Do you not know, have you not heard?
The Lord, the eternal God,
creator of earth's farthest bounds,
does not weary or grow faint;

his understanding cannot be fathomed.
He gives vigour to the weary,
new strength to the exhausted.
Young men may grow weary and faint,
even the fittest may stumble and fall;
but those who look to the Lord
will win new strength,
they will soar as on eagles' wings;
they will run and not feel faint,
march on and not grow weary.

Isaiah 40: 28 - 31

Peace has gone from my life
and I have forgotten what prosperity is.
Then I cry out that my strength has gone
and so has my hope in the Lord.

I shall wait patiently
because I take this to heart:
the Lord's love is surely not exhausted,
nor has his compassion failed;
they are new every morning,
so great is his constancy.
'The Lord,' I say, 'is all that I have;
therefore I shall wait for him patiently.'

The Lord is good to those who look to him,
to anyone who seeks him;
it is good to wait in patience
for deliverance by the Lord.

Lamentations 3: 17 - 18, 21 - 26

*The following from the Old Testament Apocrypha
may also be read:*

The souls of the just are in God's hand;
no torment will touch them.
In the eyes of the foolish
they seemed to be dead;
their departure was reckoned as defeat,
and their going from us as disaster.
But they are at peace,
for though in the sight of men
they may suffer punishment,
they have a sure hope of immortality;
and after a little chastisement
they will receive great blessings,
because God has tested them
and found them worthy to be his.

Wisdom 3: 1 - 5

The just person,
even one who dies an untimely death,
will be at rest.
It is not length of life and number of years
which bring the honour due to age;
if people have understanding,
they have grey hairs enough,
and an unblemished life is true ripeness of age.
There was once such a man who pleased God,
and God accepted him and took him
while still living from among sinners.

He was snatched away
before his mind could be perverted
by wickedness
or his soul deceived by falsehood;
in a short time
he came to the perfection of a full span of years.
His soul was pleasing to the Lord,

who removed him early from a wicked world.
People see this but give it no thought;
they do not lay to heart the truth,
that those whom God has chosen
enjoy his grace and mercy,
and that he comes to the help of his holy people.

Wisdom 4: 7 - 11, 13 - 15

PSALMS

The Lord is my shepherd; I shall not want.
He maketh me to lie down in green pastures;
he leadeth me beside the still waters.
He restoreth my soul;
he leadeth me in the paths of righteousness
for his name's sake.
Yea, though I walk through the valley
of the shadow of death,
I will fear no evil;
for thou art with me;
thy rod and staff they comfort me.
Thou preparest a table before me
in the presence of mine enemies;
thou anointest my head with oil;
my cup runneth over.
Surely goodness and mercy shall follow me
all the days of my life;
and I will dwell in the house of the Lord
for ever.   *Psalm 23 (AV)*

or

The Lord is my shepherd; I lack for nothing.
He makes me lie down in green pastures,
he leads me to water where I may rest;

he revives my spirit;
for his name's sake he guides me
in the right paths.
Even were I to walk through a valley
of deepest darkness
I should fear no harm, for you are with me;
your shepherd's staff and crook
afford me comfort.

You spread a table for me
in the presence of my enemies;
you have richly anointed my head with oil,
and my cup brims over.
Goodness and love unfailing will follow me
all the days of my life,
and I shall dwell in the house of the Lord
throughout the years to come.   *Psalm 23*

The Lord is compassionate and gracious,
long-suffering and ever faithful;
he will not always accuse
or nurse his anger for ever.
He has not treated us as our sins deserve
or repaid us according to our misdeeds.
As the heavens tower high above the earth,
so outstanding is his love
towards those who fear him.
As far as east is from west,
so far from us has he put away our offences.
As a father has compassion on his children,
so the Lord has compassion
on those who fear him.
For he knows how we were made,
he remembers that we are but dust.

The days of a mortal are as grass;
he blossoms like a wild flower in the meadow:
a wind passes over him, and he is gone,
and his place knows him no more.
But the Lord's love is for ever
on those who fear him,
and his righteousness on their posterity,
on those who hold fast to his covenant,
who keep his commandments in mind.

Psalm 103: 8 - 18

If I lift up my eyes to the hills,
where shall I find help?
My help comes only from the Lord,
maker of heaven and earth.
He will not let your foot stumble;
he who guards you will not sleep.
The guardian of Israel never slumbers,
never sleeps.
The Lord is your guardian,
your protector at your right hand;
the sun will not strike you by day
nor the moon by night.
The Lord will guard you against all harm;
he will guard your life.
The Lord will guard you as you come and go,
now and for evermore.

Psalm 121

Lord, out of the depths have I called to you;
hear my cry, Lord;
let your ears be attentive to my supplication.
If you, Lord, should keep account of sins,
who could hold his ground?

But with you is forgiveness,
so that you may be revered.

I wait for the Lord with longing;
I put my hope in his word.
My soul waits for the Lord
more eagerly than watchmen for the morning.
Like those who watch for the morning,
let Israel look for the Lord.
For in the Lord is love unfailing,
and great is his power to deliver.
He alone will set Israel free from all their sins.

Psalm 130

also

Psalm   8
                16: 8 - 11
                39: 4 - 7, 12
                42: 1 - 8
                43: 3 - 5
                46
                62: 5 - 8
                90: 1 - 6, 10, 12
                116
                118: 14 - 21, 28 - 29
                138
                139: 1 - 14, 17 - 18, 23

NEW TESTAMENT

Epistle

I reckon that the sufferings we now endure
bear no comparison with the glory,
as yet unrevealed,
which is in store for us.
In everything, as we know,

the Spirit co-operates for good
with those who love God
and are called according to his purpose.

If God is on our side, who is against us?
He did not spare his own Son,
but gave him up for us all;
how can he fail to lavish
every other gift upon us?
Who will bring a charge against those
whom God has chosen?
Not God, who acquits!
Who will pronounce judgement?
Not Christ, who died, or rather, rose again;
not Christ, who is at God's right hand
and pleads our cause!
Then what can separate us
from the love of Christ?
Can affliction or hardship?
Can persecution, hunger, nakedness,
danger, or sword?
'We are being done to death for your sake
all day long,' as scripture says –
and yet throughout it all,
overwhelming victory is ours
through him who loved us.
For I am convinced
that there is nothing in death or life,
in the realm of spirits or superhuman powers,
in the world as it is or the world as it shall be,
in the forces of the universe,
in heights or depths –
nothing in all creation
that can separate us from the love of God
in Christ Jesus our Lord.

Romans 8: 18, 28, 31 - 36a, 37 - 39

None of us lives, and equally none of us dies,
for himself alone.
If we live, we live for the Lord;
and if we die, we die for the Lord.
So whether we live or die, we belong to the Lord.
This is why Christ died and lived again,
to establish his lordship
over both dead and living.
You, then, why do you pass judgement
on your fellow-Christian?
And you, why do you look down
on your fellow-Christian?
We shall all stand before God's tribunal;
for we read in scripture,
'As I live, says the Lord,
to me every knee shall bow
and every tongue acknowledge God.'
So, you see,
each of us will be answerable to God.

Romans 14: 7 - 12

If it is for this life only
that Christ has given us hope,
we of all people are most to be pitied.
But the truth is, Christ was raised to life –
the firstfruits of the harvest of the dead.
For since it was a man
who brought death into the world,
a man also brought resurrection of the dead.
As in Adam all die,
so in Christ all will be brought to life;
but each in proper order:
Christ the firstfruits,
and afterwards, at his coming,
those who belong to Christ.

But you may ask, how are the dead raised?
In what kind of body?
What stupid questions!
The seed you sow does not come to life
unless it has first died;
and what you sow is not the body that shall be,
but a bare grain, of wheat perhaps,
or something else;
and God gives it the body of his choice,
each seed its own particular body.

So it is with the resurrection of the dead:
what is sown as a perishable thing
is raised imperishable.
Sown in humiliation, it is raised in glory;
sown in weakness, it is raised in power;
sown a physical body,
it is raised a spiritual body.

What I mean, my friends, is this:
flesh and blood can never possess
the kingdom of God,
the perishable cannot possess the imperishable.
This perishable body must be clothed
with the imperishable,
and what is mortal with immortality.
And when this perishable body
has been clothed with the imperishable,
and our mortality has been clothed
with immortality,
then the saying of scripture will come true:
'Death is swallowed up; victory is won!'
'O Death, where is your victory?
O Death, where is your sting?'
But thanks be to God!
He gives us victory

through our Lord Jesus Christ.

Therefore, my dear friends,
stand firm and immovable,
and work for the Lord always,
work without limit,
since you know that in the Lord
your labour cannot be lost.

1 Corinthians 15: 19 - 23, 35 - 38,
42 - 44, 50, 53 - 55, 57 - 58

✓ Praise be to the God and Father
of our Lord Jesus Christ,
the all-merciful Father,
the God whose consolation never fails us!
He consoles us in all our troubles,
so that we in turn may be able to console others
in any trouble of theirs,
and to share with them
the consolation we ourselves receive from God.

2 Corinthians 1: 3 - 4

✓ We wish you not to remain in ignorance, friends,
about those who sleep in death;
you should not grieve like the rest of mankind,
who have no hope.
We believe that Jesus died and rose again;
so too will God
bring those who died as Christians
to be with Jesus.
Console one another, then, with these words.

1 Thessalonians 4: 13 - 14, 18

I saw a new heaven and a new earth,
for the first heaven and the first earth
had vanished,
and there was no longer any sea.
I saw the Holy City, new Jerusalem,
coming down out of heaven from God,
made ready like a bride
adorned for her husband.
I heard a loud voice
proclaiming from the throne:
'Now God has his dwelling with mankind!
He will dwell among them
and they shall be his people,
and God himself will be with them.
He will wipe every tear from their eyes.
There shall be an end to death,
and to mourning and crying and pain,
for the old order has passed away!'
The throne of God and of the Lamb will be there,
and his servants shall worship him;
they shall see him face to face
and bear his name on their foreheads.
There shall be no more night,
nor will they need the light of lamp or sun,
for the Lord God will give them light;
and they shall reign for ever.

Revelation 21: 1 - 4; 22: 3b - 5

also

Acts	10: 34 - 43
Romans	5: 5 - 11
Romans	6: 3 - 9
Romans	8: 14 - 24a
2 Corinthians	4: 7 - 18
2 Corinthians	4: 14 to 5: 1
2 Corinthians	5: 1, 6 - 10

Ephesians	2: 4 - 9a
1 Thessalonians	4: 13 - 18
1 Thessalonians	5: 9 - 11, 23 - 24
2 Timothy	2: 8 - 13
1 Peter	1: 3 - 9
Revelation	7: 9 - 17

Gospel

Jesus said,
All that the Father gives me will come to me,
and anyone who comes to me
I will never turn away.
I have come down from heaven,
to do not my own will,
but the will of him who sent me.
It is his will that I should not lose
even one of those he has given me,
but should raise them all up on the last day.
For it is my Father's will
that everyone who sees the Son
and has faith in him
should have eternal life;
and I will raise them up on the last day.

St John 6: 37 - 40

Jesus said,
Let not your heart be troubled:
ye believe in God, believe also in me.
In my Father's house are many mansions:
if it were not so, I would have told you.
I go to prepare a place for you.
And if I go and prepare a place for you,
I will come again, and receive you unto myself;
that where I am, there ye may be also.

And whither I go ye know,
and the way ye know.
I am the way, the truth, and the life:
no man cometh unto the Father, but by me.
Peace I leave with you,
my peace I give unto you:
not as the world giveth, give I unto you.
Let not your heart be troubled,
neither let it be afraid.

St John 14: 1 - 4, 6, 27 (AV)

or

Jesus said,
Set your troubled hearts at rest.
Trust in God always; trust also in me.
There are many dwelling-places
in my Father's house;
if it were not so I should have told you;
for I am going to prepare a place for you.
And if I go and prepare a place for you,
I shall come again and take you to myself,
so that where I am you may be also;
and you know the way I am taking.
I am the way, the truth, and the life;
no one comes to the Father except by me.
Peace is my parting gift to you,
my own peace, such as the world cannot give.
Set your troubled hearts at rest,
and banish your fears.   *St John 14: 1 - 4, 6, 27*

also

St Mark	16: 1 - 8a
St Luke	7: 11 - 16
St John	11: 17 - 27
St John	20: 24 - 29

Order for use in Distressing Circumstances

The following may be added to, or substituted for, material at the appropriate places in the First or Second Order.

The Prayer at no. 4 has three parts: the general beginning, the specific thanksgivings and petitions, and the section headed 'in each circumstance'.

1   SCRIPTURE SENTENCES

> God is our refuge and our stronghold,
> a timely help in trouble;
> so we are not afraid.
>
> *Psalm 46: 1, 2*

> The Lord's love is surely not exhausted,
> nor has his compassion failed.
>
> *Lamentations 3: 22*

> God cares for you,
> so cast all your anxiety on him.   *1 Peter 5: 7*

> Gladness and joy will come upon God's people,
> while suffering and weariness flee away.
>
> *Isaiah 35: 10b*

> God has said,
> 'I will never leave you or desert you.'
>
> *Hebrews 13: 5b*

Jesus said,
'Come to me, all who are weary
and whose load is heavy;
I will give you rest.'   *St Matthew 11: 28*

2   PRAYER

God of all comfort,
in this time of distress and grief,
we have come to tell you our sorrow,
and to rest ourselves
within the circle of your love.

Your hands made us and formed us,
and you despise nothing you have made.
Set free our souls from restlessness,
and raise our downcast spirits
from perplexity and doubt
to the steadfast love
of your unchanging peace;
through Jesus Christ our Lord.

Amen.

3   SCRIPTURE READING

My God, my God, why have you forsaken me?
Why are you so far from saving me,
so far from heeding my groans?
My God, by day I cry to you,
but there is no answer;
in the night I cry with no respite.
In you our fathers put their trust;
they trusted, and you rescued them.
To you they cried and were delivered;
in you they trusted and were not discomfited.

Do not remain far away, Lord;
you are my help, come quickly to my aid.

Psalm 22: 1 - 2, 4 - 5, 19

Jesus says,
In very truth I tell you,
whoever heeds what I say
and puts his trust in him who sent me
has eternal life;
he does not come to judgement,
but has already passed from death to life.

St John 5: 24

4   PRAYERS

We praise you, O God,
we acclaim you as Lord;
all creation worships you,
the Father everlasting.
To you the angels sing in endless praise.
The glorious company of the saints praise you.
Throughout the world
the holy Church acclaims you,
Father, Son, and Holy Spirit,
one God, now and for ever.

You, Christ, are the king of glory.
In the tender compassion of God,
you came, the dawn from on high,
to shine on those who dwell in darkness
and the shadow of death.
You overcame the sting of death
and opened the kingdom of heaven
to all believers.
Chase away the darkness of our night
and restore morning to the world.

Enlighten us with the healing beams of your love
and guide our feet into the way of peace.

Eternal God,
our life is a fleeting shadow that does not endure.
Our years pass quickly,
our days are few and full of trouble.
We do not know what a day may bring forth.
You have promised that you will not fail us
nor forsake us,
and that you will hear when we call to you.

Loving God,
in whom sinners find mercy and saints find joy,
we thank you for *N* . . . ,
and for the qualities that made *him* special to us.
We remember with grateful hearts
all that *he* gave and received during *his* life.
We think especially of *his* . . .
(*appropriate attributes and activities*).

after a wasting illness

We thank you that *N* . . .
no longer has to suffer pain or fear,
grappling with death, fighting for life;
and that for *him*
limitations are ended,
weakness is overcome,
and death itself is conquered.

As *he* passes from our earthly sight,
we thank you for the years
of *his* presence among us.
And while we feel the pain of the parting,
we rejoice in the faith
that *he* has gone to be with you,

for in your presence is the fullness of joy,
at your right hand are pleasures for evermore.

Bless those who had the care of *him*,
especially doctors, nurses, and technicians.
Guide and prosper
all who are engaged in medical research:
may they never lose heart
in their search to discover
the way of health and healing.
Grant that by their vision and courage
we may advance in our understanding
of the world
and be better able to help those in need.

after a suicide

We thank you that *N* . . .
is beyond the reach of darkness and despair,
but not beyond the touch of your care and love.
The ending of *his* earthly life seems senseless.
We cannot fathom the anguish of mind
he went through.

Forgive us for those times and ways
we failed *him*.
Help us to forgive *him*
for any hurt we feel *he* has inflicted on us;
help us to forgive ourselves
for any harm we fear we may have caused *him*.

Give us grace to be content to release *him* to you,
in the assurance and hope
that you will show *him* the path of life
and lead *him* to walk in your presence
in the land of the living.

<u>*after violence*</u>

We thank you that *N* . . .
has outsoared the shadow of our night,
with its cruelty, violence, and pain.
When the trouble was near,
we could not understand
how you seemed to remain far away.
And yet it is to you we turn;
for in life and death
it is you alone whom we can trust,
and yours alone is the love that holds us fast.
We find it hard to forgive the deed
that has brought us so much grief.
But we know that, if life is soured by bitterness,
an unforgiving spirit brings no peace.
Lord, save us and help us.
Strengthen in us the faith and hope that *N* . . .
is freed from the past with all its hurt,
and rests for ever in the calm security
of your love.

<u>*in each circumstance*</u>

Gracious God,
sustain and support those
whose love for *N* . . . was dearest,
whose loss is greatest.
May they find beyond their tears
unclouded visions of your love,
and may they see beyond their darkness
the clear shining of your light.
Set their troubled hearts at rest,
banish all their fears,
and hold them in the comfort of your peace;
through Jesus Christ our Lord.   ***Amen.***

Our Father . . .

Additional Prayers for Funeral Services

APPROACH

1   Almighty God,
    in mystery you created all things;
    you made us in your own image;
    you love us with an everlasting love.
    Grant us the assurance
    of your loving presence with us now.
    Bear us gently in your gracious hands,
    and bring us in our sorrow
    the comfort for which our hearts cry out;
    through Jesus Christ our Lord.   *Amen.*

2   Gracious God,
    you made us and you love us.
    Your love is our security and our hope.
    We find our true selves, complete and whole,
    only within your love.
    And because in love you have prepared for us
    a destiny more wonderful than we can imagine,
    we trust you with our loved ones and ourselves;
    in Jesus' name.   *Amen.*

3   Eternal God,
    we come to you
    because the friend we knew and loved has died,
    and our hearts are cold,
    and our minds perplexed.

Whatever we may be thinking and feeling,
we know that you will understand.
For you made us,
and in your Son, Jesus,
you shared our life and experience.
Accept us as we are,
forgive us for our lack of faith,
inspire in us a living hope;
through the same Jesus Christ our Lord.

Amen.

4   Lord of life,
in the beginning
you formed us from the dust of the earth
and breathed life into our frame.
Your goodness and mercy
follow us all our days,
and at our departing
we return to your loving hand.
Assure us of your presence now,
and lead us to life everlasting and full of glory;
through Jesus Christ our Lord.   *Amen.*

BEFORE AND AFTER SCRIPTURE READINGS

before

5   Lord Jesus,
as we bow in the presence of death,
stand within the shadows beside us
to bring the light of your deathless love.

Lord, to whom can we go but to you?
Your words are words of eternal life.

Amen.

6   Father,
     your love is stronger than death.
     Day by day you bring us towards life at its fullest.
     Help us as we hear your promises
     to believe them
     and to receive the comfort they offer.
     Fill us with joy and peace in believing
     so that we may have hope
     through the power of your Holy Spirit.   *Amen.*

7   Eternal God our heavenly Father,
     you love us with an everlasting love
     and are able to turn
     the shadow of death into the morning.
     In the silence of this hour
     speak to us of eternal things,
     that through patience and comfort
     of the scriptures
     we may have hope,
     and be lifted above our darkness and distress
     into the light and peace of your presence;
     through Jesus Christ our Lord.
                                        Amen.

8   Gracious God,
     help us to listen for your word.
     Console us in our trouble,
     so that we in turn
     may be able to console others
     in any trouble of theirs,
     and to share with them
     the consolation we receive from you:
     that together
     we may find light in our darkness
     and faith in the midst of doubt;
     through Jesus Christ our Lord.   *Amen.*

after

9   Lord,
     we take strength from these mighty promises,
     the strong words written by those
     who experienced your faithfulness,
     and share with us their assurance.

     But you give us more than words.
     You give us Jesus Christ,
     who is himself your message,
     the guarantor of his gospel,
     present in his risen power,
     to assure us of his victory over death,
     and to share with us his triumph.

     We thank you for your readiness
     to speak with us,
     and for your grace to help us in our time of need;
     through Jesus Christ our Lord.   ***Amen.***

THANKSGIVING

10 ᵻ Gracious God,
     we praise you
     for all that you have done through Jesus Christ.
     By giving him to live and die for us,
     you showed us love without limit;
     by raising him from the dead,
     you brought us life without end.
     For the assurance and hope of our faith,
     and for those whom you have received
     into your eternal joy,
     we give you thanks and praise;
     through Jesus Christ our Lord.   ***Amen.***

11 ⯈ Heavenly Father,
       we thank you for all the gifts
       of your providence and grace.

       You have promised that
       out of darkness light shall shine,
       light which is the knowledge of your glory
       in the face of Jesus Christ.
       We thank you that his light
       dawns upon us daily,
       and brings us a grateful heart
       and a will to love and serve you
       to the end of our days.

       We thank you for your gift to us of human love;
       for the first love we know at our birth,
       a mother's love and a father's care;
       for the love that unites husband and wife;
       for the love of parents and children,
       and the family circle.

       Comfort us now with the assurance
       of the life which is beyond this life,
       and of a reunion with those
       we have loved long since
       and who wait for us in your heavenly presence;
       through Jesus Christ our Lord.   ***Amen.***

12 ⬤ We bless you, Lord,
       that Jesus came into a home like ~~ours,~~ *this.*
       and knew the loyalties and tensions
       of family living;
       that he worked as a carpenter,
       and knew the frustrations and fulfilment
       of a daily task;
       that he offered friendship,

and knew how it might be a source
of healing and courage at a time like this;
that he went about doing good,
even at the risk of being misunderstood;
that he brought glory
to ordinary tasks and relationships,
and dignity to every human being.

Above all,
we bless you that Jesus went to the lonely place,
carrying his cross;
that he died for us,
confronting all that threatened to destroy us;
that he came back from death,
making us more than conquerors,
and showing that death
shall not have dominion;
and that he leads us into his kingdom
to share with him the life everlasting.

Because he has been with us,
we shall be with him.
Because he has been like us,
we shall be like him.
Because he is for us,
who can be against us?
Thanks be to God, who gives us the victory,
through our Lord Jesus Christ! ***Amen.***

THOSE WHO MOURN

13 ⚜ Almighty God,
Lord of life and vanquisher of death,
we praise you for the sure hope of eternal life
you have given us

in the resurrection of our Lord Jesus Christ;
and we pray that all who mourn
the loss of those dear to them
may enter into his victory and know his peace;
for his name's sake.   ***Amen.***

Go with us now, as we leave this place .... and grant us Your blessing ....

14   God of hope and giver of all comfort,
we commend to your tender care
those who mourn the loss of loved ones.
Give them the peace
which is beyond all understanding,
and assure them that neither death nor life
can separate them from your love
in Jesus Christ our Lord.   ***Amen.***

OFFERING OF LIFE

15   Eternal God,
we offer you the past.
We are grateful for the memories
that will sustain us,
even if they bring us tears.
We thank you for good things shared,
and for times of contentment and affection.
We acknowledge also the unfinished business,
the vain regrets,
the guilt and anger,
bewilderment and hurt,
and thank you that in your love,
you can forgive and heal us.

We offer you the present.
You are at work
in the duties that demand our attention,
in the responsibilities that will not go away,

in the kindly words of friends,
in the sympathy and loyalty of colleagues.
We pray for grace to recognise
that these are channels of your mercy,
and to receive them as your gifts of kindness
and of love.

We offer you the future.
It is changed,
because *N* . . . is no longer with us,
and we feel uncertain and diminished.
Yet you will not fail us.
You still have gifts for us to receive,
work for us to do,
discoveries of your unfailing grace
for us to make.
And at the last you will re-unite us
with those who have gone home before us,
in the new life of your everlasting kingdom.

This offering of all our life
we make in the name of Jesus Christ our Lord,
who died for us and rose again,
and is alive and reigns
with you and the Holy Spirit,
one God, now and ever.   ***Amen.***

PETITION

16   Lord,
        we do not know whether our days
        will be many or few.
        Help us to put into each day's living
        something of worth, and kindness,
        integrity, courage, and love.

These are gifts you offer us,
gifts that will last,
for they are the sign
of your Spirit at work among us.
We ask this in Jesus' name.

Amen.

17   Risen, reigning Christ,
in you past, present, and future
are brought together in one great hope.
Renew our faith in you,
so that neither the past may hinder us,
the present overwhelm us,
nor the future frighten us.
You have brought us this far;
continue to lead us
until our hope is fulfilled
and we join all God's people
in never-ending praise;
for your name's sake.

Amen.

18   O Lord,
support us all the day long
of this troublous life,
until the shadows lengthen
and the evening comes,
and the busy world is hushed,
the fever of life is over,
and our work done.
Then Lord, in your mercy,
grant us safe lodging,
a holy rest,
and peace at the last;
through Jesus Christ our Lord.

Amen.

THE COMMUNION OF SAINTS

19   Eternal God,
        before your face
        the generations rise and pass away.
        We praise your name for all your servants
        departed this life in your faith and love,
        for those dear to us,
        and especially for your servant *N* . . .

        We thank you for your loving-kindness
        towards *him*,
        for all *he* was throughout *his* earthly life,
        and for all *he* accomplished by your grace.
        We thank you that for *him*
        sorrow and sickness are ended,
        that death itself is past,
        and that *he* lives for ever
        in your love and care.

        Encourage us by the example of your saints,
        that we may run with resolution
        the race which lies ahead of us,
        our eyes fixed on Jesus,
        the pioneer and perfecter of faith;
        till we shall come at last,
        with all whom we have loved,
        to the joy and peace of your eternal presence;
        through Jesus Christ our Lord.   ***Amen.***

20   Bring us at last to your nearer presence,
        where we shall rediscover one another
        in the light of your love,
        and be given back to one another
        in a bond that nothing shall sever;
        through Jesus Christ our Lord.   ***Amen.***

21   Almighty God,
        you have knit together your elect
        into one communion and fellowship
        in the mystical body of your Son.
        Give us grace to follow your blessed saints
        in all virtuous and godly living,
        that we may come to those joys beyond all praise
        which you have prepared
        for those who perfectly love you;
        through Jesus Christ our Lord.

Amen.

Facing Death

22   God of all hope,
        give us your continuing grace,
        that it may be joy for us when our call comes
        to commit our spirits to our heavenly Father,
        from whom we came and to whom we go;
        through Jesus Christ our Lord.

Amen.

23   Merciful Jesus Christ,
        we remember that on the cross
        you gave your spirit
        into the hands of your Father.
        By the memory of your death,
        help us to live day by day for you,
        so that, at the hour of our departing,
        we may commend ourselves trustingly
        to the same everlasting arms,
        and be received into your heavenly kingdom,
        to dwell with you for ever;
        for your endless mercies' sake.

Amen.

COMMENDATION

24   Our *brother N* . . .
          has gone forth upon *his* journey,
          in the name of God the Father who created *him,*
          in the name of God the Son who redeemed *him,*
          in the name of God the Spirit
          who sanctified *him;*
          in the company of angels and archangels
          and all the hosts of heaven.

          May *his* dwelling place be in heavenly Jerusalem,
          and all *his* portion be peace.   **Amen.**

COMMITTAL

25   *at the grave*

              We have entrusted our *brother N* . . . ,
              into the hands of God.
              We now commit *his* body to the ground,
              earth to earth, ashes to ashes, dust to dust;
              having our whole trust and confidence
              in the mercy of our heavenly Father,
              and in the victory of his Son,
              Jesus Christ our Lord,
              who died, was buried, and rose again for us,
              and is alive and reigns for ever and ever.
                                                    Amen.

      at the crematorium

              We have entrusted our *brother N* . . . ,
              into the hands of God.
              We now commit *his* body to be cremated,

ashes to ashes, dust to dust;
having our whole trust and confidence
in the mercy of our heavenly Father,
and in the victory of his Son,
Jesus Christ our Lord,
who died, was buried, and rose again for us,
and is alive and reigns for ever and ever.

Amen.

26   *at the crematorium*

We have entrusted our *brother N . . .* ,
into the hands of God.
We now commit his body to its elements,
ashes to ashes, dust to dust.
We place our confidence in the love of God
who never lets us go;
we claim the victory of Jesus Christ
who conquered death for us;
and we take to heart
the comfort of the Holy Spirit,
who carries us through life to life eternal.

We affirm that none of us
lives in vain,
labours in vain,
gives or receives or loves in vain.
Within the eternal purpose,
each of us is worth more
than we can ever calculate.
For *N . . . 's* life as it touched and enriched ours,
we give God the glory.
May he grant to all his people,
pardon, peace, and life eternal;
in the name of Jesus Christ our Lord.

Amen.

27 *In place of the Committal, when no body has been found, or recovered from the sea, some of the following may be used:*

The dust returns to the earth as it began,
and the spirit returns to God who made it.

Ecclesiastes 12: 7

Their bodies are buried in peace;
and their name lives for ever.

Ecclesiasticus 44: 14

Jesus said,
'I give them eternal life
and they will never perish.
No one can snatch them out of the Father's care.'

St John 10: 28, 29

Let us pray.

Heavenly Father,
we have lost in death our friend *N* . . .
We commend *him* to your care and keeping,
in the sure and certain hope
of the resurrection to eternal life
through Jesus Christ your Son our Lord,
who died, was buried, and rose again for us,
and is alive and reigns for ever and ever.

Amen.

Order for the Funeral of a Child

1 CALL TO WORSHIP

> We have come together to worship God,
> to thank him for his love,
> and to remember the [short] life of *N* . . . ;
> to share our grief
> and to commend *him* to the eternal care of God.

> We meet in the faith that death is not the end,
> and may be faced without fear,
> bitterness, or guilt.

> Let us worship God.

2 SCRIPTURE SENTENCES

> As a mother comforts her child,
> so shall I myself comfort you.
>
> *Isaiah 66: 13*

> As a father has compassion on his children,
> so the Lord has compassion
> on those who fear him.
>
> *Psalm 103: 13*

> Is all well with the child?
> All is well.
>
> *2 Kings 4: 26*

Jerusalem will be called the City of Faithfulness:
and the city will be full of boys and girls
playing in the streets.   *Zechariah 8: 3, 5*

The eternal God is our refuge,
and underneath are the everlasting arms.
    Deuteronomy 33: 27 (AV)

Now we see only puzzling reflections
in a mirror;
but then we shall see face to face.
Our knowledge now is partial;
then it will be whole,
like God's knowledge of us.
    1 Corinthians 13: 12

Jesus said,
Blessed are the sorrowful;
they shall find consolation.   *St Matthew 5: 4*

3   HYMN

4   PRAYERS

God of unfailing compassion,
in your creative love and tenderness
you gave us *N* . . . ,
so full of hope for the future.
You are the source of all our lives,
the strength of all our days.

You did not make us for darkness and death
but so that we should live in you
and see you face to face.
Help us to comfort one another
with the consolation

we ourselves receive from you;
through Jesus Christ our Lord.   ***Amen.***

Lord Jesus Christ,
you became a little child for our sake,
sharing our human life:
   bless us and keep us.

You grew in wisdom and grace,
learning obedience:
   bless us and keep us.

You welcomed little children,
promising them the kingdom of heaven:
   bless us and keep us.

You comforted those who mourned,
grieving for their children:
   bless us and keep us.

You took upon yourself
the suffering of us all:
   bless us and keep us.

Lord Jesus Christ,
you rose from the dead
bringing life eternal:
   bless us and keep us.   ***Amen.***

Gracious God,
speak to us now
the message of your eternal love.
Lift us above our sorrow
to the light and peace
of your presence;
through Jesus Christ our Lord.   ***Amen.***

5   SCRIPTURE READINGS

Hear the Word of God,
written for our help and comfort.

OLD TESTAMENT

As a mother comforts her son
so shall I myself comfort you;
in Jerusalem you will find comfort.

Isaiah 66: 13

Psalms

As a father has compassion on his children,
so the Lord has compassion
on those who fear him;
for he knows how we were made,
he remembers that we are but dust.
The days of a mortal are as grass;
he blossoms like a wild flower in the meadow:
a wind passes over him, and he is gone,
and his place knows him no more.
But the Lord's love is for ever
on those who fear him,
and his righteousness on their posterity,
on those who hold fast to his covenant,
who keep his commandments in mind.

Psalm 103: 13 - 17

The Lord is my shepherd; I shall not want.
He maketh me to lie down in green pastures;
he leadeth me beside the still waters.
He restoreth my soul;
he leadeth me in the paths of righteousness
for his name's sake.

Yea, though I walk
through the valley of the shadow of death,
I will fear no evil;
for thou art with me;
thy rod and staff they comfort me.
Thou preparest a table before me
in the presence of mine enemies;
thou anointest my head with oil;
my cup runneth over.
Surely goodness and mercy shall follow me
all the days of my life;
and I will dwell
in the house of the Lord for ever.   *Psalm 23 (AV)*

or

The Lord is my shepherd; I lack for nothing.
He makes me lie down in green pastures,
he leads me to water where I may rest;
he revives my spirit;
for his name's sake he guides me
in the right paths.
Even were I to walk through a valley
of deepest darkness
I should fear no harm, for you are with me;
your shepherd's staff and crook
afford me comfort.

You spread a table for me
in the presence of my enemies;
you have richly anointed my head with oil,
and my cup brims over.
Goodness and love unfailing will follow me
all the days of my life,
and I shall dwell in the house of the Lord
throughout the years to come.   *Psalm 23*

Epistle

I am convinced that there is nothing
in death or life,
in the realm of spirits or superhuman powers,
in the world as it is or the world as it shall be,
in the forces of the universe,
in heights or depths –
nothing in all creation that can separate us
from the love of God in Christ Jesus our Lord.

Romans 8: 38 - 39

Consider how great is the love
which the Father has bestowed on us
in calling us his children!
For that is what we are.
The reason why the world does not recognize us
is that it has not known him.
Dear friends, we are now God's children;
what we shall be has not yet been disclosed,
but we know that when Christ appears
we shall be like him,
because we shall see him as he is.
As he is pure,
everyone who has grasped this hope
makes himself pure.

1 John 3: 1 - 3

I heard a loud voice
proclaiming from the throne:
'Now at last
God has his dwelling with mankind!
He will dwell among them
and they shall be his people,
and God himself will be with them.
He will wipe every tear from their eyes;
there shall be an end to death,

and to mourning and crying and pain;
for the old order has passed away!'

Revelation 21: 3 - 4

Gospel

The disciples came to Jesus and asked,
'Who is the greatest in the kingdom of heaven?'
He called a child,
set him in front of them, and said,
'Truly I tell you:
unless you turn round and become like children,
you will never enter the kingdom of heaven.
Whoever humbles himself
and becomes like this child
will be the greatest in the kingdom of heaven,
and whoever receives one such child
in my name receives me.
See that you do not despise
one of these little ones;
I tell you, they have their angels in heaven,
who look continually
on the face of my heavenly Father.

What do you think?
Suppose someone has a hundred sheep,
and one of them strays,
does he not leave the ninety-nine on the hillside
and go in search of the one that strayed?
Truly I tell you: if he should find it,
he is more delighted over that sheep
than over the ninety-nine that did not stray.
In the same way,
it is not your heavenly Father's will
that one of these little ones should be lost.

St Matthew 18: 1 - 5, 10 - 14

They brought children for Jesus to touch.
The disciples rebuked them,
but when Jesus saw it he was indignant,
and said to them,
'Let the children come to me;
for the kingdom of God belongs to such as these.
Truly I tell you:
whoever does not accept the kingdom of God
like a child will never enter it.'
And he put his arms round them,
laid his hands on them,
and blessed them.

St Mark 10: 13 - 16

6 ADDRESS

7 PRAYER

Let us pray.

God of all grace and comfort,
we thank you for *N* . . . ,
and for the place *he* gained
in all our hearts.
We thank you
for the love in which *he* was conceived
and for the care with which *he* was surrounded.
As we remember times of tears and laughter,
we thank you for the love we shared
because of *him*.
We commend *him* to your safe keeping.
Rest eternal grant unto *him*.
Let light perpetual shine upon *him*.

Eternal God,
in Jesus Christ you promise eternal life

to us and to our children.
We thank you for the assurance and hope
that *N* . . .'*s* life is complete in you
and that *he* is living with you now
in the love and joy of your family in heaven.
Help us to know that together
we are enfolded in your love for ever.

God of unchanging love,
you are able
to bring good out of evil
and to raise up life from the dead.
May we know your saving peace
in the days to come,
and find new life in your eternal love.

We pray for those
to whom great sorrow and loss has come,
for *X* . . . and *Y* . . . (*parents*),
and *Z* . . . (*sister, brother*),
for the grandparents and all the family.
By the precious memories they share,
draw them closer to one another;
by the assurance that *N* . . .
is safe in your keeping,
draw them closer to you.
May they find the healing power of Christ
in all their grief and pain.

Bless us all,
friends, neighbours, (school friends and teachers),
that, by bearing one another's burdens,
we may show the love of Christ.
Gather us, with all your children,
into your everlasting arms,
so that, even when we cannot understand,

we may be filled with the light and comfort
of your presence.

God our Father,
you know our thoughts and share our sorrows.
Lead us out of desolation
to the caring comfort of your love.
When we forget what happiness is,
renew in us fresh springs of hope.
When we feel bereft of peace,
restore our hearts and calm our fears.
And when we come at last to our departing,
bring us home with you forever,
the family of God complete;
through Jesus Christ our Lord.

Amen.

Our Father ...

8   BLESSING   *if the Committal is elsewhere*

9   COMMITTAL

At the place of committal, all stand.

The minister says:

Jesus said,
It is not your heavenly Father's will
that one of these little ones should be lost.
I am the resurrection and the life.
Whoever has faith in me shall live,
even though he dies;
and no one who lives and has faith in me
shall ever die.

at the grave

N . . . is in the care of almighty God.
We now commit *his* body to the ground,
earth to earth, ashes to ashes, dust to dust,
in sure and certain hope of eternal life;
through Jesus Christ, who died, was buried,
and rose again for us,
and is alive and reigns for evermore.

Amen.

in the crematorium

N . . . is in the care of almighty God.
We now commit *his* body to the elements,
ashes to ashes, dust to dust,
in sure and certain hope of eternal life;
through Jesus Christ, who died, was buried,
and rose again for us,
and is alive and reigns for evermore.   **Amen.**

The Lamb who is at the centre of the throne
will be their shepherd
and will guide them
to springs of the water of life;
and God will wipe every tear from their eyes.
Revelation 7: 17

God will show us the path of life:
in his presence there is fullness of joy,
and at his right hand
there are pleasures for evermore.   *Psalm 16: 11*

10   PRAYER

Let us pray.

Loving God,
your Son our Saviour
put his arms around the children
and blessed them.
We thank you that you have received *N* . . .
into your never-failing care,
and welcomed him into the light and love
of your presence.

or

Heavenly Father,
we bless you for the assurance that *N* . . .
is safe in your keeping
and that you have welcomed *him*
into the light and love of your presence.

Comfort all who have loved *him* here on earth,
with the knowledge that you have called *him*
to yourself
and will keep *him* safe now and for ever;
and bring us at the last
to your everlasting kingdom;
through Jesus Christ our Lord.

Living God,
though our thoughts may linger here,
we believe that *N* . . .
has made a new beginning,
with your mercy and love still around *him*.
Strengthened by this assurance,
help us to return to the tasks that await us,
resolved to be faithful to you
and true to one another;
for the sake of Jesus Christ our Lord.

Amen.

Almighty God,
we commend ourselves and all dear to us,
wherever they may be,
to your gracious protection.
Guard us in life and in death,
that whether we wake or sleep,
we may live together with you;
through Jesus Christ our Lord.

Amen.

11   HYMN

12   BLESSING

The peace of God,
which is beyond all understanding,
guard your hearts and your thoughts
in Christ Jesus.

And the blessing of God almighty,
the Father, the Son, and the Holy Spirit,
be with you.

Amen.

Order for the Funeral of a Still-born Child

1 INTRODUCTION

These, or similar words, may be used.

> We gather here
> on what is for all of us a sad occasion.
> We were looking forward
> to a time of joy and happiness,
> and now there are tears and grief.
> We are left with a feeling of emptiness.
> All that has happened seems futile and pointless.
> Our minds are filled with questions
> to which there appear to be no answers:
> so many things we do not know;
> so many things we do not understand.
>
> But there are some truths we do know.
> We know that the God who made us, loves us;
> that he loves us always;
> that, through his Son Jesus Christ,
> he has promised never to leave us
> nor forsake us.
> And we know also,
> as others before us have found,
> that his strength is available for us,
> especially at those times when we feel
> that we have no strength of our own.
> These promises are found in God's Word.

2 SCRIPTURE READINGS

Some of these Lessons may be read:

Like a shepherd he will tend his flock
and with his arm keep them together;
he will carry the lambs in his bosom.

Isaiah 40: 11

The Lord is my shepherd,
I lack for nothing.
He makes me lie down in green pastures,
he leads me to water where I may rest;
he revives my spirit;
for his name's sake he guides me
in the right paths.
Even were I to walk
through a valley of deepest darkness
I should fear no harm,
for you are with me;
your shepherd's staff and crook
afford me comfort.

You spread a table for me
in the presence of my enemies;
you have richly anointed my head with oil,
and my cup brims over.

Goodness and love unfailing
will follow me all the days of my life,
and I shall dwell in the house of the Lord
throughout the years to come.

Psalm 23

Love is patient and kind.
Love envies no one,

is never boastful,
never conceited, never rude;
love is never selfish, never quick to take offence.
Love keeps no score of wrongs,
takes no pleasure in the sins of others,
but delights in the truth.
There is nothing love cannot face;
there is no limit to its faith,
its hope, its endurance.
Love will never come to an end.
At present we see only puzzling reflections
in a mirror,
but one day we shall see face to face.
My knowledge now is partial;
then it will be whole,
like God's knowledge of me.
There are three things that last for ever:
faith, hope and love;
and the greatest of the three is love.

1 Corinthians 13: 4 - 8, 12 - 13

God has said,
'I will never leave you or desert you.'
So we can take courage and say,
'The Lord is my helper, I will not fear;
what can man do to me?'

Hebrews 13: 5, 6

Jesus says,
It is not your heavenly Father's will
that one of these little ones should be lost.

St Matthew 18: 14

Jesus says,
Let the children come to me;
for the kingdom of God belongs to such as these.

Truly I tell you:
whoever does not accept the kingdom of God
like a child will never enter it.
And he put his arms round them,
laid his hands on them, and blessed them.

St Mark 10: 13 - 16

These reassuring words
have brought comfort and strength
to the friends of God through the ages.
May we also know the truth of his promises,
and find in him the strength and peace we need.

3   PRAYERS

Let us pray.

*Some of these prayers may be said,
ending with the prayer at e.:*

a.   Gracious God,
we thank you for the love
in which *N* . . . was conceived,
and for the love of the home
into which *he* was to be born.

We pray that the love
which *his* parents have for each other
may grow and deepen
as a result of this experience.

Give us grace, in patience and understanding,
to listen to each other,
and to help one another
in the days to come.

b. Lord Jesus Christ,
   you took little children into your arms
   and laid your hands upon them
   and blessed them.

   Assure us that you have taken our child *N* . . .
   into your arms and into your care,
   and that *he* and we together
   are enfolded in your love.

c. Almighty God, creator and keeper of life,
   we acknowledge that our child *N* . . .
   is your child,
   loved since before the foundation of the world.

   Grant us such trust
   in the finished work of your Son our Saviour
   that we shall look with hope
   towards a full knowledge of *N* . . . ,
   whose earthly life we have so little shared
   but who is now complete with Christ in you.

   We commend *him* to your safe keeping.
   Rest eternal grant unto *him*.
   Let light perpetual shine upon *him*.

d. Heavenly Father,
   you alone can heal our broken hearts;
   you alone can wipe away the tears
   that well up inside us;
   you alone can give us the peace we need;
   you alone can strengthen us to carry on.

   We ask you to be near those
   whose time of joy has been turned into sadness.

Assure them that with you
nothing is wasted or incomplete,
and uphold them with your tender love.

Supported by your strength,
may our love for one another
be deepened by the knowledge
of your love for us all.

e. Loving God,
amid all our questions,
help us to trust you.
In our time of darkness,
shine into our lives
with the light of your presence.

Our Father . . .

4 COMMITTAL

at the grave
We have entrusted (this little child) *N* . . .
into the hands of God.
We now commit *his* body to the ground,
earth to earth, ashes to ashes, dust to dust,
in sure and certain hope
of the resurrection to eternal life;
through Jesus Christ, who died, was buried,
and rose again for us,
and is alive and reigns for evermore.   ***Amen.***

in the crematorium
We have entrusted (this little child) *N* . . .
into the hands of God.
We now commit *his* body to be cremated,
ashes to ashes, dust to dust,

in sure and certain hope
of the resurrection to eternal life;
through Jesus Christ, who died, was buried,
and rose again for us,
and is alive and reigns for evermore.

Amen.

5   BLESSING

The peace of God,
which is beyond all understanding,
guard your hearts and your thoughts
in Christ Jesus.

And the blessing of God almighty,
the Father, the Son, and the Holy Spirit,
be with you.

Amen.

Order for the Interment or Scattering of Ashes

1 SCRIPTURE SENTENCES

The eternal God is our refuge,
and underneath are the everlasting arms.

Deuteronomy 33: 27 (AV)

Trust in the Lord at all times;
pour out your hearts before him;
God is our shelter.

Psalm 62: 8

God so loved the world
that he gave his only Son,
that everyone who has faith in him
may not perish but have eternal life.

St John 3: 16

There is nothing in death or life,
in the world as it is or the world as it shall be,
nothing in all creation that can separate us
from the love of God in Christ Jesus our Lord.

Romans 8: 38, 39

Praised be the God and Father
of our Lord Jesus Christ!
In his great mercy
by the resurrection of Jesus Christ from the dead,
he gave us new birth into a living hope,

the hope of an inheritance,
reserved in heaven for you,
which nothing can destroy or spoil or wither.

1 Peter 1: 3 - 4

The souls of the righteous are in God's hand;
no torment will touch them.
They are at peace.   *Wisdom 3: 1, 3*

2   PRAYERS

God, the Lord of life and conqueror of death,
you are our help in every time of trouble.
We thank you for the assurance of the Gospel,
that in your keeping
the souls of the faithful
find lasting peace and joy,
and that though we see our loved ones no more
they are safe with you.

Comfort all who mourn.
May our memories of *N* . . .
be a consolation for the present
and a strength for the future.
By the glorious resurrection of your Son,
confirm in us the hope of eternal life,
and enable us to put our whole trust
in your goodness and mercy;
through the same Jesus Christ our Lord.

Amen.

3   SCRIPTURE READINGS

If it is for this life only
that Christ has given us hope,
we of all people are most to be pitied.

But the truth is,
Christ was raised to life –
the firstfruits of the harvest of the dead.
For since it was a man
who brought death into the world,
a man also brought resurrection of the dead.
As in Adam all die,
so in Christ all will be brought to life;
but each in proper order:
Christ the firstfruits,
and afterwards, at his coming,
those who belong to Christ.
Then comes the end,
when he delivers up the kingdom
to God the Father,
after deposing every sovereignty,
authority, and power.
For he is destined to reign
until God has put all enemies under his feet;
and the last enemy to be deposed is death.

1 Corinthians 15: 19 - 26

There are heavenly bodies and earthly bodies;
and the splendour of the heavenly bodies
is one thing,
the splendour of the earthly, another.
The sun has a splendour of its own,
the moon another splendour,
and the stars yet another;
and one star differs from another in brightness.
So it is with the resurrection of the dead:
what is sown as a perishable thing
is raised imperishable.
Sown in humiliation, it is raised in glory;
sown in weakness, it is raised in power;
sown a physical body,

it is raised a spiritual body.

1 Corinthians 15: 40 - 44

No wonder we do not lose heart!
Though our outward humanity is in decay,
yet day by day
we are inwardly renewed.
Our troubles are slight and short-lived,
and their outcome is an eternal glory
which far outweighs them,
provided our eyes are fixed,
not on the things that are seen,
but on the things that are unseen;
for what is seen is transient,
what is unseen is eternal.
We know that if the earthly frame
that houses us today is demolished,
we possess a building which God has provided –
a house not made by human hands,
eternal and in heaven.

2 Corinthians 4: 16 - 5: 1

4   INTERMENT *or* SCATTERING

The Lord says,
'Do not be afraid.
I am the first and the last,
and I am the living One;
I was dead
and now I am alive for evermore.'

Revelation 1: 18

We have entrusted *N* . . .
to God's eternal keeping.
We now commit *his* ashes to the ground
(*to the elements*),

in sure and certain hope
of the resurrection to eternal life
through Jesus Christ our Lord,
who died, was buried, and rose again for us,
and is alive and reigns for ever and ever.

Amen.

5 PRAYERS

Let us pray.

Eternal God,
by your dear Son's rising from the dead
you have destroyed the power of death.
In you the dead find life for ever,
and the faithful
who served you on earth
praise you for all eternity in heaven.

As we return to our tasks,
cheer us by the hope of everlasting life
and support us by the sure love
of your guiding hand.
Bring us at the last,
with all the faithful,
to the full knowledge of your love
and the unclouded vision of your glory;
through Jesus Christ our Lord.   *Amen.*

6 BLESSING

The peace of God,
which is beyond all understanding,
guard your hearts and your thoughts
in Christ Jesus.

And the blessing of God almighty,
Father, Son, and Holy Spirit,
be with you.

Amen.

Order for the Ordination and Admission of Elders

The Kirk Session is constituted before public worship. The (ordination and) admission takes place during the service, at an appropriate point after the sermon.

If the readings for the day are not used, Lessons may be drawn from the following:

Exodus	18: 13 - 26
Isaiah	6: 1 - 9a
Romans	12: 3 - 18
1 Corinthians	12: 4 - 14, 27 - 31
Ephesians	4: 1 - 8, 11 - 16
1 Thessalonians	5: 12 - 24
1 Peter	5: 1 - 4, 10b - 11
St Mark	10: 42 - 45
St Luke	12: 35 - 40
St John	15: 9 - 17

1 PROLOGUE

The minister and people say responsively:

There are different gifts,
but it is the same Spirit who gives them.

There are different ways of serving God,
but it is the same Lord who is served.

God works through different people
in different ways,
**but it is the same God who achieves
his purpose through them all.**

Each one is given a gift by the Spirit,
to use it for the common good.

from 1 Corinthians 12: 4 - 11

The minister says:

We have the joy of using our gifts
as members of the Church of Christ,
which is his body
continuing his ministry in the world today.

Those who are chosen
for the office of the eldership
have the particular responsibility
of caring for God's people
and exercising oversight and leadership.

Today, the Kirk Session is met

either

to ordain *A, B, C,* and *D*
to the office of the eldership
and to admit them as elders
in this congregation.

or

>   to ordain *A, B, C,* and *D*
>   to the office of the eldership
>   and to admit them,
>   together with *E, F, G,* and *H*
>   as elders in this congregation.

or

>   to admit *E, F, G,* and *H*
>   as elders in this congregation.

Due notice has been given,
no objection has been made,
and we therefore proceed.

2   PREAMBLE

The minister says:

>   In the name of the Lord Jesus Christ,
>   the King and Head of the Church,
>   who, being ascended on high,
>   has given gifts
>   for the building up of the body of Christ,
>   we are met

either

>   to ordain to the office of the eldership
>   and admit to that office in this congregation
>   *A, B, C,* and *D.*

or

>   to ordain to the office of the eldership
>   and admit to that office in this congregation

A, B, C, and *D;*
and to admit to the office of the eldership
in this congregation
E, F, G, and *H.*

or

to admit to the office of the eldership
in this congregation
E, F, G, and *H.*

In this act,
the Church of Scotland,
as part of the holy catholic or universal Church,
worshipping one God,
Father, Son, and Holy Spirit,
affirms anew its belief
in the Gospel
of the sovereign grace and love of God,
wherein through Jesus Christ,
his only Son, our Lord,
incarnate, crucified, and risen,
he freely offers to all,
upon repentance and faith,
the forgiveness of sins,
renewal by the Holy Spirit,
and eternal life,
and calls them to labour
in the fellowship of faith
for the advancement of the kingdom of God
throughout the world.

The Church of Scotland
acknowledges the Word of God,
contained in the Scriptures
of the Old and New Testaments,

to be the supreme rule of faith and life.
The Church of Scotland
holds as its subordinate standard
the Westminster Confession of Faith,
recognising liberty of opinion
on such points of doctrine
as do not enter into the substance of the Faith,
and claiming the right,
in dependence on the promised guidance
of the Holy Spirit,
to formulate, interpret,
or modify its subordinate standards:
always in agreement with the Word of God
and the fundamental doctrines
of the Christian faith
contained in the Confession,
of which agreement
the Church itself shall be sole judge.

3   AFFIRMATION

The minister says:

In view of this Declaration
you are now required to answer this question:

Do you believe
the fundamental doctrines of the Christian faith;
do you promise
to seek the unity and peace of this Church;
to uphold its doctrine, worship,
government and discipline;
and to take your due part
in the administration of its affairs?

I do.

The Lord bless you
and enable you faithfully to keep this promise.

The elder-elect signs the prescribed Formula.

4   PRAYER

The elder-elect may kneel or stand

The minister says:

Let us pray.

Loving God,
you have chosen for yourself a Church
in which your Holy Spirit
inspires men and women
to serve your purposes of love.
We give you thanks
that by your grace you have called
A, B, . . . G, and *H* (*or* these your servants
whom we have named before you)
to lead and care for your people
as elders in your Church.

We commend them to you now
as we (*ordain and*) admit them
to the office of the eldership
within the Church of your dear Son.

Grant them the gift of your Holy Spirit,
that their hearts may be set on fire
with love for you
and for those committed to their care.
Make them pure in heart
as those who have the mind of Christ.

Give them vision to discern your purpose
for the Church and for the world you love.
Keep them faithful to the end in all their service,
that, when the chief shepherd appears,
they may receive glory,
a crown that never fades.

Blessed be God for all his goodness,
and blessed be his Son Jesus Christ,
and blessed be his Holy Spirit,
endowing the Church with the fullness of grace
and making her words the word of life,
her bread the bread of heaven,
her shepherding of the flock of God
his own shepherd work.

And to you, Father, Son, and Holy Spirit,
be glory for ever.   ***Amen***.

5   DECLARATION AND WELCOME

The minister says:

In the name of the Lord Jesus Christ,
the King and Head of the Church,
*(I declare you to have been ordained
to the office of the eldership, and)*
I admit you to office as elders
in this congregation and parish.

As a sign of our welcome
we give you the right hand of fellowship.
The grace of the Lord Jesus Christ be with you.

*The elders follow the minister in offering the right
hand of fellowship.*

6 RENEWAL OF COMMITMENT

The minister says:

> Christ calls us all to share in his ministry.
> Let us, then, dedicate ourselves anew
> to his service.

> Let all stand.

to all:

> Members and elders of this congregation:
> putting your whole trust in Jesus Christ
> as Saviour and Lord,
> do you commit yourselves
> to love and serve his Church and Kingdom?

> **We do.**

to the congregation:

> As members of this congregation,
> will you encourage and support your elders,
> surround them with your love,
> and remember them in your prayers?

> **We will.**

to the elders:

> In your service as elders,
> will you promise to carry out all your duties
> faithfully and cheerfully,
> God being your helper?

We will.

The minister says:

Let all sit.

7   WORDS OF COUNSEL

The minister may offer suitable words of counsel to encourage both
 (a)   the elders in the cheerful fulfilment of their duties as they represent Christ in the community, and
 (b)   the congregation as they welcome the elders into their homes and share with them the task of the Church;

concluding with a reading, such as Romans 12: 9 - 18, or Ephesians 4: 4 - 8, 11 - 16.

8   PRAYER

The minister says:

Let us pray.

All say:

> **God of grace,**
> **you have called us**
> **to be servants of Christ Jesus,**
> **and to share in his ministry of love**
> **to all people.**
>
> **Renew our zeal,**
> **give us joy in your service.**

Direct us by your Spirit of wisdom
and fill us with the gifts of your grace,
that together we may declare
your wonderful deeds
and show your love to the world;
through Jesus Christ our Lord.

Amen.

9   *The service continues in the customary manner.*

Following the service, the Kirk Session resumes its meeting, and the newly-admitted elders are welcomed as members of the Kirk Session.

If preferred, the signing of the Formula and the giving of the right hand of fellowship may take place at this point rather than during the service.

Order for a Covenant Service

Days which might be considered appropriate for this service are:

> *St Andrew's Day,*
> *or the Sunday nearest to St Andrew's Day;*
> *the first Sunday in January;*
> *the Saturday before Easter Day which, by tradition,*
> *is linked to the renewal of baptismal vows;*
> *a Sunday in the early autumn, marking the*
> *beginning of a new year in church organisations.*

1 CALL TO WORSHIP

The minister says:

> Grace and peace to you
> from God our Father
> and the Lord Jesus Christ. *1 Corinthians 1: 3*

> Let us worship God.

2 HYMN

3 SCRIPTURE SENTENCE

The minister says:

Lord God of Israel,
there is no God like you
in heaven above or on earth beneath,
keeping covenant with your servants
and showing them constant love
while they continue faithful to you
with all their hearts.   *1 Kings 8: 23*

4   PRAYERS

The minister says:

Let us pray.

Gracious God,
through Christ you call us
to share in your covenant.

In baptism, you brought us
into union with Christ
within the family of his Church.

In bread and wine, you bring us
the fruit of his obedience.

Give us the power of your Spirit,
that we may put to death our evil desires,
and rise to newness of life in Christ,
with thoughts aspiring to the realm above,
and wills eager to live his Gospel.   **Amen.**

   Heavenly Father,
   at all times you have shown
   singular favour to all who fear you.
   Look not upon the many sins
   by which we offend you,

> *seeing we are so fragile and weak;*
> *but remember the covenant*
> *you made with our forebears*
> *and ratified in your Son Jesus Christ.*
> *By its virtue, may we assure ourselves*
> *of your eternal salvation;*
> *and with your angels*
> *praise and glorify you for ever.*   *Amen.*

Collect of the Day

5   HYMN

6   OLD TESTAMENT

7   PSALM *said or sung*

8   EPISTLE

9   GOSPEL

10   ALLELUIA *or* HYMN

11   INVOCATION OF THE HOLY TRINITY
     SERMON
     ASCRIPTION OF PRAISE TO THE HOLY TRINITY

12   CREED

13   COVENANT

The people still standing, the minister says:

> In the old covenant,
> God chose Israel to be his people
> and to obey his laws.

We stand within the new covenant
made by the death
and resurrection of Jesus Christ,
and we bear his name.

We are initiated into this covenant by baptism,
dying with Christ,
being buried with Christ,
and rising with Christ
to a life of faith and hope and love.

The covenant is renewed
each time we meet at the Lord's Table.

In the strength of the covenant,
which he has made with his people,
let us bind ourselves anew to God
who has so graciously bound himself to us.
And let us gladly
take the yoke of Christ upon us.

The following may be read,
not necessarily by the minister:

Christ has many services to be done;
some are easy, some are difficult;
some bring sorrow, others bring reproach;
some are suited to our natural inclinations
and material interests,
others are contrary to both.
In some we please Christ and please ourselves,
in others we cannot please Christ
except by denying ourselves.
Yet the power to do all things
is given us in Christ who strengthens us.

The minister says:

Let us pray.

God of love and faithfulness,
you have appointed our Lord Jesus Christ
as mediator of a new covenant.
Give us grace to join ourselves
in a perpetual covenant with you,
as with joy we take upon us
the yoke of glad obedience,
and engage ourselves
to seek and do your perfect will.
We are no longer our own, but yours.

> *We are no longer our own, but yours.*
> *Put us with what you will,*
> *rank us with whom you will;*
> *put us to doing, put us to suffering;*
> *let us be employed for you*
> *or laid aside for you,*
> *exalted for you or brought low for you;*
> *let us be full, let us be empty;*
> *let us have all things, let us have nothing;*
> *we freely and wholeheartedly*
> *yield all things*
> *to your pleasure and disposal.*
>
> *And now, glorious and blessed God,*
> *Father, Son, and Holy Spirit,*
> *you are ours, and we are yours.*
> *May this covenant, now made on earth,*
> *be ratified in heaven,*
> *to the glory of your name.*
> *Amen.*

14   *The service continues with Holy Communion,*
    beginning with the Invitation;
    or continues with the Prayers of Intercession.

    The Dismissal and Blessing may be in this form:

    The minister says:

      Go in peace.

      And may the God of peace,
      who brought back from the dead
      our Lord Jesus,
      the great Shepherd of the sheep,
      through the blood of an eternal covenant,
      make you perfect in all goodness,
      so that you may do his will;
      and may he create in you
      what is pleasing to him.

      And the blessing of God almighty,
      Father, Son, and Holy Spirit,
      be with you.   **Amen.**

Order for Laying
the Foundation Stone
of a Church

*The service is planned in co-operation with representatives
of the wider church and of the civic community.*

*When all have gathered at the prepared site, a procession
is formed (the architect, surveyor, builder, representatives
of the civic community, representatives of local churches,
officiating ministers) and goes to the stone.*

1 CALL TO WORSHIP

The presiding minister says:

> Who is able to build a house for God
> when heaven itself, the highest heaven,
> cannot contain him?
>
> *2 Chronicles 2: 5 - 6*

> Unless the Lord builds the house,
> its builders labour in vain.   *Psalm 127: 1*

> Our help is in the name of the Lord,
> maker of heaven and earth.   *Psalm 124: 8*

> Let us worship God.

2 PRAYERS

The minister says:

Let us pray.

Living God,
you are present everywhere
in heaven and on earth,
and your glory rests on places
where you have set your name.
Hallow this place,
where a house of prayer will rise
for the worship of your name
and the service of your kingdom;
through Jesus Christ our Lord.

Amen.

Guide us, Lord,
in all our doings with your gracious favour,
and further us with your continuing help;
that in all our works,
begun, continued, and ended in you,
we may glorify your holy name,
and by your mercy attain everlasting life;
through Jesus Christ our Lord.

Amen.

3 HYMN

4 SCRIPTURE READINGS

5 ADDRESS

6 APOSTLES' CREED

7 HYMN

8 PRAYER

The minister says:

Let us pray.

Almighty God,
your Son Jesus Christ is the living stone,
chosen by you and of great worth to you.
Build us up as living stones
into a spiritual temple,
and form us into a holy priesthood
to offer spiritual sacrifices acceptable to you.

Establish this stone
which we place here in your name.
Give us the continual presence of your Spirit,
that this work undertaken for your service
may be completed to your praise and glory;
through Jesus Christ our Lord,
who lives and reigns
with you and the Holy Spirit,
one God, now and for ever.

Amen.

9   LAYING OF THE STONE

*After the usual articles, such as documents and coins,
have been deposited in their place, the stone is laid by
the person appointed.*

The minister places his hand on the stone and says:

In the name of the Father, and of the Son,
and of the Holy Spirit,
we lay this foundation stone of *N* . . . Church.

Amen.

Glory to the Father, and to the Son,
and to the Holy Spirit:
as it was in the beginning, is now,
and will be for ever.   *Amen.*

The minister may say:

These are the words of the Lord God:
I am laying a stone in Zion,
a precious corner-stone, well founded;
he who has faith will not waver.
I shall use justice as a plumb-line
and righteousness as a plummet.

Isaiah 28: 16, 17

There can be no other foundation
than the one already laid:
I mean Jesus Christ himself.

1 Corinthians 3: 11

10   PRAYERS

The minister says:

Let us pray.

Gracious God,
you have built your Church
on the foundation of the apostles and prophets,
with Christ Jesus himself as the corner-stone.
Confirm and bless
what we have now done in your name
and prosper the work
to which we have set our hands.
Give us grace to accomplish it,
and by your inspiration

make it beautiful and good;
through Jesus Christ our Lord.   *Amen.*

Almighty God,
protect and shield
those who will work on this site.
Guide those who will plan and oversee
the building of the church;
bless those who will contribute to its costs;
prepare the hearts and minds of those
who will minister and worship here
in days to come.
And grant that in due time
your house of prayer may stand complete,
for the glory of your name
and the proclaiming of your Kingdom;
through Jesus Christ our Lord,
who lives and reigns
and is worshipped and glorified,
with you and the Holy Spirit,
one God, now and for ever.   *Amen.*

Our Father ...

11   HYMN

12   DISMISSAL AND BLESSING

The minister says:

Now to the One who can keep you from falling,
and set you in the presence of his glory,
jubilant and above reproach,
to the only God our Saviour,
be glory and majesty, power and authority,
through Jesus Christ our Lord.

Go in the strength of God.

And the blessing of God almighty,
the Father, the Son, and the Holy Spirit,
be with you all.   ***Amen.***

Scripture Lessons may be chosen from the following:

OLD TESTAMENT

Genesis	28: 10 - 22
1 Chronicles	29: 10 - 18
Ezra	3: 10 - 11 (12 - 13)

EPISTLE

1 Corinthians	3: 5 - 11
1 Peter	2: 1 - 7
Revelation	21: 1 - 6

GOSPEL

St Matthew	16: 13 - 18
St Mark	12: 1 - 12
St John	2: 12 - 22

Order for
the Dedication
of a Church

The congregation, including representatives of the wider church and of the civic community, meets inside the church by the appointed time.

The presbytery meets in the hall or vestry of the church, and in due course proceeds into the church.

The choir proceeds into the church to its appointed place.

The doors are closed two minutes before the hour at which the service is to begin.

1   OPENING OF THE DOORS

The Moderator of the presbytery and the officiating ministers proceed from the hall or vestry and, if the weather allow, make a circuit of the building before approaching the main door of the church.

The Moderator knocks three times on the closed door, and says:

> Lift up your heads, you gates,
> lift yourselves up, you everlasting doors,
> that the king of glory may come in.

From inside the church, the congregation says:

Who is this king of glory?

The Moderator answers:

The Lord of hosts, he is the king of Glory.

Psalm 24: 7, 8, 10

*The doors are opened (to a flourish of trumpets),
and the Moderator says:*

Peace to this house,
from God the Father and the Lord Jesus Christ.

Amen.

Let us pray.

Enter your house, O God,
and the hearts of your faithful people.
Establish for yourself a dwelling-place for ever,
that we may be glorified
by the indwelling of him
whose building we are;
through Jesus Christ our Lord.

Amen.

*A representative of the congregation delivers the
keys of the church to the Moderator and says:*

This parish church has been built
for the glory of God
and the proclaiming of the gospel of Christ.
As Moderator of the Presbytery of *N* . . . ,
and representing the Church of Scotland,
will you accept these keys,

and will you dedicate this church
to the worship of almighty God?

The Moderator answers:

In the name of the Presbytery of *N* . . .
and of the Church of Scotland,
I accept these keys
as a token of the trust committed to us,
and we proceed now to the dedication.

*The Moderator proceeds through the doors into the
church and says to the congregation:*

Grace and peace be yours in fullest measure,
through knowledge of God and of Jesus Christ.
                                        Amen.

Peace be to this house and all who worship in it.
Peace be to those who enter it,
and to those who go out from it.
Peace be to those who love it,
and who love the name of Jesus Christ our Lord.
                                        Amen.

Let us pray.

Almighty and ever-living God,
you are the source of every good and perfect gift.
Accept the offerings of the many people
whose gifts and labours have enabled us
to complete and furnish this building.
Use it for your purposes
and hallow it with your blessing.
Dwell in this house
and brighten it with your glory,

that it may be to all who seek you here
a temple of the living God,
none other than the gate of heaven;
through Jesus Christ our Lord.

Amen.

2   HYMN

While the hymn is being sung, the Moderator and those with him go to their places.

3   OFFERING OF THE KEYS

The Moderator lays the keys of the church on the Holy Table and says:

Let us pray.

Lord Jesus Christ,
you are the beginning and the ending
of all things,
the first and the last.
You have the key of the house of David;
what you open none will shut,
and what you shut none will open.
Give your power to your servants,
that this house, now opened for your service,
may always be filled with your presence,
and bring strength and inspiration
to those who worship here;
for the glory and praise of your holy name.

Amen.

4   SCRIPTURE SENTENCES

The minister says one or more of the following:

Unless the Lord builds the house,
its builders labour in vain.   *Psalm 127: 1*

Our help is in the name of the Lord,
maker of heaven and earth.   *Psalm 124: 8*

The Lord says,
Wherever I cause my name to be invoked,
I will come to you and bless you.

Exodus 20: 24

God, within your temple
we meditate on your steadfast love.

Psalm 48: 9

Blessed be the glorious name
of the Lord for ever;
may his glory fill the whole earth.

Psalm 72: 19

Glorify the Lord with me;
let us exalt his name together.   *Psalm 34: 3*

5   PRAYERS

The minister says:

Let us pray.

Blessed are you, God our Father.
Blessed are you, Christ our Peace.
Blessed are you, Holy Spirit our Comforter.

Blessed are you in the temple of your glory.
Blessed are you on the throne of your kingdom.
Blessed are you in the hearts of your people.

Glory to the Father, and to the Son,
and to the Holy Spirit:
as it was in the beginning, is now,
and will be for ever.   *Amen.*

Holy and merciful God,
in your presence we confess our sin
and acknowledge we have fallen
short of your glory.
We have wandered from your ways,
we have wasted your gifts,
we have forgotten your love.

Lord have mercy.
    Christ have mercy.
Lord have mercy.

May God almighty freely pardon
all who repent and turn to him.
May he fulfil in every contrite heart
the promise of his redeeming grace,
absolving us from our sins
and delivering us from a guilty conscience;
through the merits and mediation
of Jesus Christ our Lord.   *Amen.*

Blessed and glorious God,
you make perfect and illumine all things.
Your loving-kindness never fails.
Enable us with your grace
as with humbleness of heart
and readiness of will
we come to dedicate this place
entirely to your service.
Accept at our hands this house,
for the reading of your Word

and the preaching of your gospel,
for celebrating your Sacraments
and offering to you our sacrifice
of praise and thanksgiving,
for the blessing of the people in your name
and the glory of your everlasting kingdom;
through Jesus Christ our Lord,
who is alive and reigns
with you and the Holy Spirit,
one God, now and for ever.

Amen.

6   OLD TESTAMENT

7   PSALM

8   EPISTLE

9   GOSPEL

10   APOSTLES' CREED

11   HYMN *Veni Creator Spiritus*

12   DEDICATION

The congregation standing, the Moderator says:

This house has been built
for the honour and service of almighty God,
to fill our minds
with greater reverence for his glory,
and to inspire our hearts with devotion and joy.

Let us now pray
for God's blessing upon this work

and dedicate this building
to the honour of his glorious name.

In the name of the Lord Jesus Christ we do this.
To the glory of God the Father,
who has called us by his grace:
to the glory of Christ his Son,
who loves us and gave himself for us:
to the glory of the Holy Spirit,
who illumines and sanctifies us:
     we dedicate this house.   *Amen.*

For the worship of God in praise and prayer:
for the preaching of the gospel of Jesus Christ,
incarnate, crucified, risen, and exalted:
for the celebration of the holy Sacraments
of his grace:
     we dedicate this house.   *Amen.*

For the giving of comfort to all who mourn:
of strength to all who are tempted:
of light to those who seek the way:
     we dedicate this house.   *Amen.*

For the hallowing of family life:
for the teaching and guiding of the young:
for the equipping of God's people
for work in his service,
and the building up of the body of Christ:
     we dedicate this house.   *Amen.*

> *And now, as a people*
> *within the household of God:*
> *in the unity of the faith,*
> *in the communion of saints,*
> *in love and goodwill to all,*

in remembrance of those
who have finished their course in this life,
in gratitude for the gift of this house
to be a dwelling-place of God
through the Spirit,
we dedicate ourselves anew
to the worship of God
and the service of his kingdom:
In the name of the Father,
and of the Son,
and of the Holy Spirit.   **Amen.**

13 PRAYERS

The people may sit.

The Moderator says:

The Lord be with you.
    And also with you.

 Lift up your hearts.
    We lift them to the Lord.

Let us give thanks to the Lord our God.
    It is right to give our thanks and praise.

It is indeed right, it is our duty and our joy,
at all times and in all places,
to give you thanks and praise,
holy Father, heavenly King,
almighty and eternal God.

Heaven itself, the highest heaven,
cannot contain you,
how much less this house that we have built!

Yet you promised by Jesus Christ our Lord
to be present in the prayers and faithful service
of your servants who call upon you.
Hear us, merciful Father,
creating all that is good;
hear us, Christ our Saviour,
entering into glory by the Cross;
hear us, Holy Spirit,
quickening and renewing all thought and life.
Holy and glorious Trinity,
hear us as we call upon you;
satisfy us with the goodness of your house
and the abundance of your grace.

Fill this house,
which now we dedicate to your glory,
with the radiance of your presence:
that it may be a sanctuary
and a shrine for all people;
a place of strength for the weak,
of refuge for the troubled;
a place where your truth is taught and learned;
a place where prayer is fulfilled
according to your will,
and the worship and service
of your faithful people here on earth
is caught up in the worship
and service of heaven.
Bless us with the vision of your everlasting light
and fill us with the knowledge
of your eternal love;
through Jesus Christ our Lord,
who lives and reigns
with you and the Holy Spirit,
one God, now and for ever.

Amen.

*To dedicate the furnishings, the Moderator may go
to each place in turn, and as he moves, the choir
and/or congregation may sing, or instrumentalists
may play.*

at the lectern

> Grant that your holy Word, read in this place,
> may be received into honest and good hearts,
> and bring forth fruit
> worthy of the gospel of grace and truth;
> through Jesus Christ our Lord.　　**Amen.**

at the font

> Grant that those who in this house
> are baptized into your name
> and made members of Christ's Church
> and sanctified by his Spirit,
> may ever remain
> in the number of your faithful children;
> through Jesus Christ our Lord.　　**Amen.**

at the chancel steps

> Grant that those who in this place
> reaffirm their baptism and renew their vows
> may be confirmed and strengthened
> by your Holy Spirit,
> and grow in grace
> till they come to your everlasting kingdom;
> through Jesus Christ our Lord.　　**Amen.**

at the Holy Table

> Grant that those who receive in this house
> the blessed Sacrament
> of the body and blood of Christ
> may come to that holy mystery
> with a penitent heart,

a lively faith,
and a perfect love.
So fill them with your grace
and heavenly benediction
that with all the benefits of Christ's passion
they may obtain remission of their sins,
and be made partakers of the living Bread
and heirs through hope of eternal life;
through Jesus Christ our Lord.   ***Amen.***

at the chancel steps

Grant that those who in this place
make their marriage covenant together
may grow strong in your holy love
and faithfully and joyfully
keep their sacred vows;
through Jesus Christ our Lord.   ***Amen.***

at the pulpit

Grant that those who preach in this house
may be so filled with the Holy Spirit,
that the Word of the Lord
may have swift and glorious success
and bring light and inspiration to all who hear;
through Jesus Christ our Lord.   ***Amen.***

at the choir stalls or organ

Grant the grace of reverence and joy
to those who in this place
make music by voice or instrument:
that they may catch
the glory of eternal harmony,
and we may learn on earth
to keep in tune with heaven;
through Jesus Christ our Lord.   ***Amen.***

at the nave among the people
>Grant that those who worship in this house
may have an answer to their prayers.
Refresh and quicken them by your Holy Spirit
and lead them into all truth,
and with all truth into all love;
that as the years pass by
your love and mercy may radiate from them
into the homes and lives of this parish
and into the wider community;
through Jesus Christ our Lord.   ***Amen.***

at the main inner door
>Grant that there may go forth from this place
a great company of men and women
to serve you faithfully
for the good of their neighbours
and the glory of your name.
And when the day of our worship
in your Church on earth is ended,
receive us into the blessed company
of the Church in heaven,
to praise and honour you for ever;
through Jesus Christ our Lord,
who is alive and reigns
with you and the Holy Spirit,
one God, now and for ever.

>   ***Amen.***

>### *Our Father . . .*

14 PROCLAMATION

The people stand.

The Moderator says:

I now declare *N . . . Parish Church*
to be consecrated and set apart
for the worship and service of almighty God.
In the name of God,
Father, Son, and Holy Spirit.   ***Amen.***

Now to him who is able
through the power which is at work among us
to do immeasurably more
than all that we can ask or conceive,
to him be glory in the Church
and in Christ Jesus
from generation to generation for evermore.
                                            Amen.

15 HYMN

16 SERMON

*with Invocation of the Holy Trinity before, and
Ascription of Glory after, the sermon.*

17 THANK-OFFERING

*Offerings are received and placed on the Holy
Table.*

18 PRAYERS

The minister says:

Let us pray.

God most holy,
your gifts are beyond measure, above price.
Not to us, Lord, not to us,

but to your name be the praise and the glory
for your love, for your faithfulness.

Accept the offerings we present
and dedicate to you;
save us, and strengthen us for your service.

Receive our prayers:
for the peace that comes from above,
and for the salvation of our souls;
for the peace of the world,
and for the welfare of the Church;
for the nations of the world
and peoples of every race;
for our Queen, our country,
and for those who bear responsibility
for the affairs of this, and every land;
for all who are in trouble,
who are poor, who are broken;
for those who love this church,
who have helped to build it up,
and especially for those who cannot be here now
but whose thoughts and prayers are with us;
for the minister and people
of this parish and congregation:
Holy God, holy and mighty, holy and immortal,
have mercy upon them
and upon all for whom we have prayed;
through Jesus Christ our Lord.   *Amen.*

Eternal God,
you are the strength of those who labour
and the repose of the blessed dead.
We thank you for all your faithful servants
departed this life in your faith and fear,
whom we remember in silence before you . . .

As we dedicate ourselves to your service,
lift us into light and love;
and give us at the last a place
with those who trusted your word
and sought to do your will,
that we with them be made partakers
of the saints in light.
And to your name, Father, Son, and Holy Spirit,
one God for ever,
with the Church on earth
and the Church in heaven,
we ascribe honour and glory,
now and for ever. *Amen.*

19   HYMN

20   DISMISSAL AND BLESSING

The Moderator says:

Truly the Lord is in this place.
This is none other than the house of God;
it is the gateway to heaven.

You are God's temple,
where the Spirit of God dwells.
May he keep you sound in faith,
steadfast in hope, and strong in love.

Go forth in the peace of God.
And the blessing of God almighty,
Father, Son, and Holy Spirit,
be with you all.

Amen.

Scripture Lessons may be chosen from the following:

OLD TESTAMENT

Genesis	28: 10 - 22
Exodus	25: 8 - 22
1 Kings	8: 22 - 30
2 Chronicles	5: 1 - 7, 11, 13, 14

PSALMS

24
27: 1 - 10, 13 - 14
43: 3 - 5
48: 9 - 14
68: 18 - 20, 24 - 29, 32 - 35
84: 1 - 7, 10 - 12
122

EPISTLE

Ephesians	1: 3 - 23
Ephesians	2: 13 - 22
Philippians	2: 1 - 11
Colossians	3: 1 - 4, 12 - 17
1 John	4: 7 - 21
Revelation	21: 9 - 27

GOSPEL

St Matthew	21: 12 - 17
St John	10: 1 - 18
St John	15: 1 - 17

Dedication
of Church
Furnishings

The Basic Order is used on each occasion whenever a dedication takes place.

The section of Particular Dedications provides a Scripture Sentence and Particular Prayers to be used at no. 1, no. 2, and no. 6. The Sentence and the Prayers should be incorporated in the Basic Order at the places indicated.

The dedication takes place immediately before that point in the service when the item to be dedicated would normally be used.

At the appropriate point, the minister (and those with him) goes to the part of the church where the Particular Dedication is to take place.

BASIC ORDER

The congregation stands.

1   SCRIPTURE SENTENCE

The minister says:

> May the favour of the Lord our God be on us.
> Establish for us all that we do.   *Psalm 90: 17*

add appropriate Particular Sentence no. 1.

2 PRAYERS

The minister says:

Let us pray.

Almighty God,
without you nothing is strong,
nothing is holy;
with you everything is good,
and true, and beautiful.
May your hand rest on us,
that all we do
may show the honour of your name.

All things have their beginning
in your creative power;
all things are made perfect
in your redeeming love.
In your Son Jesus Christ our Saviour,
we look with hope to a new heaven
and a new earth,
when all creation
will be free to praise its Maker.

Lord of heaven and earth,
every good and perfect gift comes from you.
Send us now your Holy Spirit,
that our gifts may truly witness
to our faith and hope and love;
through Jesus Christ our Lord.   ***Amen.***

or

Glorious Lord,
all things are sanctified, enlightened,

and made perfect by your love and power.
Be merciful to us and bless us.
Cause your face to shine upon us,
that what we do now may please you
and show forth the honour of your name;
through Jesus Christ our Lord.　　　　***Amen.***

add appropriate Particular Prayer no. 2.

3　NARRATIVE

*A statement may be made about the memorial
(or gift and its donor).*

4　THE GIFT

The representative (or donor of the gift) asks:

As minister of this parish,
will you receive this . . .
(in memory of *N . . . , or* in the name of *N . . .*)
and dedicate it to the glory of God?

The minister responds:

On behalf of this congregation
I gratefully accept this memorial (*or gift*).

5　DEDICATION

The minister says:

In the faith of our Lord Jesus Christ
I dedicate this . . .
to the glory of God
(and in memory of his servant N . . .)

(and declare it to be set apart
for use in this place).
In the name of the Father, the Son,
and the Holy Spirit.

Amen.

6   PRAYERS

The minister says:

Let us pray.

The appropriate Particular Prayers no. 6a and no.
6b are said (together with what immediately follows,
if relevant).

When the article to be dedicated is a memorial, the
following prayers are said between the Particular
Prayers a and b:

God of love and power,
you hold all souls in life,
and bind together all your people
in heaven and on earth
in one holy fellowship of service and love.
We praise you for those who in their generation
have been lights in the world,
in whose lives we have seen reflections
of your goodness and love.

We thank you for all that was pure and true,
beautiful and good,
in the *life* commemorated today;
and for the grace you gave *him*
of thoughtful generosity;
for the example *he* has left

of faith and hope and duty,
and of love for your Church;
and for the assurance we have, through Christ,
that *he* has entered into glory,
through the same Jesus Christ our Lord.   *Amen.*

*When the article to be dedicated is a gift, this prayer
is said between Particular Prayers a and b:*

We thank you that you inspired your servant(s)
to offer this gift
for the use and beauty of your sanctuary.
Accept *his* devotion,
comfort *him* with your favour,
and reward *him* for the kindness
he has shown to your house and its worship,
through Jesus Christ our Lord.   *Amen.*

PARTICULAR DEDICATIONS

at the Dedication of a **Font**

1 SCRIPTURE SENTENCE

Because God our Saviour was merciful,
he saved us through the water of rebirth
and the renewing power of the Holy Spirit,
which he lavished upon us through Jesus Christ.

Titus 3: 5 - 6

2 PRAYER

Gracious God,
we love you because you loved us first.
In baptism you claimed us for your own

and set your seal upon our heart.
Your grace reached us before we could respond;
and day by day we grow in grace,
learning to walk more closely
to our Lord Jesus Christ.
Renew us by the power of your Spirit,
that he who started the good work in us
may bring it to completion
by the day of Christ Jesus,
who lives and reigns
with you and the Holy Spirit,
one God, now and for ever.

Amen.

6   PRAYERS

a. God of love and mercy,
with you is the fountain of life.
Accept and bless this font
which we have set apart
for its holy use in the worship
and service of your house.
Grant that those who are baptised into Christ
by the Spirit of Pentecost,
and received into the ark of the Church,
may ever remain
among the number of your loving children.

May this font be a witness to us
of the covenant of grace
into which we have entered,
that upheld by your Spirit
we may live day by day
as the sons and daughters
of our heavenly Father,
and be made fit to share the heritage

of God's people
in the realm of light;
through Jesus Christ our Lord.   ***Amen.***

b.   Faithful God,
by water and the Spirit
you bring us from bondage to freedom,
from darkness to light,
from death to life.
Keep far from us the spirit of fear,
and grant us the courage
which you give to all who know your love.
By the power of the Spirit
make us true sons and daughters
of your grace
and faithful witnesses to the glory of the gospel;
through Jesus Christ our Lord.

     Amen.

*at the Dedication of a **Holy Table***

1   SCRIPTURE SENTENCE

I am satisfied as with a rich feast
and there is a shout of praise on my lips.

Psalm 63: 5

2   PRAYER

All praise and thanks to you, O God!

You redeemed the world
by giving your Son;
by feeding on him we have life evermore.
Keep us in the covenant
he made with his disciples

when, at his last supper,
he broke the bread and gave it,
took the cup and reached it to them,
and through them to us
and to all who by his grace
are called to sit at his Table.

All praise and thanks to you, O God!

Amen.

6   PRAYERS

a. Eternal God, Father of our Lord Jesus Christ,
every family in heaven and on earth
takes its name from you.
Accept and bless this Holy Table
which we have dedicated to your glory
and consecrated for its holy use.
Grant that your people may come here
in joyful obedience to their Saviour's command,
with humble penitence
and in full assurance of forgiveness.
As they offer you the sacrifice of thanksgiving
and receive the Sacrament
of the body and blood of your dear Son,
may they be filled
with your grace and heavenly benediction,
and be made partakers of eternal life;
through Jesus Christ our Lord.   *Amen.*

b. Almighty God,
may this Holy Table in the midst of your house
be a witness to your redeeming love,
pointing us to Christ,
in whom you come to us
and through whom we offer ourselves to you,

a living sacrifice,
dedicated and fit for your acceptance.
Whenever we feed on Christ by faith,
confirm our vows,
receive our longings,
comfort our sorrows,
heal our wounds,
and answer all our prayers;
through the same Jesus Christ our Lord.

Amen.

at the Dedication of Communion Vessels

1 SCRIPTURE SENTENCE

When we bless the cup of blessing,
is it not a means of sharing
in the blood of Christ?
When we break the bread,
is it not a means of sharing
in the body of Christ?

1 Corinthians 10: 16

2 PRAYER

Creator God,
your name is blessed for ever!
You fashioned us in your image
and remade us by your love in Jesus Christ.
You inspire artists with your creative skill
to work in the service of the sanctuary.
Refresh us by the beauty of their offerings,
and make us also, by your grace,
living works of art;
through Jesus Christ our Lord.

Amen.

6 PRAYERS

a. Almighty God,
   receive these vessels
   which we have set apart from all common use
   and dedicated for the service of your house
   in the Sacrament of the Holy Supper of our Lord.
   We thank you that
   Christ who died upon the Cross for our salvation
   gives himself to be our spiritual food.
   Grant that whenever your people use these vessels
   in the Communion of his body and blood,
   they may be made glad by the Saviour's love,
   quickened by his Spirit,
   and made partakers of his glorious resurrection
   to eternal life;
   through the same Jesus Christ our Lord.
                                                           Amen.

b. God of heaven and earth,
   you have made everything
   that is good and lovely, pure and true.
   We thank you for these gifts
   which generosity and art have made
   for the adornment of your sanctuary
   and for use in the holy Sacrament.
   Illuminate us with your presence
   and set your beauty upon us,
   that, though we be but earthen vessels,
   we may be fit for our Master's use
   and tell the treasure of his love;
   for his name's sake,
   who lived and died and rose again,
   and is alive and reigns
   with you and the Holy Spirit,
   one God, now and for ever.   ·   *Amen.*

*at the Dedication of a **Pulpit** or **Lectern**
or a **Lectern Bible***

1 SCRIPTURE SENTENCE

Happy are those who hear the word of God
and keep it.   *St Luke 11: 28*

2 PRAYER

Almighty God,
you enlighten the minds of your servants
with the knowledge of your truth.
Illumine our minds
by the clear shining of your Spirit,
and lead us to the brightness of your Son,
the Word made flesh, full of grace and truth.
Grant that your Word
(read and) proclaimed here
may not return to you empty
without accomplishing its purpose
and succeeding in the task for which you sent it;
that those who speak and those who listen
may know you more truly
and love you more dearly;
through Jesus Christ our Lord.   **Amen.**

6 PRAYERS

a. Blessed God,
you caused all holy scriptures
to be written for our learning,
that by patience and comfort of your Word
we might embrace and for ever hold fast
the hope of everlasting life.
Set your blessing upon this place (*this Bible*)

from which your holy Word
will be delivered (*read*).
Bring to life the written word
by the power of him
who reveals your loving nature,
calls your people to holiness,
and offers them new life
in the gospel of his grace,
even Jesus Christ, the Word of Life himself,
who lives and reigns
with you and the Holy Spirit,
one God, now and for ever. **Amen.**

b. Living God,
satisfy the hunger in our hearts
with the nourishment of your Word.
Fill us with the faith of the gospel
that we may be strong
to walk in the ways of Christ,
eager to listen for his voice,
and ready to respond to his Spirit.
So may our lives themselves be a gospel,
telling everyone who reads them
the story of your matchless love in Christ;
for his name's sake.

Amen.

*at the Dedication of a **Prayer Desk***

1 SCRIPTURE SENTENCE

The priests stood to bless the people,
and their voice was heard
when their prayer
reached God's dwelling-place in heaven.

2 Chronicles 30: 27

2 PRAYER

God of all grace,
we make our approach to you
in sincerity of heart
and the full assurance of faith,
because the blood of Jesus Christ your Son
makes us free
to enter the sanctuary with confidence.
Let your ear be attentive and your eyes open
to the humble prayers
which we make in your presence
on behalf of all your people.
By the power of your Holy Spirit,
lift our prayers into the eternal prayer of Jesus,
our great high priest,
who is always alive to plead on our behalf,
and who reigns with you and the Holy Spirit,
one God, now and for ever.

Amen.

6 PRAYERS

a. Almighty God,
you are more ready to hear than we to pray,
and more ready to give
than we either desire or deserve.
Receive this Prayer Desk
which we have set apart for your glory,
and bless its use in the service of your Church.
Remember not our unworthiness
but only the merits of Jesus Christ
your Son our Saviour,
and grant that our prayers
being offered in his name
may be accepted for his sake,

who lives and reigns
with you in the unity of the Holy Spirit,
now and for ever. **Amen.**

b.   God of wisdom and might,
you never fail to hear and answer
the prayers of your faithful people.
Give us the grace of prayer:
make us ready both to desire
and to do your will,
that our prayers may not end on our lips,
but go forth with power
to accomplish your purpose in the world;
through Jesus Christ our Lord.

Amen.

*at the Dedication of an **Alms Dish**, **Offering Plates**
or **Offering Bags***

1   SCRIPTURE READING

Ascribe to the Lord the glory due to his name.
Bring an offering and enter his courts.

Psalm 96: 8

2   PRAYER

Heavenly Father,
you are the giver of all good things.
You did not spare your own Son,
but gave him up for us all,
and with him you lavished
every other gift upon us.
You have taught us that
happiness lies more in giving than in receiving.
Make us ready of heart and cheerful of spirit

to give all that we ought
for the good of your house,
the growth of your kingdom,
and the glory of your name;
through Jesus Christ our Lord.   *Amen*.

6 PRAYERS

a. God our Father,
we praise you for the sacred life and death
of Jesus Christ your Son our Lord.
His is the only offering perfect in your eyes.
By his sacrifice we are saved;
with his sacrifice we identify;
to his sacrifice we respond with our offerings.
Move us by his great love
to devise great things for your glory.
Receive and bless this alms dish (*or . . .*)
which we have set apart for your service,
and grant that our offerings
may be pleasing to you,
since we make them in the name
and by the Spirit of your Son,
the same Jesus Christ our Lord.   *Amen.*

b. Lord Jesus Christ,
we praise you for your generosity.
Though you were rich,
yet for our sake you became poor,
so that through your poverty
we might become rich.
You ask nothing of us but our heart.
Enable us to give it without hesitancy,
without limit, and holding nothing back;
for your love's sake.

                            Amen.

*at the Dedication of a **Window(s)***

1 SCRIPTURE READING

Put me to the proof, says the Lord,
and see if I do not open windows in the sky,
and pour a blessing on you
as long as there is need.   *Malachi 3: 10*

2 PRAYER

Almighty God,
you are the light of the minds that know you
and the joy of loving hearts.
Grant that the life of your Church on earth
may be so loving,
the wisdom of its leaders so pure,
the lives of its members so winning,
that the power of your gospel
may shine through
and be known in all the world,
and your love be for ever adored;
through Jesus Christ our Lord.   **Amen.**

6 PRAYERS

a. Eternal God,
you are the source of light,
you nourish and gladden
all things in heaven and on earth.
Accept and bless this gift of a window(*s*).
May your light stream through *it*
and shine into our hearts,
to chase away any darkness of sorrow or sin.
Help us to walk
without stumbling in the path of life;

and may the bright beams of your love
illumine our way
and lighten the lives of your people;
through Jesus Christ our Lord.

Amen.

b. Lord Jesus Christ,
you are the Son of the living God,
the brightness of his glory
and the express image of his person.
Fill us with thoughts
that are translucent and lovely
and draw us to the vision and love
of heavenly things.
Make us more and more in your image,
and when sign and symbol have passed away
may we see you face to face,
and in that moment of unclouded vision
be changed at last into your perfect likeness;
for your name's sake.

Amen.

At the Dedication of an **Organ**

The Dedication takes place before the organ is used.

*The service may begin by the people singing
unaccompanied:*

> **Praise God, from whom all blessings flow;**
> **praise him, all creatures here below;**
> **praise him above, ye heavenly host;**
> **praise Father, Son, and Holy Ghost.**
>
> *Amen.*

1   SCRIPTURE SENTENCE

> Let everything that has breath praise the Lord!
>
> *Psalm 150: 6*

2   PRAYER

> Heavenly Father,
> your gift of free grace
> puts a new song in our mouth.
> We praise you that through music
> we can express something
> of the glory we have seen,
> the victory we share,
> and the joy we know.
> Bless your people as they sing,
> that as our offering of praise and prayer
> is enriched by the music of a new organ,
> so the Holy Spirit
> may always be present to breathe upon us,
> lifting our song into the worship of heaven;
> through Jesus Christ our Lord.   **Amen.**

6   PRAYERS

> *a.*   God of grace,
> in the glory of your presence
> there is neither noise nor silence
> but one equal music.
> We on earth would worship you
> with undiscording voice,
> answering the melodious sound of heaven.
> Set your blessing on this organ
> now dedicated to your glory.
> Grant that its music may inspire us
> to sing with grace in our hearts;

and when words fall into silence,
may its harmonies bring
all heaven before our eyes;
through Jesus Christ our Lord.   *Amen.*

b. Holy and eternal God,
all the hosts of heaven proclaim your glory.
Sanctify and bless the music of our worship
and all who make it.
Give us the will and power
to devote to your service
all the music that is in us.
Make us and all your people joyful,
and grant that the praise and service we offer
may be perfected
when we come to your heavenly kingdom;
through Jesus Christ our Lord.   *Amen.*

Suggested Lections:

FONT

Romans	6:	3 - 11
Colossians	2:	8 - 12
Titus	3:	3 - 8
St Matthew	28:	18 - 20

HOLY TABLE

1 Kings	8:	6 - 11
Hebrews	9:	11 - 12, 24
Hebrews	10:	19 - 25
St John	17:	13 - 21

COMMUNION VESSELS

Exodus	37:	1 - 16
2 Corinthians	4:	1 - 7
St John	13:	3 - 17

PULPIT/LECTERN/BIBLE

Nehemiah	8: 1 - 4a, 5 - 6
1 Corinthians	13: 1 - 11
2 Timothy	3: 14 - 17
St Matthew	13: 3 - 7, 18 - 23
St Luke	4: 16 - 21

PRAYER DESK

1 Kings	8: 27 - 30 (- 53)
1 Peter	5: 6 - 11
St Luke	11: 1 - 10

ALMS DISH

Malachi	3: 8, 10
2 Corinthians	8: 1 - 9
St Luke	21: 1 - 4

WINDOW

Isaiah	60: 1 - 5a
Revelation	1: 10 - 11a, 12-18
St Matthew	5: 14 - 16

ORGAN

2 Chronicles	29: 25 - 29
Revelation	14: 1 - 3
St Luke	19: 37 - 40

Order for the Dedication of a Churchyard or Burial Ground

1   SCRIPTURE SENTENCES

The people having assembled at the main gateway,
or on the ground to be dedicated, the minister says:

> 'O Death, where is your victory?
> O Death, where is your sting?'
> The sting of death is sin,
> and sin gains its power from the law.
> But, thanks be to God!
> He gives us victory
> through our Lord Jesus Christ.
> *1 Corinthians 15: 55 - 57*

> What is sown as a perishable thing
> is raised imperishable.
> Sown in humiliation,
> it is raised in glory;
> sown in weakness,
> it is raised in power;
> sown a physical body,
> it is raised a spiritual body.
> *1 Corinthians 15: 42 - 44*

2   HYMN

3   STATEMENT

The minister says:

> We learn from scripture
> that, since the time of Abraham,
> God's people have set apart holy ground
> for the burial of the dead.

> Our Lord Jesus Christ was himself interred
> in accordance with Jewish burial customs
> before his resurrection
> and ascension to the right hand of God.

> We now gather in his name,
> that, by the reading of God's word
> and by prayer,
> we may set apart and dedicate this ground
> as a resting-place
> for the earthly remains
> of those departed this life.

4   SCRIPTURE LESSONS

One or more of the following may be read:

Genesis	23: 1 - 4, 17 - 20
Psalm	23
Psalm	39: 4 - 7, 12 - 13
1 Corinthians	15: 1 - 27
1 Thessalonians	4: 13 - 18
St Mark	15: 42 - 47
St Mark	16: 1 - 8
St John	11: 25 - 26
St John	14: 1 - 6, 27

5   DEDICATION

The minister says:

> In the name of the Father, and of the Son,
> and of the Holy Spirit.   **Amen.**

> I dedicate this ground to the glory of God,
> to be set apart from common uses,
> to be God's Acre within this parish,
> for the Christian burial of the dead.

>> ***Christ has died.***
>> ***Christ is risen.***
>> ***In Christ shall all be made alive.***

>> ***Blessing and honour and glory and power***
>> ***be to our God for ever and ever.***   ***Amen.***

6   PRAYERS

The minister says:

> Let us pray.

> Eternal Lord, our heavenly Father,
> you are God not of the dead
> but of the living.
> We ask your blessing on this resting-place,
> dedicated to your glory
> and appointed for its sacred purpose;
> that set apart from common use
> it may be held in honour,
> respected with reverence,
> and cared for with love;
> through Jesus Christ our Lord.   **Amen.**

Lord Jesus Christ
crucified for our sins
but crowned for our salvation,
you broke the power of darkness
and rose triumphant from the tomb.
Grant that those
who have fallen asleep in your faith
may waken in your love,
and that the gates of this holy place
may be for them
the gates of life eternal.   *Amen.*

Holy Spirit of God,
you strengthen us in weakness,
and wipe all tears from our eyes.
Comfort those who sorrow here,
that by your power
they may find light in darkness,
hope in distress,
and faith in the midst of doubt.
Assure them that the souls of our loved ones
who lie buried in peace
are safe in your everlasting arms;
through Jesus Christ our Lord.   *Amen.*

Almighty God,
your people are united in one holy Church,
the body of Christ our Lord.
Give us grace to follow your saints
in the life of faith and fellowship,
and to find at the last the heavenly joys
prepared for those who love you;
through Jesus Christ our Lord,
who is alive
and reigns with you and the Holy Spirit,
one God, now and for ever.   *Amen.*

Our Father . . .

7 HYMN

8 BLESSING

The minister says:

> May the God of peace,
> who brought again from the dead
> our Lord Jesus,
> the great Shepherd of the sheep,
> by the blood of an eternal covenant,
> make you perfect in all goodness
> so that you may do his will;
> and may he create in you
> what is pleasing to him,
> through Jesus Christ,
> to whom be glory for ever and ever!

Amen.

> And the blessing of God almighty,
> Father, Son, and Holy Spirit,
> be with you.

Amen.

Order for a Service of Healing

1 INTRODUCTION

The service of healing is a public act of worship in which the ministry of healing proclaims and offers the wholeness of the gospel of grace to people (body, mind, and spirit) and to their communities.

In the ministry of Christ, healing was central as a sign of the kingdom. Our Lord commissioned his disciples to proclaim the kingdom and heal the sick. The healing power of Christ is proclaimed and looked for in the regular acts of confession and intercession of the worshipping Church. At Holy Communion, Christ stands among us in his risen and healing power, assuring us of the ultimate victory over suffering.

It is therefore fitting that the ministry of healing should take place within the context of the regular services of the Church, including the service of Holy Communion. For some, however, a service of healing without Communion offers a more informal atmosphere and a readier opportunity for shared spiritual experience; it also encourages the participation of those without formal church connection.

Within the Christian tradition, liturgical acts of healing have included the laying on of hands, absolution, exorcism, and anointing. At the present time, a service of healing usually includes:

Ministry of the Word	*(the healing gospel)*
Prayers	*(shared or open intercession, mentioning those in need)*
Ministration	*(with laying on of hands)*

Within this pattern, it is desirable that services should be altered or adapted to meet local needs.

2 PRACTICAL SUGGESTIONS

Where congregations have not been familiar with this type of service, explanation and guidance should be given in advance.

Before the service, names to be read out during the intercessions should be gathered and grouped and given to the minister or the person leading the prayers. Otherwise, those present may name aloud at an appropriate time people who are brought to mind during the prayers.

When people come forward or are brought forward to receive the laying on of hands, they may be accompanied for (moral or physical) support.

The laying on of hands is normally the action of the presiding minister, who may invite others to share in the exercise of this ministry.

People may come forward or be brought forward without saying who they are or why they are there, giving an element of privacy and anonymity where this is desired.

Form
and Order
of Service

Prayers for healing, and the ministry of the laying on of hands, should normally take place within the regular church service, morning or evening. It is assumed that:

> *they occur at a point after the ministry of the Word, and before Holy Communion if it is celebrated;*

> *there has been some opportunity of expressing penitence and assurance of Divine grace either in the previous prayers or in the preaching or in both;*

> *some explanation has been given, both about procedures and about what people might properly expect to happen.*

1 SCRIPTURE SENTENCES

The minister says some of the following:

> Wait quietly for the Lord,
> be patient till he comes. *Psalm 37: 7*

> Blessed is anyone who trusts in the Lord,
> and rests his confidence in him.
> Heal me and I shall be healed,
> save me and I shall be saved;
> for you are my praise.
> *Jeremiah 17: 7, 14*

The Lord is near, do not be anxious,
but in everything
make your requests known to God
in prayer and petition with thanksgiving.
Then the peace of God,
which is beyond all understanding,
will guard your hearts and your thoughts
in Christ Jesus.

Philippians 4: 5a - 7

Christ himself suffered on your behalf,
and left you an example
in order that you should follow in his steps.
By his wounds you have been healed.

1 Peter 2: 21, 24

God cares for you,
so cast all your anxiety on him.

1 Peter 5: 7

Jesus says,
Come to me, all who are weary
and whose load is heavy;
I will give you rest.
Take my yoke upon you, and learn from me,
for I am gentle and humble-hearted;
and you will find rest for your souls.
For my yoke is easy to wear, my load is light.

St Matthew 11: 28 - 30

Jesus says,
Where two or three meet together in my name,
I am there among them.

St Matthew 18: 20

2   PRAYERS FOR HEALING

Leader
Christ our Lord,
long ago in Galilee
many who were sick and suffering
needed friends
to bring them to your side.
Confident of your goodness,
we now bring to you
those who need your healing touch.

All
Look on our faith,
even our little faith.

Leader
We name before you
those who are ill in body:
whose illness is long,
or painful,
or difficult to cure;
who suffer restless days
and sleepless nights.
here names may be said aloud

Leader
Lord Jesus Christ, lover of all,
All
bring healing, bring peace.

Leader
We name before you
those who are troubled in mind,
distressed by the past,
or dreading the future;
those who are trapped
and cast down by fear.
here names may be said aloud

Leader
Lord Jesus Christ, lover of all,
All
bring healing, bring peace.

Leader	We name before you
	those for whom light
	has been turned to darkness:
	by the death of a loved one;
	the breaking of a friendship;
	the fading of hope.
	here names may be said aloud

Leader	Lord Jesus Christ, lover of all,
All	***bring healing, bring peace.***

Leader	In silence we name before you
	those whose names
	we may not say aloud.
	here silence is kept

Leader	Lord Jesus Christ, lover of all,
All	***bring healing, bring peace.***

Leader	We ask your blessing
	on doctors and nurses;
	on all who look after
	those who are ill,
	who give friendship
	to those who are distressed,
	or sit with those
	who are near to death.

Leader	Lord Jesus Christ, lover of all,
All	***bring healing, bring peace.***

Leader	We ask your guidance
	for those who are engaged
	in medical research,
	that they may persevere
	with vision and energy;
	and for those who administer
	the agencies of health and welfare,
	that they may have
	wisdom and compassion.

Leader	Lord Jesus Christ, lover of all,
All	***bring healing, bring peace.***

Leader	Loving God,
	the care of every soul
	is in your hands,
	the cure of every sickness
	comes from you.
	We do not know
	your will for us.
	If by our lives
	your grace may be made known,
	then in us, through us,
	or even in spite of us,
	your kingdom come,
All	***your will be done.***
	Amen.

3 HYMN *during which people who wish the ministry of laying on of hands may come forward and kneel or sit at the appropriate place.*

4 LAYING ON OF HANDS

*In turn, hands are laid on each one kneeling or
sitting, and this or a similar prayer is said:*

> May the Spirit of the living God,
> present with us now,
> heal you of all that harms you,
> in body, mind, or spirit.
>
> In the name of Jesus Christ.
> ***Amen.***

5 *When all who require the laying on of hands have
received this ministry, and the service does not
proceed to Holy Communion, the following prayer
is said:*

> Watch now, dear Lord,
> with those who wake, or watch, or weep tonight,
> and give your angels charge
> over those who sleep.
> Tend your sick ones, O Lord Christ;
> rest your weary ones,
> bless your dying ones,
> soothe your suffering ones,
> pity your afflicted ones,
> shield your joyous ones;
> and all for your love's sake.
> ***Amen.***

6 THE GRACE

All ***The grace
of our Lord Jesus Christ,
and the love of God,***

> ***and the fellowship***
> ***of the Holy Spirit,***
> ***be with us all evermore.***
>
> ***Amen.***

7   HYMN *during which all return to their seats.*

8   DISMISSAL AND BLESSING

If the Lessons for the day are not used, the following readings may be suitable for this service:

OLD TESTAMENT

Isaiah	35	
	40:	1 - 11
	53:	4 - 12
	54:	7 - 10
Ezekiel	47:	1 - 12

PSALMS

23	
27	
30	
43	
46	
51	
86	
91	
103	
116	
121	
139	
143:	1 - 11

EPISTLE

Acts	3:	1 - 16
	28:	7 - 10
2 Corinthians	12:	7 - 10
St James	5:	13 - 16

GOSPEL

St Matthew	5:	1 - 12
	6:	25 - 34
St Mark	1:	21 - 34
	2:	1 - 12
	9:	14 - 29
St Luke	7:	18 - 23
	9:	1 - 6
	10:	1 - 9, 38 - 42
	11:	5 - 13
St John	9	
	14:	12 - 27

Order for Remembrance Day

1 to 10 in the first section may be used where a separate Act of Remembrance is held at a War Memorial outwith the church.

AT THE WAR MEMORIAL

1   SCRIPTURE SENTENCES

The minister says:

> The grace of the Lord Jesus Christ
> be with you.   *1 Corinthians 16: 23*

> Our help is in the name of the Lord,
> maker of heaven and earth.   *Psalm 124: 8*

2   PRAYERS

The minister says:

> Let us pray.

> Most gracious God, Father of all mercies,
> we offer our thanks
> for the bounty of your providence
> and the renewing liberty of your grace.
> We rejoice in our inheritance in holy things,

and in the freedom and peace in which we live.
Especially on this day we give thanks
for the remembrance
we are privileged to make
of those companions of our way
whose lives were given in time of war
(*whose names are written here*).

3   THE TRYST

The minister says:

'They shall grow not old,
as we that are left grow old;
Age shall not weary them,
nor the years condemn.
At the going down of the sun
and in the morning,
We will remember them.'

We will remember them.

[4   THE LAST POST

   5   LAMENT]

   6   THE SILENCE

Silence is kept for two minutes.

[7   REVEILLE]

   8   PRAYERS

The minister says:

Let us in honesty of heart
seek the Lord's renewing grace,
to deepen our wisdom and our peace,
and to equip us as instruments of his kindness.

Let us pray.

God of goodness and truth,
we offer our broken spirits for your healing,
our searching for your guiding light;
through Jesus Christ our Lord.

God of light and love,
you desire that all your people
should live in your peace.
Grant us the humility to seek your forgiveness
and the will to practise it
in our dealings with others.

Help us in days to come
to seek the good of the world,
to work for the increase of peace and justice,
and to show tolerance and open-mindedness
towards those whose character and customs
differ from ours.

Grant that our remembrance this day
may be consecrated for practical service,
and the world made better
for our children's children.

Receive our prayers
for the well-being of all people,
especially those who mourn and are sad,
and for all in distress,
both known to us and unknown.

Hear us for the peace of the world,
for the wise resolution of conflicts,
and the release of captive
and oppressed people everywhere.
Grant that the people of the world
may do your will and live in your spirit;
through Jesus Christ our Lord. ***Amen.***

Our Father . . .

9   LAYING OF THE WREATHS

10   BLESSING

IN THE CHURCH

1   CALL TO WORSHIP

The minister says:

We are met this day
to glorify God whose power sustains the world;
to remember with thanksgiving
those who lived and died
in the service of our country;
and to ask for God's help and blessing,
that we may be worthy of their sacrifice
each day of our life.

Let us worship God.

2   SENTENCES

The minister says:

God is our refuge and our stronghold,
a timely help in trouble.   *Psalm 46: 1*

Those who look to the Lord
will win new strength,
they will soar as on eagles' wings;
they will run and not feel faint,
march on and not grow weary.

Isaiah 40: 31

3 HYMN

4 PRAYERS

The minister says:

Let us pray.

Eternal God,
you are the shepherd of our souls,
the giver of life everlasting.

On this day
when we commemorate and commend to you
those who lived and died
in the service of others,
we are glad to remember
that your purposes for us are good,
that you gave Jesus Christ
for the life of the world,
and that you lead us by his Holy Spirit
into the paths of righteousness and peace.

Merciful and faithful God,
your purpose is to fold both earth and heaven
in a single peace.

With sorrow we confess
that in our hearts we keep alive
the passions and pride
that lead to hatred and to war.
We are not worthy of your love,
nor of the sacrifice made by others on our behalf.

Lord, have mercy.
>   ***Christ, have mercy.***
Lord, have mercy.

Almighty God,
pardon and deliver us from all our sins,
confirm and strengthen us in all goodness,
and keep us in life eternal;
through Jesus Christ our Lord.   ***Amen.***

God of unbounded grace,
you declared your reconciling love and power
in the death and resurrection
of our Saviour Jesus Christ.
Teach us, who live only in your forgiveness,
to forgive one another.
Heal our divisions,
cast out our fears,
renew our faith in your unchanging purpose *to bring*
~~of~~ goodwill and peace on earth;
through Jesus Christ our Lord,
who lives and reigns
with you and the Holy Spirit,
one God, now and for ever.   ***Amen.***

5   CALL TO REMEMBRANCE

The minister says:

Will the congregation please stand.

All or part of the following may be said:

Let us remember the kindness of God,
and his favour to us in our time of need.

Let us remember the courage,
devotion to duty,
and the self-sacrifice
of the men and women in our armed forces;
the toil, endurance, and suffering
of those who were not in uniform;
the support of those who sent us help from afar,
or came and stood by our side.

Let us remember those
who were wounded in the fight;
those who perished in air-raids at home;
those who fell in battle,
and are buried at sea
or in some corner of a foreign field;
and especially those
whom we have known and loved,
whose place is for ever in our hearts.

Let us remember those who were our enemies,
whose homes and hearts are as bereft as ours,
whose dead lie also
in a living tomb of everlasting remembrance.

Let us remember those who came back;
those whose lives still bear the scars of war;
those who lost sight or limbs or reason;
those who lost faith in God
and hope for humanity.

Let us remember the continuing grace of God,
whose love holds all souls in life,
and to whom none is dead
but all are alive for ever.

6   THE TRYST   – *Binyon's Ode.*

The minister says:

'They shall grow not old,
as we that are left grow old;
Age shall not weary them,
nor the years condemn.
At the going down of the sun
and in the morning,
We will remember them.'

We will remember them.

[7   THE LAST POST

   8   LAMENT]

   9   THE SILENCE

Silence is kept for two minutes.

[10   REVEILLE]

  11   PRAYER

The minister says:

In memory of those who died,
may we be better men and women;
and in gratitude to God,

may we live as those who are not their own
but who are bought with a price.   ***Amen.***

12   HYMN

13   OLD TESTAMENT LESSON

14   PSALM

15   NEW TESTAMENT LESSONS

16   APOSTLES' CREED

17   HYMN

18   SERMON

19   OFFERING

20   PRAYERS

The minister says:

Let us pray.

God of power and love,
bless our country and commonwealth.
Give wisdom and strength to the Queen,
govern those who make the laws,
guide those who direct our common life,
and grant that together we may fulfil our service
for the welfare of the whole people
and for your praise and glory.

Bless all members of the armed forces.
Defend them in danger.

Give them courage to meet
all occasions with discipline and loyalty.
So may they serve
the cause of justice and peace,
to the honour of your name.

Bless our young people.
May they never see the flames of war,
or know the depths of cruelty
to which men and women can sink.
Grant that in their generation
they may be faithful soldiers
and servants of Jesus Christ.

Bless our friends
and those who were our enemies,
who suffered or are still suffering from war.
Grant that your love
may reach out to the wounded,
the disabled, the mentally distressed,
and those whose faith has been shaken
by what they have seen and endured.
Comfort all who mourn the death of loved ones,
and all who this day
miss the comradeship of friends.

Bless those who are homeless,
those who are refugees,
those who are hungry,
those who have lost their livelihood or security.
Help us to pledge ourselves
to comfort, support, and encourage others,
80 that all may live in a world
where evil and poverty are done away with –
and where human life
reflects the radiance of your kingdom.
To that end we give our offerings – with ourselves –
for Jesus' sake AMEN.

Bless those in authority in every land,
and give them wisdom to know
and courage to do what is right.
Encourage those who work for peace,
who strive to improve international relations,
who seek new ways of reconciling
people of different race, colour, and creed.

Bless your Church throughout the world.
By your Holy Spirit,
draw the scattered flock of Christ
into a visible unity,
and make your Church
a sign of hope to our divided world.
Grant that we who bear your Son's name
may be instruments of your peace,
bringing peace to our homes,
our nation, and our world.

And now, rejoicing in the communion of saints,
we remember those whom you have gathered
from the storm of war
into the peace of your presence,
and give you thanks
for those whom we have known,
whose memory we treasure.
May the example of their devotion inspire us,
that we may be taught to live
by those who learned to die.
And at the last, grant that we,
being faithful till death,
may receive with them
the crown of life that never fades;
through Jesus Christ our Lord.   *Amen.*

Our Father . . .

21   HYMN

22   NATIONAL ANTHEM

23   BLESSING

The minister says:

Let us pray.

God grant to the living, grace;
to the departed, rest;
to the Church, the Queen, the Commonwealth,
and all people,
peace and concord;
and to us and all his servants
life everlasting.

And the blessing of God almighty,
Father, Son, and Holy Spirit,
be with you all.   ***Amen.***

Scripture Lessons may be chosen from the following:

OLD TESTAMENT

2 Samuel	23: 13 - 17	
Isaiah	2: 1 - 5	
Isaiah	25: 1 - 9	
Isaiah	26: 1 - 4	
Micah	4: 1 - 5	

EPISTLE

Romans	8: 31 - 39	
Ephesians	4: 25 - 5: 2	
Ephesians	6: 10 - 18	
Revelation	21: 1 - 7	

GOSPEL

St Matthew	5: 1 - 12	
St John	15: 9 - 17	

Order for the Blessing of a New Home

1   INTRODUCTION

The minister says:

> Peace be to this house
> and with all who live here.
>
> When Christ took flesh and dwelt among us,
> he made his home in Nazareth;
> and by his life with Mary and Joseph,
> he sanctified the life of home.
>
> When he came to Jericho
> he said to Zacchaeus,
> 'I must stay at your house today.
> Today salvation has come to this house.'

2   PRAYERS

The minister says:

> Let us pray
> that Christ will be at home in this house
> and bless it with his presence.
>
> May Christ always be here with you.
> May he share in your joys,
> and comfort you in your sorrows.

May he inspire and help you
to make your home
a dwelling-place of love,
offering the kindly hospitality of God.

Peace and joy be to this house.   **Amen.**

All say:

> **Guide us, Lord,**
> **in all our doings with your gracious favour,**
> **and further us with your continuing help:**
> **that in all our works,**
> **begun, continued, and ended in you,**
> **we may glorify your holy name,**
> **and by your mercy attain everlasting life;**
> **through Jesus Christ our Lord.**
>
>   **Amen.**

> **Our Father . . .**

3   SCRIPTURE READING

The minister says:

Listen for the Word of God
in the Holy Gospel according to St Luke:

By this time they had reached the village
to which they were going,
and Jesus made as if to continue his journey,
but they pressed him:
'Stay with us, for evening draws on,
and the day is almost over.'
So he went in to stay with them.
And when he had sat down with them at table,

he took bread and said the blessing;
he broke the bread, and offered it to them.
Then their eyes were opened,
and they recognized him;
and he vanished from their sight.
They said to one another,
'Did we not feel our hearts on fire
as he talked with us on the road
and explained the scriptures to us?'

St Luke 24: 28 - 32

All say:

> **Stay with us, Lord,**
> **and dwell in this home;**
> **that we may honour you as our Friend,**
> **and serve you as our Saviour.**
>
> **Amen.**

4   PRAYERS

The minister says:

God our Father,
your presence makes every dwelling
a holy temple.
Enter this home,
to hallow it in pureness and beauty of love,
and surround it
with contentment and joy.

Lord Jesus Christ,
you taught us to build
the house of our life
upon the solid rock of your truth.
Grant that your servants, *A* . . . and *B* . . . ,

may hold fast to your teaching,
and be built up in faith,
in hope, and in love.

Holy Spirit of God,
you desire to find a home in each of us.
So dwell with *A* . . . and *B* . . .
that you will be their shelter when at home,
their companion when away,
and their welcome guest when they return.

Father, Son, and Holy Spirit,
one God, blessed for ever:
expel and put away from this house
all power and presence of darkness.
Watch over and defend this home,
and let no evil come near your servants,
that they may be guarded by your angels
and folded in your eternal love.

Amen.

5   BLESSING

The minister says:

The peace and blessing of almighty God,
rest upon this house,
upon all who enter it and go out from it,
and upon all who dwell under this roof.

In the name of the Father,
and of the Son,
and of the Holy Spirit.

Amen.

[6 EVENING PRAYER

Later that night (and thereafter, every night),
the occupant(s) of the house may say:

>The sacred Three
>my fortress be,
>encircling me.
>Come and be round
>my hearth, my home.]

IV
PRAYERS
for the
SEASONS
of the
CHRISTIAN YEAR

Prayers
for the Seasons
of the Christian Year

ADVENT 1

Lord Jesus Christ,
your world awaits you.
In the longing of the persecuted for justice;
in the longing of the poor for prosperity;
in the longing of the privileged
for riches greater than wealth;
in the longing of our hearts for a better life;
and in the song of your Church:
expectation is ever present.

> *O come, Lord,*
> *desire behind our greatest needs.*
> *O come, Lord, liberator of humanity.*
> *O come, Lord, O come, Immanuel.*
>
> *Amen.*

ADVENT 2

God of faithfulness and truth,
you sent your servant John the Baptist
to preach in the desert
and summon the people to repentance.
Make us and all things new,
that in the wilderness of our hearts
we too may prepare a way
over which your Son may walk.   *Amen.*

ADVENT 3

God of eternity,
when the voice of the prophet was silent
and the faith of your people low;
when darkness had obscured light
and indifference displaced zeal:
you saw that the time was right,
and prepared to send your Son.
Set us free from fear and faithlessness
that we may be ready to welcome him
who comes as Saviour and Lord.   ***Amen.***

ADVENT 4

God and maker of all,
to redeem the world
you chose the most unsuspecting of women
to mother your Son
and by your choice gave new glory
to human flesh and earthly parenting.

With the joy that was Mary's,
may our souls magnify the Lord,
and our bodies be the means
through which you continue
the mighty work of salvation
for which Christ came.   ***Amen.***

CHRISTMAS DAY

Today, O God,
the soles of your feet
have touched the earth.

Today,
the back street, the forgotten place
have been lit up with significance.
Today,
the households of earth
welcome the King of heaven.
For you have come among us,
you are one of us.
So may our songs rise to surround your throne
as our knees bend to salute your cradle.
                                    Amen.

EPIPHANY

Holy Jesus,
before your infant form
sages bowed the knee
and acknowledged your lordship
over all power and wisdom.
Grant us also clear vision and courage,
that in the light of your light
we may devote our power and potential
to your service,
even when that requires us
to go home by another way.   ***Amen.***

LENT *General*

God of all seasons,
in your pattern of things
there is a time for keeping
and a time for losing,
a time for building up
and a time for pulling down.

In this holy season of Lent,
as we journey with our Lord to the cross,
help us to discern in our lives
what we must lay down
and what we must take up;
what we must end
and what we must begin.
Give us grace to lead a disciplined life,
in glad obedience
and with the joy
which comes from a closer walk with Christ.

Amen.

Holy Jesus,
in body, mind, and soul
you faced every temptation
of our common humanity.
Throughout this sacred season
help us to lean on you and learn from you.
May we do nothing
to defile our body, the temple of the Holy Spirit.
May we think nothing
to displace the mind of Christ in us.
May we admit nothing into our souls
except the goodness of God our Father.

Amen.

Heavenly Father,
your Son Jesus Christ was like us in all things,
tempted as we are,
yet without sin.
We, who know our frailty,
yet share his flesh and blood,
ask that the mind of Christ may be in us.

In this time of Lent,
enable us both to examine our conscience
and to inform it;
both to examine our faith
and to deepen it;
and to watch and pray,
as Christ would have us do,
so that we recognise temptation and spurn it.

Amen.

Jesus Christ,
vulnerable and alone,
in the desert
you faced the force of evil
yet withstood temptation.
Be with us
in our struggles with temptation,
that by your strength
we may reject the devil
in whatever form he comes.

Amen.

Almighty God,
conscious of the frailty of our faith
and the fickleness of our wills,
we offer ourselves to you
as those whose living and believing
need to be better modelled on your Son,
our Lord and Saviour, Jesus Christ.

Amen.

LENT 1

The prayers for Lent may be said by two voices,
a. and b.

a.　　Lord Jesus Christ,
　　　you refused to turn stones into bread.
b.　　Save us from using our power,
　　　however little,
　　　to satisfy the demands of selfishness
　　　in the face of the greater needs of others.

a.　　Lord Jesus Christ,
　　　you refused to leap from the temple top.
b.　　Save us from displaying our skills,
　　　however modest,
　　　to win instant popularity
　　　in the face of nobler calls on our abilities.

a.　　Lord Jesus Christ,
　　　you refused to bend the knee to a false god.
b.　　Save us from offering our devotion,
　　　however weak,
　　　to cheap or easy religion
　　　in the face of the harder path
　　　on which you bid us follow you.

a.　　Saviour of the World,
　　　you saw Satan masquerading as an angel of light
　　　and shunned him.
b.　　Give us wisdom
　　　to discern behind each subtle temptation
　　　the ploy of the prince of darkness;
　　　and in the face of all that is hellishly attractive,
　　　help us to choose the will of God.

Amen.

LENT 2

a.   Lord Jesus Christ,
on the mountain top Peter, James, and John
looked upon the majesty of your glory,
and from the mystery of a cloud
heard a voice declaring you to be God's Son.

b.   Though we do not live on mountain tops,
grant that we too may glimpse your glory.
In the mundane predictability of our life,
may there be for us moments
when sight gives way to insight,
and the paths of earth
become the road to heaven.   ***Amen.***

LENT 3

a.   Lord God,
in this world where goodness and evil
continue to clash with each other,
instil in us, and in all your people,
discernment to see what is right,
faith to believe what is right;
and courage to do what is right.

All   ***Keep us aware of the subtlety of sin,***
and preserve us, body, mind, and soul,
through the power of your Holy Spirit.
     Amen.

Lent 4

a.   Lord Jesus Christ,
you called your disciples to go forward with you
on the way to the cross.
Since you first walked that road
countless millions have followed you.

b.   In all that we do as your disciples,
save us from false familiarity with your journey.
May we never presume to step into your shoes,
but make us small enough to fit our own,
and to walk in love and wonder behind you.

Amen.

Lent 5

a.   Saviour of the world,
though easier paths beckoned
and friends pleaded for you to stay with them,
you turned your face resolutely
towards Jerusalem,
determined to go all the way to Calvary.

b.   Take us with you now, Lord,
and show us how through your sufferings
evil is conquered and the world is saved.

Amen.

Palm Sunday

Humble and riding on a donkey,
we greet you;
acclaimed by crowds and carolled by children,

>   *we cheer you;*
> moving from the peace of the countryside
> to the corridors of power,
>   *we salute you:*
>   ***CHRIST OUR LORD.***

> You are giving the beast of burden
>   *a new dignity;*
> you are giving majesty
>   *a new face;*
> you are giving those who long for redemption
>   *a new song to sing.*
> With them, with heart and voice,
>   *we shout:*
>   *'HOSANNA!'*
>   *Amen.*

HOLY WEEK

> Lord Jesus Christ,
> in this sacred and solemn week
> when we see again the depth and mystery
> of your redeeming love,
> help us
> to follow where you go,
> to stop where you stumble,
> to listen when you cry,
> to hurt as you suffer,
> to bow our heads in sorrow when you die,
> so that when you are raised to life again
> we may share your endless joy.
>   *Amen.*

Almighty God,
you loved the world so much
that you sent your Son
not to condemn the world
but that through him the world might be saved.

We who are quicker to judge than to bless
fall silent at the extravagance of your grace.

As we are confronted again
with the depth of human wickedness
and the greater depth
of your divine compassion,
may we not remain unmoved.
As Christ's arms are stretched out
and his body lifted up,
may we confess our part in the sin of the world,
repent of it,
know the reality of your forgiveness,
and be transformed.   *Amen.*

Lord God,
maker and lover of all,
as we contemplate again
the pageant of our Lord's betrayal,
suffering, and death;
may neither the history, ritual,
nor sentiment of this season
in themselves fascinate us.
Rather may our souls be grasped
by what our minds alone cannot contain –
that this was all for us.

And so, Lord, may we be all for you.   *Amen.*

GOOD FRIDAY

Saviour of the world,
what have you done to deserve this?
And what have we done to deserve you?
Strung up between criminals,
cursed and spat upon,
you wait for death,
and look for us,
for us whose sin has crucified you.

To the mystery of undeserved suffering,
you bring the deeper mystery of unmerited love.
Forgive us for not knowing what we have done;
open our eyes to see what you are doing now,
as, through wood and nails,
you disempower our depravity
and transform us by your grace.   ***Amen.***

EASTER

Jesus Christ, we greet you!
Your hands still have holes in them,
your feet are wet from the dew;
and with the memory of our names
undimmed by three days of death
you meet us,
risen from the grave.

We fail to understand how;
we puzzle at the reason why.

But you have come:
not to answer our questions,
but to show us your face.

You are alive,
and the world can rejoice again.
    Hallelujah!   *Amen.*

Glory be to you,
God, our strength and our redeemer.

The vacant cross and the empty tomb
vindicate your claim
that the love which suffers
is the love which saves.

So fill your people with joy
and your Church with celebration
that the world may know
that your holy Son Jesus
is not a dead hero we commemorate
but the living Lord we worship,
to whom with you and the Holy Spirit
be our praise for ever.   *Amen.*

Lord Jesus Christ,
we greet you.

The cross has not defeated you,
the grave has not kept you silent.
At the first dew of the morning,
you met our sister, Mary,
and called her by her name.

We are your family and friends,
and though numbed by your death
and aware of our complicity in it,
we come hesitantly but gladly,

to confirm the rumour
that you are alive.

Meet us as you met Mary,
with gentleness and resolution.
Speak our names quietly
in our hearts,
that we may proclaim your name boldly
on our lips.

Amen.

Almighty God,
through the rising of your Son from the grave,
you broke the power of death
and condemned death itself to die.
As we celebrate this great triumph
may we also make it the model for our living.

Help us to identify in our lives
all that should rightly die –
redundant relationships,
tired habits,
fruitless longings.
Resurrect in our lives faith, hope, and love,
as surely as you raised Jesus Christ
from the grave.

Amen.

ASCENSION

Risen Christ,
glorious you now ascend into heaven,
there to take your seat
and be acclaimed by angels.

In vain we seek to imagine
the heights to which you aspire.
Higher than high,
further than our most perceptive thoughts,
closer to God than our best imagining,
you reign, celestial, and supreme.
Yet here on earth,
your footprints are still seen
and your words are still warm.
Hallowed be your name in heaven
and followed be your way on earth.   *Amen.*

Lord Jesus Christ,
you have ascended
beyond horizons which our eyes can see,
and further than the limits
which our minds can reach.

No longer restricted to one place,
you are seated on the throne of heaven,
and present in all places.

We praise you,
our glorious Lord and Saviour,
and are for ever glad
that now there is in heaven
one who understands and intercedes for us.

Hallowed be your name!
hallowed on earth as now in heaven.   *Amen.*

Almighty God,
in sorrow you saw your Son crucified,
but with deeper joy

saw him raised from the dead.
And now we celebrate his return to heaven,
to his Father's embrace
and the acclamation of the angels.

Grant that we may learn to suffer as he did,
that we may also experience resurrection,
and finally be received in heaven by him,
with you and the Holy Spirit,
to whom be glory for ever.   ***Amen.***

Blessing and honour and glory and power!
Our words echo the praise of heaven
as you, Jesus Christ,
rise above the limitations of earth,
to sit for ever on the right hand side of God.

Though now we cannot ascend
to where you are,
still raise our hopes and hearts,
that our discipleship in this world
may be touched with the glory of heaven,
and our lives be signs and promises
of the fullness of the life to come.   ***Amen.***

PENTECOST

Come, Holy Spirit,
lamplighter, midwife of change,
comforter, disturber, inspirer, and advocate.

Come, fill the church
with the gifts earth
can neither produce nor afford.

Come, fill our lives
with that rich mixture of peace and restlessness,
calm and enthusiasm,
which are the hallmarks of holiness.

Come, promised Spirit of God,
find your way and make your home among us.
Amen.

Gracious God,
you keep your promises.
This day we receive the Spirit
of which Jesus spoke,
and we rejoice that now and for ever
this world is filled with your presence.

As the Spirit came in wind and fire,
blow through us and enflame us,
that our lives may bear witness
to your liveliness,
and to the passion
with which you love your people. **Amen.**

Lord Jesus Christ,
your promised comforter, advocate, and inspirer
is sent among us.

Pray for us to the Father,
that we may discern and receive
the richness of the Spirit's gifts.

Bestow on your church the diversity of skill
needed to further your purpose in the world.
Give us, not the gifts we long for,

but the gifts you know we need,
until our hearts and homes
become welcoming places
where your Holy Spirit may rest,
and his presence renew us.   ***Amen.***

Come, Holy Spirit:
come, breath of life,
come, fire of love,
come, power of hope,
come, catalyst of God's kingdom,
come, heavenly friend.

Come and confront us
with the truth from which we turn;
come and reveal to us
the way of Christ we dimly see;
come and nurture in us the spiritual gifts
on which life in all its fullness relies.   ***Amen.***

TRINITY

Holy, holy, holy – let angels cry
who see and know you face to face.

Blessed are you, maker of all from nothing;
Blessed are you, saviour of all from sin;
Blessed are you, spirit of all,
in all, and through all.
Blessed are you,
God alone, yet God in community.

Bless, O God, your Church on earth
with the harmony and diversity of heaven,
that we may be one, as you are one.   ***Amen.***

Holy are you, God our maker;
Holy are you, Christ our saviour;
Holy are you, Spirit and sanctifier.

Surrounded by the communion of saints,
you live in community,
three yet one,
diverse yet united.

Be a model for us
of how the Church must live;
be a model for us
of how our communities must be healthy;
be a model for us
of how, in ourselves,
we must be whole and holy.

God our father, mother,
creator, and protector,
made in your image, we adore you.

Christ our brother, friend,
servant, and saviour,
converted by your love, we adore you.

Holy Spirit, our inspirer, comforter,
counsel, and defender,
blessed by your presence, we adore you.

God, three in one,
whose nature we acknowledge as mystery,
we praise you for every sign of your care,
for your variety of gifts,
and for every way
in which you help, heal, and uphold us.

Amen.

Holy, holy, holy is God, our sovereign Lord,
who was, and is, and is to come!
Before your unfathomable mystery, O God,
all eloquence of form and language is facile.
We cannot encompass you,
for you encompass us.

So we fall silent,
and let the child deep within us
be content in the knowledge
that we are known, wanted, and loved
by One infinitely greater than we shall ever be.

Amen.

ALL SAINTS

Eternal God,
in every age you have summoned
men and women to serve you,
and in serving to reflect
your truth and glory.

We bless you for Paul and Peter,
for Martha and Mary,
for Augustine and Theresa,
for Ninian, Columba, and Margaret,
for all the saints of history and heaven,
and for those whom we met here and loved,
whose lives won people for Christ
and confronted their societies
with the claims of the gospel.

As they enjoy the company of heaven,
inspire us by their example
to answer your summons as they did,
and so come ever closer to Christ.   *Amen.*

High King of Heaven,
in the early days when your Church was young,
in the wake of the apostles
you called princes and common folk
to carry the gospel to unbelieving lands.

For all the saints of long ago
who brought Christ's word to Celtic lands,
we praise you.
For Patrick and Columba,
for Bride and Cuthbert,
for all who nurtured communities of faith,
we praise you.

We pray that in the present day
the zeal of early pioneers
may still enthuse your Scottish Church.

Amen.

Lord Jesus Christ,
you built your Church
on the rock of redeemed humanity;
and through Peter and Paul,
through Augustine and Francis,
through Luther, Calvin, and Knox,
through all the saints of every age,
you extended, reformed, and diversified
the household of faith.

We who inherit their witness today
and reap what others have sown
bless you for our fathers and mothers in God.
Like them,
may we so love and serve your Church
that those yet unborn

may benefit from our labour;
and when the grace of life on earth is past,
may we enjoy, with them,
the company of heaven.

Amen.

Lord God almighty,
you surround us with a great cloud of witnesses.
Only sight prevents us from seeing them
while daily we enjoy the freedoms,
insights, and fruits of compassion
which they, following Christ,
achieved for all ages.

They, who once sat at your table on earth,
are now hosted by your Son in heaven.
For that company we praise you,
asking that we, like them,
may put your will before our own
and follow them in following Christ
through this life
and into the life everlasting.　　　*Amen.*

God of all people,
not only the achievements of the great,
but also the kindness of the humble
has touched and influenced our lives for good.
For the ordinary saints
who helped your kingdom
take root and grow among us,
we praise you:
mothers and grandmothers,
fathers and grandfathers,
common heroes

and unsung servants of the kingdom,
who have let us see Jesus.
We bless you for our fellowship with those
whom you have called to greater life,
and we prize the company
of those who still live around us.
Lord, find a place for all of them in paradise,
and bring us with your saints
to glory everlasting. *Amen.*

St Andrew

Lord Jesus Christ,
your apostle Andrew
inspires us as patron of our land.
May we show today
the same enthusiasm for your gospel
which he displayed.
Make our lives as attractive as his,
that the vitality of our faith
and the warmth of our love
may always point beyond us to you.
Like him, may we become
not only disciples
but witnesses;
not only your followers
but also your friends. *Amen.*

V
PRAYERS
for
OCCASIONAL USE

Prayers for Occasional Use

for new year

> Eternal God,
> your everlasting mercy *and Grace*
> rises new in the morning of another year.
> Give us grace to arise with Christ
> who is our morning light.
> In this new year of our life's journey,
> may we walk by faith in him,
> and with a willing spirit
> persevere to the end;
> through the same Jesus Christ our Lord.
>
> ***Amen.***

for harvest

> God of faithfulness,
> your generous love supplies us
> with the fruits of the earth in their seasons.
> Give us grace to be thankful for your gifts,
> to use them wisely,
> and to share our plenty with others;
> through Jesus Christ our Lord.
>
> ***Amen.***

in time of an election

Almighty God,
you are the source of wisdom and justice.
Guide those who at this time are called
to choose representatives to serve
in the High Court of Parliament
(*or the Council of this Region or District*),
that they may cast their vote
with a true sense of their responsibility.
Give those who are elected
the spirit of wisdom and of understanding,
that they may provide conditions
for a good and honest life for all the people;
through Jesus Christ our Lord.

Amen.

in time of industrial unrest

God of righteousness,
you have taught us through your Son
to set our minds on your kingdom and justice
before everything else.
Give us courage and energy at this time
to think for ourselves clearly and fairly,
to seek for the truth
and to follow it whatever the cost.
Help us to believe
that whatever is right is always possible,
and that what accords with the mind of Christ
is upheld by his almighty power.

Grant that in us and in others
suspicion may give place to trust,
and stridency to peace,

that we may live and work together
in unity and love;
through Jesus Christ our Lord.   *Amen.*

after a disaster

Gracious God,
through your Son you have taught us
that nothing in life or in death
is able to separate us from your love.
Look in mercy on all
to whom great sorrow has come
through the *A* . . . in *X* . . .
Help those who are injured,
support those who are dying.
Strengthen the members
of the emergency services
(*the appropriate services may be mentioned*)
and all who bring relief and comfort.
Console and protect
those who have lost loved ones.
Give your light in darkness
to all who are near to despair,
and assure them that you hold all souls in life;
through Jesus Christ our risen Lord.

Amen.

in time of war

God of infinite mercy,
we trust in your good purposes
of peace for all your children.
We pray for those who at this time
face danger in the defence of justice.

Watch over those in peril;
support those who are anxious for loved ones;
gather into your eternal purpose
those who will die.
Remove from the hearts of all people
the passions that keep alive the spirit of war,
and in your goodness restore peace among us;
for the sake of the Prince of peace,
Jesus Christ our Lord.   **Amen.**

*thanksgiving for peace
and for deliverance in any danger*

Almighty God,
you are our refuge and our stronghold,
a timely help in trouble.
We give you praise and thanks
for our deliverance from those great dangers
which threatened (*or* compassed) us,
(and for your precious gift of peace).
Not to us, Lord, not to us
but to your name be glory,
for your goodness alone kept and preserved us.

Continue your mercies to us, we pray,
that we may always acknowledge
that you are our Saviour
and our mighty deliverer;
through Jesus Christ our Lord.   **Amen.**

VI
PRAYERS
for
SPECIFIC GRACES

Prayers for Specific Graces

for absolution

Almighty God,
you gave your Son to be the sacrifice
to atone for the sins of the whole world.
Spare your servants who confess their faults,
and mercifully absolve them from their sins;
through Jesus Christ our Lord.

Amen.

Almighty God,
you have promised in your mercy
to forgive the sins of all who turn to you
with hearty repentance and true faith.
Have mercy upon us, we pray;
pardon and deliver us from all our sins;
confirm and strengthen us in all goodness;
and bring us to everlasting life;
through Jesus Christ our Lord.   *Amen.*

Almighty and merciful God,
you are more ready to hear than we to pray,
and you give more
than either we desire or deserve.
Pour down upon us
the abundance of your mercy.

Forgive us those things
of which our conscience is afraid,
and give us those good things
which we are not worthy to ask,
save through the merits and mediation
of Jesus Christ, your Son, our Lord.   ***Amen.***

Holy God,
bring us to the cross of Jesus,
that we may find salvation.
Help us to know our sins and repent of them.
Give us your pardon and peace in our hearts;
and on the day of judgement,
show us your mercy;
through Jesus Christ our Lord.   ***Amen.***

for cheerfulness

God of hopefulness and joy,
give us a cheerful sense of our blessings.
Make us content with all that you provide for us.
Teach us that nothing can hurt us
since you hold us in your kind and loving hands.
Chase from our hearts all gloomy thoughts,
and make us glad with the brightness of hope;
through Jesus Christ our Lord.
       Amen.

for courage

God of might and valour,
your grace is all we need.
In our weakness give us strength:

support us in temptation;
make us bold in time of danger;
give us fresh vigour when we lose heart;
and help us to do your work
with a good courage,
for the sake of Jesus Christ our Lord.

Amen.

for courtesy

Loving God,
you call us to follow the pattern of graciousness
we see in the life of your Son.
Help us to be courteous and considerate
to all with whom we share our lives.
Fill us with respect for others,
save us from self-conceit,
and grant that no rivalry,
no flare of temper,
may spring up among us.
May your holy peace rest upon us,
through Jesus Christ our Lord.

Amen.

for diligence

God of faithfulness and love,
your Son taught us that while daylight lasts
we must carry on your work,
for night is coming, when no one can work.
Keep us from sloth and idleness,
and from the misuse of the talents
you have entrusted to us.
Help us to perform our duties

with cheerfulness and care,
and to do everything with single-mindedness,
out of reverence for the Lord,
Jesus Christ, your Son, our Saviour.

Amen.

for enthusiasm

Teach us, good Lord,
to serve you as you deserve;
to give and not to count the cost;
to fight and not to heed the wounds;
to toil and not to seek for rest;
to labour and not to ask for any reward
save that of knowing that we do your will;
through Jesus Christ our Lord.   ***Amen.***

for faith

Almighty and eternal God:
our eyes cannot see you,
our hands cannot touch you.
You are beyond the understanding of our minds.

Yet you have breathed your Spirit
into our spirits.
You have formed our minds to seek you,
inclined our hearts to love you,
called us to be heirs of your eternal kingdom.
Give us faith to lay hold of things unseen,
to live as those who see the invisible God.

Bring us at the last
to those things beyond our seeing,

beyond our hearing,
beyond our imagining,
to the vision of your glory
when we shall see you face to face;
through Jesus Christ our Lord.

Amen.

for fortitude

God of grace and glory,
you have called us to take hold of eternal life.
Help us to run with resolution
the race that lies before us,
our eyes fixed on Jesus,
the pioneer and perfecter of faith.
May he always be to us
the pattern we follow,
the redeemer we trust,
the master we serve,
and the friend to whom we turn.
Keep us faithful till death,
and bring us at the last
into your eternal presence
to receive the crown of life;
through Jesus Christ our Lord.

Amen.

for a generous spirit

Loving God,
you are a generous giver,
neither grudging nor reproachful.
Keep us from envying
the good enjoyed by others.

Teach us to be thankful
for what they have and we have not,
and to delight in
what they can achieve and we cannot.
Make us generous of praise
and slow to criticize,
in the Spirit of Jesus Christ, your Son, our Lord.

Amen.

for grace

Spirit of love and gentleness,
shed abroad in our hearts
the cheering light of your sevenfold grace.
You know our faults,
our failings,
our necessities,
the dullness of our understanding,
the waywardness of our affections,
the perverseness of our will.
When we neglect to practise what we know,
visit us with your grace.
Enlighten our minds,
rectify our desires,
correct our wanderings,
so that, guided by your grace,
we may be preserved
from making shipwreck of faith,
and at length be landed safe
in the haven of eternal rest;
through Jesus Christ our Lord.

Amen.

for guidance and protection

God of light and love,
in your tender compassion you sent your Son
to shine on those who sit in darkness
and to guide our feet into the way of peace.

Grant us, in our doubts and uncertainties,
the grace to ask what you would have us do.
By your Spirit of wisdom,
save us from false choices.
And since it is by your light
that we are enlightened,
lead us and protect us,
and give us a straight path to follow,
that we may neither stumble nor fall;
through Jesus Christ our Lord.

Amen.

Guide us, Lord,
in all our doings with your gracious favour,
and further us with your continual help;
that in all our works,
begun, continued, and ended in you,
we may glorify your holy name,
and by your mercy attain everlasting life;
through Jesus Christ our Lord.

Amen.

for hope

God, ground of our hope,
when we are cast down or dismayed,
keep alive in us your spirit of hope.

Fill us with all joy and peace
as we lead the life of faith,
until, by the power of the Holy Spirit,
we overflow with hope;
through Jesus Christ our Lord.   ***Amen.***

for inner peace

Set free, O Lord, the souls of your servants
from all restlessness and anxiety.
Give us your peace and power,
and so keep us that,
in all perplexity and distress,
we may abide in you,
upheld by your strength
and stayed on the rock of your faithfulness;
through Jesus Christ our Lord.   ***Amen.***

O God,
you are the author of peace
and lover of concord.
To know you is eternal life,
to serve you is perfect freedom.
Defend us your servants
from all assaults of our enemies;
that we may trust in your defence,
and not fear the power of any adversaries;
through Jesus Christ our Lord.   ***Amen.***

O God,
you are the source of all good desires,
all right judgements, and all just works.
Give to your servants that peace

which the world cannot give;
that our hearts may be set
to obey your commandments,
and that, freed from fear of our enemies,
we may pass our time in rest and quietness;
through Jesus Christ our Lord.   ***Amen.***

for joy

Creator God,
you have made the heavens and the earth
and all that is good and lovely in them.
You have shown us through Jesus our Lord
that the secret of joy
is a heart set free from selfish desires.
Help us to find delight in simple things,
and always to rejoice
in the richness of your bounty;
through Jesus Christ our Lord.   ***Amen.***

for kindness

Lord Jesus Christ,
your kindly Spirit sets us free
from hastiness and angry tempers,
from harshness and ill-will.
Help us so to live
in the brightness of your presence,
that we may bring your sunshine
into cloudy places.

Take our hands and work with them;
take our lips and speak through them;
take our minds and think with them;

take our hearts and set them on fire
with love for you and all your people;
for your name's sake.   *Amen.*

for knowledge of God

Almighty God,
in you we live and move and have our being.
You have made us for yourself,
so that our hearts are restless
till they rest in you.
Give us such purity of heart
and strength of purpose,
that no selfish passion
may hinder us from knowing your will
and no weakness prevent us from doing it.
In your light may we see light,
and in your service find our perfect freedom;
through Jesus Christ our Lord.

                                                        Amen.

God of grace and truth,
you are the light of the minds that know you,
the life of the souls that love you,
and the strength of the hearts that serve you.
Help us so to know you
that we may truly love you,
and so to love you that we may fully serve you,
whom to serve is perfect freedom;
through Jesus our Lord.

                                                        Amen.

for love

> God of all goodness and grace,
> you are worthy of a greater love
> than we can either give or understand.
> Fill our hearts with such love for you,
> that nothing may seem too hard for us
> to do or to suffer
> in obedience to your will.
> And grant that, loving you,
> we may daily become more like you,
> and finally obtain the crown of life
> which you have promised
> to those who love you;
> through Jesus Christ our Lord.   ***Amen.***

> God of love,
> through your Son
> you gave us a new commandment,
> to love one another as he loved us.
> In his Spirit we ask you
> for a mind forgetful of past injury,
> a will to seek the good of others
> and a heart full of love to all;
> through Jesus Christ our Lord.   ***Amen.***

for an open mind

> God of eternal truth and goodness,
> keep us alert to the least hint of your will,
> that we may welcome all truth,
> however it comes,
> bless every good deed,
> whoever does it,

and receive new thoughts with grace,
from whatever source they spring;
through Jesus Christ our Lord.   *Amen.*

for patience

Bless us, O God,
with the vision of your being and beauty,
that in the strength of it
we may be neither hasty
nor slothful in our work.
And give us the grace to be patient with others
as you are patient with us,
that we may gently bear with their faults
while we strive at all times to root out our own;
for your mercy's sake.

                                        Amen.

for purity

Holy God,
your eyes are too pure to look on evil,
you cannot countenance wrongdoing.
Fill us entirely with your love,
that our thoughts may be sincere,
our words true,
our deeds kind,
and all our life be pure.
Help us so to overcome
the temptations of this present world
that we shall be made partakers
of the glories of the world to come;
through Jesus Christ our Lord.

                                        Amen.

for reverence

God of goodness, beauty, and truth,
grant us sound judgement
to search out and praise what pleases you best
and to prize what is precious to you.
Give us a devout reverence for all your works,
and make us day by day
more aware of your presence,
till we come to see you face to face in heaven;
through Jesus Christ our Lord.

Amen.

for self-control

Almighty God,
through Jesus Christ your Son
you call us to refuse the evil
and to choose the good.
Grant us eagerness to hear his teaching,
readiness to obey his commandments,
and devotion to give ourselves to his service,
with no reserve and no delay.

Amen.

for selflessness

To you, merciful God,
we commend ourselves
and all who need your help.
Where there is hatred, give love;
where there is injury, pardon;
where there is doubt, faith;
where there is despair, hope;

where there is sadness, joy;
where there is darkness, light.

Grant that we may not seek so much
to be consoled as to console,
to be understood as to understand,
to be loved as to love.
For in giving we receive,
in pardoning we are pardoned,
in dying we are born into eternal life.   *Amen.*

for a spiritual mind

Almighty God,
you alone can bring order
to the unruly wills and passions of sinful people.
Give us grace to love what you command
and to desire what you promise,
that, in all the changes and chances of this world,
our hearts may be surely fixed
where true joys are to be found,
in Jesus Christ our Lord.   *Amen.*

for strength

God of might and power,
you support us in danger
and carry us through temptation.
Give us grace to trust in you
that, though by nature we are frail and weak,
we may stand upright in any time of trial;
through the strength of him
who makes us more than conquerors,
even Jesus Christ our Lord.   *Amen.*

for temperance

Almighty and gracious God,
you open your hand
and fill the world with plenty.
Teach us to use your gifts
with gladness and care,
that no goodness of yours may become for us
an occasion of selfishness and greed,
and that in the strength of your provision
we may faithfully serve you here
and be counted worthy to be made partakers
of your eternal kingdom;
through Jesus Christ our Lord.   ***Amen.***

for a tranquil spirit

Lord,
support us all the day long of this troublous life,
until the shadows lengthen
and the evening comes,
the busy world is hushed,
the fever of life is over,
and our work done.
Then, Lord, in your mercy,
grant us safe lodging,
a holy rest,
and peace at the last;
through Jesus Christ our Lord.   ***Amen.***

for truthfulness

God, the Father of Jesus Christ and our Father,
you sent your Spirit of truth to us

to guide us into all the truth.
Rule our lives by your love and power,
that no fear of danger, no hope of reward
may make us false in act or speech or thought.
Save us from all that would make us
love a lie or practise deceit,
and make us truthful
with the truth that sets us free;
through Jesus Christ our Lord.   *Amen.*

for zeal

God of unfailing power,
you give vigour to the weary,
fresh hope to the exhausted.
We look to you to win new strength,
that we may soar as on eagles' wings,
run and not feel faint,
march on and not grow weary.
Keep us aglow with your Spirit,
that with unflagging zeal
we may serve the Lord.   *Amen.*

VII
SPECIFIC
INTERCESSIONS

Specific
Intercessions

for our absent friends

God our Father,
you are present to your people everywhere.
We pray for those we love who are far away.
Watch over them and protect them.
Keep far from them
all that would hurt the body and harm the soul.
Give to them and to us
the assurance of the strength and peace
of your presence,
and keep us all so near to you
that we will be for ever near to one another.
In your good time,
may we renew our fellowship on earth,
and at the last
come to the unbroken fellowship
of the Father's house in heaven;
through Jesus Christ our Lord. **Amen.**

for agriculture and fishing

Almighty God, Creator of all,
you have blessed land and sea
and made them fruitful:
we depend on your bounty for our daily food.
We thank you for your goodness,

and seek your blessing on those who work
at sea or on the land.
As they fulfil the duties
and face the dangers of their calling
may they know the strength of your protection.
By the good results of their labours,
may our needs be met,
our lives nourished,
and our hands opened in generosity
to the needs of others;
through Jesus Christ our Lord.   ***Amen.***

for all people

God of all nations,
your love is without limit and without end.
Enlarge our vision
of your redeeming purpose for all people.
By the example of your Son,
make us ready to serve the needs
of the whole world.
May neither pride of race nor hardness of heart
make us despise any
for whom Christ died
or injure any in whom he lives;
through the same Jesus Christ our Lord.
                                        Amen.

for the arts

God of light and love,
your Spirit leads us to desire you,
the perfection of goodness,
the fountain of truth,

the vision of beauty.
We aspire to your perfection,
we seek your truth,
we rejoice in your beauty.
We praise you for every way the arts
reflect your loveliness
and lift the human spirit into heaven.
Continue to inspire thinkers and writers,
artists and authors, composers and craftsmen,
directors and performers,
that they may play their part
in making the heart of the people wise,
their mind sound, and their will just;
to the honour of Jesus Christ our Lord. ***Amen.***

for Christian Unity

Lord God,
we thank you for calling us
into the company of those who trust in Christ
and seek to obey his will.
You have made us strangers no longer
but pilgrims together
on the way to your kingdom.
Guide us closer to you and to one another
in the unity of the Spirit and the bond of peace,
and strengthen us together
in mission and service to your world;
through Jesus Christ our Lord. ***Amen.***

for the Church

Most gracious God,
we humbly pray for your holy catholic Church.

Fill it with all truth;
in all truth with all peace.
Where it is corrupt, purge it;
where it is in error, direct it;
where anything is amiss, reform it;
where it is right, strengthen and confirm it;
where it is in want, furnish it;
where it is divided, heal it,
and unite it in your love;
through Jesus Christ our Lord.   ***Amen.***

for civic occasions

Lord of our life and God of our salvation,
we ask your blessing on all that is best about us,
and your forgiveness
for anything that has fallen short
of the greatness of the past,
the hopes of the present,
and the call to higher things in the future.

Guide those who direct the affairs
of this Region (*or District*).
Sustain them in their work,
support them in their anxieties,
and strengthen them in their resolve
to seek and pursue
the well-being of all the people.
Give them joy in their service,
due pride in their successes,
and the approval of a good conscience
in all their endeavours.
And so work among us
by your good and kindly Spirit,
that our community

(*or city, town, Region, District*)
may be renewed in beauty and order,
in happiness and peace;
through Jesus Christ our Lord.   ***Amen.***

for the coming of Christ's kingdom

Lord God, Sovereign over all,
bring in the day
of the splendour of your kingdom
and draw the whole world
into willing obedience to your reign.
Cast out the evil things that cause war,
and send your Spirit to rule the hearts of people
in righteousness and love.
Repair the desolations of many generations,
that the wilderness may rejoice,
and the city be made glad with your law.
Confirm every work that is founded on truth,
and fulfil the desires and hopes of your people,
through the victory of Christ our Lord.
                                          Amen.

for the Commonwealth

Eternal God,
bless our Commonwealth of nations.
Give us, of whatever race or tongue,
peace and prosperity,
sound government and just laws,
simplicity and justice
in our relations with one another,
and a spirit of service to all the world;
through Jesus Christ our Lord.   ***Amen.***

for those in the Community Services

God of all life,
you call us to live in community
and teach us to care for one another
after the pattern
of Jesus Christ your Son our Lord.
We pray for those whose position and authority
affect the lives of others.
Inspire them with a vision
of the community as it might be,
where love of neighbour
and concern for one another
drive out discontent and strife, anxiety and fear.
Help us all to work together
with one heart and will,
with sympathy and understanding,
to serve the common good,
to minister to people in trouble and despair,
and to multiply true happiness among us;
through Jesus Christ our Lord.   **Amen.**

for education and learning

God of truth and love, the only wise God,
you have commanded us to love you
with all our mind.
So bless the work of schools
and colleges and universities,
that in them the truth may never be denied,
betrayed, concealed,
but be honoured, followed, and obeyed.
Guide teachers and students in their endeavours
to seek and serve the truth:
may their learning

never cut them off from the community,
but lead them towards
enlarged and selfless service.
Grant that learning may flourish among us,
as a means both of enriching our lives
and of drawing us nearer to you
from whom all truth proceeds;
through Jesus Christ our Lord.   **Amen.**

for the environment

Creator God,
you made all things
and all you made was very good.
Show us how to respect
the fragile balance of life.
Guide by your wisdom those who have power
to care for or to destroy the environment,
that by the decisions they make
life may be cherished
and a good and fruitful earth
be preserved for future generations;
through Jesus Christ our Lord.

                                        Amen.

for the Forces of the Crown

Almighty God,
in you alone we find safety and peace.
We commend to your gracious keeping
all the men and women who serve
in the Navy, the Army, or the Air Force,
who face danger and put their lives at risk
so that others might live in safety.

Defend them day by day
by your heavenly power;
and help them to know
that they can never pass
beyond the reach of your care.
Keep alive in them and in us
your vision of that peace
which alone we must seek and serve;
through Jesus Christ our Lord.   ***Amen.***

for the General Assembly

Almighty God,
your Son promised his disciples
that he would be with them always.
Hear the prayer we offer for your servants
now (*to meet*) met in General Assembly.
May your Holy Spirit rest on them:
a spirit of wisdom and understanding,
a spirit of counsel and power,
a spirit of knowledge and fear of the Lord.
Grant them vision and courage;
unite them in love and peace;
teach them to be trustworthy stewards
of your truth.
And so guide them in all their doings
that your kingdom may be advanced,
your people confirmed in their most holy faith,
and your unfailing love
declared to all the world;
through Jesus Christ our Lord.
                                        Amen.

for home and family

Lord,
you have been our home
in every generation.
Defend our homes against all evil;
surround them with your presence,
and make them sanctuaries
of your peace and joy.
Bless those dear to us, wherever they may be,
and grant that they and we
may dwell together in the shelter of your love,
until we come at last
into the Father's house in heaven,
the family of God complete;
through Jesus Christ our Lord.

Amen.

for those who are homeless

Almighty God,
your Son had nowhere to lay his head.
Have compassion on those who are homeless
or who live in overcrowded conditions.
Give them strength and hope,
and keep them close to you.
Help us to work and pray
for the day when all your children
are housed and healthy
and free to live full and happy lives;
through Jesus Christ our Lord.

Amen.

for hospitals and healing

God of love,
your Son brought healing to the sick
and hope to the despairing.
We pray for all who suffer pain,
or who bear the burden of illness,
or who have to undergo an operation.
Give them the comfort and strength
of your presence,
and surround them
with your healing love and power.
May they know the fellowship of Christ
who bore pain and suffering for us,
and at the last won victory over death.

Bless those who share with Christ
a healing ministry,
researchers, doctors, surgeons, nurses.
Use their sympathy and skill
for the relief of suffering,
the conquest of disease,
and the restoration of health;
and crown all their efforts with good success;
through Jesus Christ our Lord.   ***Amen.***

for those who are hungry

God our Father,
in the name of him
who gave bread to the hungry,
we remember all
who through our human ignorance,
folly, and sin
are condemned to live in want.

Show us, who have so much,
what we can do
to help those who have so little;
and bless the efforts of those
who work to overcome poverty and hunger,
that sufficient food may be found for all;
through Jesus Christ our Lord.   *Amen.*

for industry and commerce

Living God,
you are the source of wisdom and power.
You have given us the resources of the earth,
and the skills to use them.
By your wisdom, we manufacture and distribute
all that is necessary for our daily lives.
We pray for the industry of our land.
Increase understanding and co-operation,
that differences may be resolved
fairly and without bitterness,
our commerce prosper in equity and peace,
and the ordered life of our country
be maintained justly
for the benefit of all the people;
through Jesus Christ our Lord.   *Amen.*

for the mission of the Church

Loving God,
you sent your Son into the world
that all might live through him.
You gave your Holy Spirit to the apostles
to empower them
to preach the message of your truth.

Pour out the same Spirit on your Church,
that she may proclaim to all people
the gospel of the love of Christ,
till all are gathered into your kingdom,
and your glory covers the earth
as the waters fill the sea.

Amen.

Eternal God,
you have shown yourself
to the world in many ways
and have never left yourself
without witness in human lives.
Hear our prayer for people
whose faith and customs differ from ours.
Make us eager to learn from them,
as well as ready to share with them
the truth you have given us
in Jesus Christ our Lord.

Amen.

for the Nation

God of righteousness,
hear our prayer for the life of our country.
Bless the Queen
and those in positions of authority.
Bless the people:
rule their hearts and encourage
their endeavours for good.
Help us to seek service before privilege,
public prosperity before private gain,
and the honour of your name
before the popularity of our own.

Give us liberty, peace, and joy,
and bind us in service to the community
and in loyalty to you;
through Jesus Christ our Lord.   ***Amen.***

for those in need

God of all grace and comfort,
hear our prayer for those who are unhappy,
who are lonely or neglected,
who are damaged or abused,
or whose life is darkened
by fear or pain or sorrow.

Give us grace to help them when we can.
Give them faith
to look beyond their troubles to you,
their heavenly Father and unfailing friend,
that they may take up the threads of life again
and go on their way with fresh courage
and renewed hope;
through Jesus Christ our Lord.
                                    Amen.

for peace

Almighty God,
all thoughts of truth and peace
proceed from you.
Kindle in the hearts of all people
the true love of peace.
Guide with your pure and peaceable wisdom
those who (*at this time*) take counsel
for the nations of the earth;

that in tranquillity your kingdom
may go forward,
till the earth is filled
with the knowledge of your love;
through Jesus Christ our Lord.   ***Amen.***

Almighty God,
your Son came to be the Saviour of the world
and the Prince of peace.
Give us grace to follow in his ways
and to fulfil our calling
as peacemakers in his name.
May his Holy Spirit
so move in the hearts of all people
and among the nations of the world,
that the barriers of fear, suspicion, and hatred
which separate us may crumble and fall,
and the peoples of the world
be united in justice and peace;
through Jesus Christ our Lord.   ***Amen.***

for racial harmony

God and Father of all,
in your love
you made all the nations of the world
to be a family,
and your Son taught us to love one another.
Yet our world is riven apart
with prejudice, arrogance, and pride.
Help the different races
to love and understand one another better.
Increase among us sympathy,
tolerance, and goodwill,

that we may learn to appreciate the gifts
that other races bring to us,
and to see in all people
our brothers and sisters for whom Christ died.
Save us from jealousy, hatred, and fear,
and help us to live together
as members of one family at home in the world,
sons and daughters of one Father
who live in the liberty of the children of God;
through Jesus Christ our Lord.   *Amen.*

for scientists

Almighty God, Creator and Lord of all,
we praise you for the knowledge given to us
to search out and harness
the hidden forces of nature.
Bless the work of those
who carry on the work of science
in all its many forms.
Grant with increasing knowledge
increasing wisdom,
that they may use
their discoveries and inventions
for the welfare of us all
and the glory of your name;
through Jesus Christ our Lord.   *Amen.*

for space research

Eternal God,
your creative power makes the universe,
and your loving wisdom
gives us intelligence to explore it.

We pray for the safety
of those whose scientific skill
allows them to travel into space
and to probe infinity.
May space research be guided
by profound respect
for the integrity of creation,
that planet earth may be preserved
as a home for future generations,
and the universe resound with praise for you;
through Jesus Christ our Lord.   *Amen.*

for those who are unemployed

God of mercy and grace,
we commend to you
those who suffer through unemployment,
who would work but find no work to do,
whose gifts and energies seem not to be needed.
Support and strengthen them and their families.
May no bitterness of mind
blot out your love from their lives,
and may no hopelessness of heart
quench their spirits
or threaten their relationships.
In your love and by your mercy,
help those in authority to provide for them
the means of livelihood
that they may be set free from anxiety and fear
and be enabled to work in security and peace;
through Jesus Christ our Lord.   *Amen.*

VIII
ADDITIONAL
PRAYERS
for
PUBLIC WORSHIP

Additional Prayers for Public Worship

1   Holy God, righteous and merciful,
cleanse our minds and free our consciences
from the things that divide us from you.
We have shut our eyes to your glory,
our minds to your truth,
and our hearts to your Spirit.

And yet we want to love you, Lord,
to offer you true worship and joyful service.
Pardon and deliver us from all our sins;
and since all your paths are loving and sure,
guide us in the way we should go,
and lead us to life everlasting;
through Jesus Christ our Lord.

Amen.

2   God of mercy and of grace,
you know the secrets of our hearts:
how blind we are to our own faults,
yet harsh in judging others;
how swift we are to take for gain,
yet slow to give for others;
how proud we are of our success,
yet grudging in our praise of others.

Remember, Lord,
your tender care and love unfailing.
Do not remember our sins and offences,
but remember us in your goodness,
in accordance with your endless mercy;
through Jesus Christ our Lord.

Amen.

3   Father in heaven,
your love brings
life to dead souls,
light to darkened minds,
strength to weak wills.

Help us to believe and trust
that no wrong we have done,
no good we have failed to do,
is too great for you to pardon
through the merits of Jesus Christ your Son.

Amen.

4   God of all mercy,
give us grace to make a fresh start today.
We know we have not loved you
with our whole heart,
nor have we loved our neighbour as ourselves.

As we hope to be forgiven,
teach us also to forgive;
and lead us forward in a new life
where neither grudges
nor resentment have a part;
through Jesus Christ our Lord.

Amen.

5   God of mercy and truth,
       we seek your forgiveness
       for the sinful way we live.
       We are unworthy to be your children,
       unfit to be your servants.
       We are burdened with memories
       of things undone
       that ought to have been done,
       and of things done
       that ought not to have been done.

       Bring us afresh
       the healing and cleansing power of your Spirit,
       that we may lay hold of the salvation you offer
       and walk in newness of life,
       to the glory and praise of your name;
       through Jesus Christ our Lord.   ***Amen.***

THANKSGIVING

1   God of kindliness and grace,
       we thank you for the joy we have in our homes;
       for the comradeship of our colleagues at work;
       for the delight we have in nature,
       the refreshment we find in good company,
       the renewal we gain from the arts;
       for the patience and courage
       of those who in the past fought for human rights,
       and for the continuing service of those
       who have a vision of the world
       made fair and lovely.

       In praising you for the service of others
       and for your mercy given through them,
       we offer you the service of our own lives;
       through Jesus Christ our redeemer.   ***Amen.***

2 Almighty God, we give you thanks
   for this life and all its blessings,
   for joys great and simple,
   for gifts and powers more than we deserve,
   for love at the heart of your purpose
   and surpassing wisdom in all your works,
   for light in the world
   brought once in Jesus Christ
   and shining ever through his Spirit.

   We pray, through Jesus Christ our Lord,
   for that light to dawn upon us daily,
   that we may always have a grateful heart,
   and a will to love and serve you
   to the end of our days.
   Lord, hear our prayer and praises:
     Alleluia, we bless you, O God. ***Amen.***

3 Almighty God, Father of all mercies,
   we, your unworthy servants,
   give you most humble and hearty thanks
   for all your goodness and loving kindness
   to us and to all people.

   We bless you for our creation, preservation,
   and all the blessings of this life;
   but above all for your immeasurable love
   in the redemption of the world
   by our Lord Jesus Christ,
   for the means of grace,
   and for the hope of glory.

   Give us, we pray,
   such a sense of all your mercies,
   that, with truly thankful hearts,

we may show forth your praise,
not only with our lips but in our lives,
by giving up ourselves to your service,
and by walking before you in holiness
and righteousness all our days;
through Jesus Christ our Lord,
to whom, with you and the Holy Spirit,
be all honour and glory,
for ever and ever.   *Amen.*

4   Lord our God,
     source and giver of all good things,
     we thank you for all your mercies
     and for your loving care over all creation.

     We bless you for the gift of life:
     for your protection around us,
     your guiding hand upon us,
     your steadfast love within us.
     We thank you for friendship and duty,
     for good hopes and precious memories,
     for joys that cheer us
     and trials that teach us to trust in you.
     Most of all, we thank you
     for the saving knowledge
     of your Son our Saviour,
     for the living presence of your Spirit,
     the comforter,
     for the Church, the body of Christ,
     for the ministry of word and sacrament
     and all the means of grace.

     In all these things,
     make us wise in the right use of your blessings,
     that we may render an acceptable thanksgiving

all the days of our life;
through Jesus Christ our Lord.   *Amen.*

5   Let us praise and thank God
      for all great and simple joys:
      for the gift of wonder, the joy of discovery,
      and the everlasting freshness of experience;
      for all that comes to us
      through sympathy and through sorrow;
      for the joy of work attempted and achieved;
      for musicians, poets, artists,
      all who work in form and colour
      to increase the beauty of life;
      for the likeness of Christ in ordinary people,
      their forbearance, courage, and kindness,
      and for quiet and faithful service
      cheerfully given.

      Glory to the Father, and to the Son,
      and to the Holy Spirit:
            as it was in the beginning,
            is now, and will be for ever.   *Amen.*

INTERCESSION

1   O God, the creator and preserver of all,
      we pray for people of all sorts and conditions.
      Make your purpose known in the earth,
      your saving power among the nations.

      We pray for the well-being
      of the catholic Church.
      So guide and guard it by your good Spirit,
      that all who profess

and call themselves Christians
may be led into the way of truth,
and hold the faith in the unity of the Spirit
and in righteousness of life.

We commend to your generous goodness
all those who are in any way
afflicted or distressed,
in mind, body, or circumstances.
Comfort and relieve them
according to their individual needs;
give them patience under their sufferings,
and a happy release out of all their afflictions.

All this we ask for the sake of Jesus Christ.
                                    Amen.

2   Lord Jesus Christ,
     we acknowledge your rule
     over every realm of life:
     subdue the world by the might of your love.

     Son of Mary:
     consecrate our homes.
     Son of David:
     cleanse our politics.
     Son of God:
     grant us eternal life.

     Jesus the Carpenter:
     hallow our daily work.
     Jesus the Saviour:
     save us from ourselves.
     Jesus the Life-giver:
     renew your Church.

Jesus the Crucified:
reveal your love and power to all who suffer.
Jesus the King:
raise us to live and reign with you for ever.
Jesus the Word of God:
perfect your creation
and bring the world
to the knowledge of your love.

> *For the kingdom,*
> *the power, and the glory are yours,*
> *for ever and ever.*   *Amen.*

3   Mighty and merciful God,
      may your kindness be known to all.

      Hear the prayers of all who cry to you;
      open the eyes of those
      who never pray for themselves;
      have mercy on those who are in misery;
      deal gently with those who sit in darkness;
      increase the number of those
      who love and serve you daily.

      Preserve our land from all things hurtful,
      preserve our Church from all dangerous error,
      preserve our people from forgetting
      that you are their Lord and Saviour.

      Be gracious to those countries
      that are made desolate
      by war, famine, disease, or persecution,
      and grant that the course of the world
      may be so ordered in obedience to your will
      that the people may live in security

and freedom from want,
and their children grow up
to be makers of peace;
through Jesus Christ our Lord.

Amen.

4   Loving and Holy Spirit of God, we pray:

that we and all people
may increasingly work together
to establish on earth
the rule of the kingdom of heaven;

that the resources of the world
may be gathered,
distributed, and used
with unselfish motives and scientific skill
for the greatest benefit of all;

that beauty may be given
to our towns and cities,
and left untarnished in the countryside;
that children may grow up strong in body,
sound in mind, and trained in spirit;

that there may be open ways,
and peace, and freedom,
from end to end of the earth;

and that people everywhere
may learn to live in love
through keeping the company
of Jesus Christ our Lord,
in whose great name we pray.

Amen.

5   For the peace of the world,
the welfare of the Church,
the unity of all people:
let us pray to the Lord.

silence

For the Queen and her government,
the leaders of the world,
and all in authority:
let us pray to the Lord.

silence

For those who are oppressed,
or destitute, or hungry,
and for those who are unemployed:
let us pray to the Lord.

silence

For those whom we love, at home or far away,
neighbours and friends and colleagues at work,
all those whose lives are closely linked with ours:
let us pray to the Lord.

silence

For the glory of your name, O God,
turn us from all that is evil,
and grant us grace
to put our whole trust and confidence
in your loving purpose for the world.
Strengthen us by your Spirit
to serve you with a willing heart
and a cheerful spirit;
through Jesus Christ our Lord.   ***Amen.***

DEDICATION OF THE OFFERINGS

1   Accept, O Lord,
      the offering we seek to make,
      of ourselves and our money;
      and grant that we may ever work and pray
      to build a world of peace
      and joy and freedom;
      through Jesus Christ our Lord.

                                            Amen.

2   Lord our God,
      we acknowledge that
      you are our Father,
      we are your children,
      our neighbours
      are our brothers and sisters in Christ.
      To their service and to your glory
      we dedicate ourselves,
      our hearts and minds, our wills and works.

      Strengthen our resolve
      to stand fast in your faith,
      to seek the help of your Holy Spirit,
      and to work willingly for your perfect kingdom,
      in the name of Jesus Christ our Lord.

                                            Amen.

3   Gracious and loving God,
      if we have gifts to bring,
      it is of your free mercy;
      for all things are yours,
      and what we have comes from you.

Accept the offerings we make,
and grant that gifts which can never be worthy
may yet be hallowed by your blessing
and used in your service;
through Jesus Christ our Lord.

Amen.

4 We bring our gifts to you, Lord God,
with cheerfulness and a joyful heart.
Grant that with our gifts
we may also offer
a ready mind and a willing spirit
to show forth in our lives
the truth of the gospel;
through Jesus Christ our Lord.

Amen.

5 God of all goodness and grace,
give us such confidence,
such peace, such happiness in you,
that your will
may always be dearer to us
than our will,
and your pleasure than our pleasure.
All that you give is your free gift to us,
all that you take away is your grace to us.
May you be thanked for all,
praised for all,
loved for all;
through Jesus Christ our Lord.

Amen.

IX
A
DAILY
SERVICE

A Daily
Service

From early in her history, the Church has developed forms of daily prayer and worship, consisting at first of the saying or singing of psalms and prayers of intercession.

At the Reformation, the people were encouraged to join in daily worship in their parish churches, and the 1564 Book of Common Order made provision for daily services of prayers and readings.

Ministers in following their own spiritual discipline may welcome the opportunity to encourage others to join with them in daily worship wherever possible.

Where it is physically impossible to join in a daily service in church, this service may be used at home or elsewhere. It is mutually encouraging to both minister and people to know that they are joining in the same act of worship.

The Readings may be taken from a lectionary, such as that provided by the Joint Liturgical Group in 'The Daily Office Revised' (SPCK 1978). Other patterns of regular reading of the Scripture may take the form of an Old Testament Lesson in the morning, and a Lesson or Lessons (Epistle and Gospel) in the evening; or over a period of time a whole book may be read consecutively.

1   SCRIPTURE SENTENCE

The minister and people say responsively:

> Lord, open my lips,
> > ***that my mouth may proclaim your praise.***
> Make haste and save me, God;
> > ***Lord, come quickly to my help.***

2   INVOCATION

> The world belongs to God,
> > ***the earth and its people are his.***
> How good and lovely it is
> > ***to live together in unity.***
> Love and faith come together,
> > ***justice and peace join hands.***
> If the Lord's disciples keep silent,
> > ***these stones would shout aloud.***
> Lord, open our lips;
> > ***and our mouths***
> > ***shall proclaim your praise.***

> Glory to the Father, and to the Son,
> and to the Holy Spirit:
> > ***as it was in the beginning,***
> > ***is now, and will be for ever.***   ***Amen.***

3   HYMN (*where appropriate*)

4   PRAYER

> *either*

> God our Creator,
> your kindness has brought us

the gift of a new day.
Help us not to cling to yesterday,
nor covet tomorrow,
but to accept the uniqueness of today.

silence

By your love,
celebrated in your Word,
seen in your Son,
brought near by your Spirit,
take from us all we need carry no longer,
that we may be free again to choose to serve you
and be served by each other.

> *We believe that God forgives*
> *and sets us free,*
> *and at the day's beginning*
> *we commit ourselves*
> *to follow where Christ calls*
> *and to love one another.*   **Amen.**

or

Almighty God, maker of all,
  Lord, have mercy on us.
Jesus Christ, Son of God,
  Christ, have mercy on us.
Holy Spirit, breath of life,
  Lord, have mercy on us.

Let us in silence remember
our own faults and failings . . .

silence

I confess to God almighty,
and in the presence of all God's people,
that I have sinned in thought, word and deed,
and I pray God almighty to have mercy on me.

> *May almighty God have mercy on you,*
> *pardon and deliver you from all your sins,*
> *and give you time to amend your life.*

Amen.

> *We confess to God almighty,*
> *and in the presence of all God's people,*
> *that we have sinned in thought,*
> *word and deed,*
> *and we pray God almighty*
> *to have mercy on us.*

May almighty God have mercy on you,
pardon and deliver you from all your sins,
and give you time to amend your life.   ***Amen.***

5 PSALM

The Psalm for the day, said responsively,
or sung together

6 CANTICLE

One of the following Canticles may be said
antiphonally, or sung

Monday:	*Te Deum Laudamus*	(Hymn 345)
Tuesday:	*Magnificat*	(Hymn 163)
Wednesday:	*Benedictus*	(Hymn 161)
Thursday:	*Gloria in Excelsis*	(Hymn 62)

| Friday: | *Trisagion and Reproaches* | (Hymn 240) |
| Saturday: | *Venite, exultemus* | (Hymn 20) |

7   SCRIPTURE

Bible reading(s) for the day

   silence

8   APOSTLES' CREED

9   HYMN (*where appropriate*)

10   PRAYERS

Satisfy us with your love in the morning,
and we will live this day in joy and praise.

Use either a. or b. or other prayers of intercession

Let us pray.

a.   Eternal God,
your Son is King
and Head of the Church.
We pray for your people across the world,
that what is divided
by doctrine or race,
by class or creed,
may be united in your praise.

Lord, in your mercy,
hear our prayer.

Eternal God,
your Son is Ruler of nations.

We pray for all in authority,
that those who lead us
may establish right priorities,
and that by your wisdom and their vision
the world may reflect your kingdom.

Lord, in your mercy,
    hear our prayer.

Eternal God,
your Son is Prince of peace.
We pray for a peaceful world,
where children grow up without fear,
where security rests on trust rather than threats,
and where nations fight against poverty
rather than against each other.

Lord, in your mercy,
    hear our prayer.

Eternal God,
your Son is Saviour of the poor.
We pray for those born into poverty,
that we may strive
to make this world a place of plenty,
where the riches of creation are shared by all.

Lord, in your mercy,
    hear our prayer.

Eternal God,
your Son is healer of our sickness.
We pray for those who are ill
or who are passing through difficult times,
that they may know
the power of Christ to sustain them

and the love of friends to support them.

Lord, in your mercy,
   hear our prayer.

Eternal God,
your Son is the Resurrection and the Life.
Confirm our faith in the communion of saints,
that, inspired by dear ones gone before us,
we may seek those things that are above
and live on earth the life of heaven.

Lord, in your mercy,
   hear our prayer.

b. Let us pray for the whole Church,
for the fellowship of the faithful here
and throughout the world;
that the Lord may give us
the grace of lives consecrated to his will:

   Lord, hear our prayer.

Let us pray for all who hate us
or persecute us for Christ's sake;
that the Lord may calm their hatred,
filling their hearts
and ours with his generous love:

   Lord, hear our prayer.

Let us pray for all who are lonely,
overworked or depressed,
for all who are destitute
and have no one to turn to;

that the Lord may protect and save in his love
all who can hope only in him:

Lord, hear our prayer.

Let us pray for one another,
and for all who are absent from us now;
that the Lord in his grace
may keep us from falling,
preserve us to the end,
and gather us together in his kingdom:

Lord, hear our prayer.

Remembering all the witnesses
and martyrs of the faith
and all who have given their lives for God,
and in communion
with all our brothers and sisters
who have fallen asleep in Christ,
let us commit ourselves and one another
to the living God through his Christ:

Lord, hear our prayer.   **Amen.**

Collect of the day or season

11 FREE PRAYER

*This time of prayer varies according to circumstances;
it brings before God the concerns of each day,
including the needs of the local community or of the
time; and ends with the General Collect and the
Lord's Prayer.*

12 GENERAL COLLECT

Monday

God most holy,
we give you thanks
for bringing us out of the shadow of night
into the light of morning.
We ask you
for the joy of spending this day in your service,
so that, when evening comes,
we may once more give you thanks,
through Jesus Christ, your Son, our Lord.

Amen.

Tuesday

Eternal God and Father,
you create us by your power
and redeem us by your love:
guide and strengthen us by your Spirit,
that we may give ourselves today
in love and service to one another and to you;
through Jesus Christ our Lord.

Amen.

Wednesday

Vulnerable God,
you challenge the powers
that rule this world,
through the needy,
the compassionate,
and those who are filled with longing.
Make us hunger and thirst to see right prevail,
that we may see your face
and be satisfied in you,
through Jesus Christ.

Amen.

Thursday

Lord Christ,
we are strangers and pilgrims on the earth,
disconcerted by the world's violence
and its sorrow,
distracted by our inward doubts and fears.
Wherever we are on this day's journey,
breathe on us your gentle Spirit,
that we may be oases
of quietness and refreshment,
bringing to your uneasy world
reconciliation and peace.

Amen.

Friday

Almighty God,
your beloved Son, for love of us,
willingly offered himself to endure the cross,
its agony and shame.
Remove from us all coldness
and cowardice of heart,
and give us grace to take up our cross
and follow him in humility and love;
through the same Jesus Christ
our Saviour and Lord.

Amen.

Saturday

Almighty Father,
whose Son Jesus Christ
is the Way, the Truth, the Life:
keep us upright in the way,
faithful to the truth
and eager for the life;
until our lives
are a perfect image

of his eternal love,
who is alive and reigns with you
in the unity of the Spirit,
one God, now and for ever.

Amen.

Our Father . . .

13   THE TRYST

either

Lord, set your blessing on us
as we begin this day together.
Confirm in us the truth
by which we rightly live;
confront us with the truth
from which we wrongly turn.
We ask not for what we want
but for what you know we need,
as we offer this day and ourselves
for you and to you;
through Jesus Christ our Saviour.

Amen.

The Lord be with you
    And also with you.

or

This is the day that God has made.
    We will rejoice and be glad in it.

We will not offer to God
    offerings that cost us nothing.

Go in peace and serve the Lord.
We will seek peace and pursue it.

Glory to the Father, and to the Son,
and to the Holy Spirit:
as it was in the beginning,
is now, and will be for ever.

Amen.

14   DISMISSAL AND BLESSING

Come, Lord Jesus.
We are open to your Spirit.
We await the fullness of your presence.
Our world finds rest in you alone.

Let us bless the Lord.
Thanks be to God

Go in peace to love and serve the Lord.

And the blessing of God almighty,
the Father, the Son, and the Holy Spirit,
be with you.

Amen.

X
An
ORDER
for
DAILY DEVOTION

Order for Daily Devotion: Morning and Evening

This Order for Daily Devotion offers a structure to encourage the discipline of daily private devotion. It may be used alone, or in a family or other small group. What is said about Readings, in the introductory rubrics to the Daily Service, is relevant here.

The structure of the Daily Office is:

1 SCRIPTURE SENTENCE

2 COLLECT OF THE DAY

3 SONG OF PRAISE

4 PSALM(S) *said or sung*

5 SCRIPTURE READING(S)

6 SILENCE

7 SONG OF PRAISE

8 APOSTLES' CREED

9 THANKSGIVINGS AND INTERCESSIONS
   LORD'S PRAYER

10 FINAL COLLECT

11 CONCLUSION

The SONG OF PRAISE, *at 3 and at 7, is usually from a biblical text, and is set out for responsive or antiphonal reading by a family or other group. It may, of course, be said alone. A hymn or song may be substituted for it.*

The CONCLUSION *is sometimes in the form of a prayer for blessing. A minister may use it as a benediction by changing the first person pronouns in italics to the second person.*

Sunday Morning

1   SCRIPTURE SENTENCE

> Awake sleeper;
> rise from the dead,
> and Christ will shine upon you.

Ephesians 5: 14

2   COLLECT OF THE DAY

3   SONG OF PRAISE

The Spirit of the Lord   *Isaiah 61: 1 - 3, 10, 11*

1   The spirit of the Lord God is upon me
    because the Lord has anointed me;
    he has sent me to announce
    good news to the humble,

2   to bind up the broken-hearted,
    to proclaim liberty to captives,
    release to those in prison;

3   to comfort all who mourn,
    to give them garlands instead of ashes,

4   oil of gladness instead of mourners' tears,
    a garment of splendour
    for the heavy heart.

5   They will be called trees of righteousness,
     planted by the Lord for his adornment.

6   Let me rejoice in the Lord
     with all my heart,
     let me exult in my God;

7   for he has robed me in deliverance
     and arrayed me in victory.

8   As the earth puts forth her blossom
     or plants in the garden burst into flower,

9   so will the Lord God
     make his victory and renown
     blossom before the nations.

> *Glory to the Father, and to the Son,*
> *and to the Holy Spirit:*
> *as it was in the beginning, is now,*
> *and will be for ever.*   **Amen.**

4   PSALM(S) *said or sung*

5   SCRIPTURE READING(S)

6   SILENCE

7   SONG OF PRAISE

    A joyful assembly   *Hebrews 12: 22 - 24, 28*

1   You have come to mount Zion,
     the city of the living God,
     the heavenly Jerusalem,
     to myriads of angels,

2 *to the full concourse*
   and assembly of the firstborn
   who are enrolled in heaven,

3 and to God the judge of all,
   and to the spirits of good men made perfect,

4 *and to Jesus*
   the mediator of a new covenant,
   whose sprinkled blood has better things to say
   than the blood of Abel.

5 The kingdom we are given is unshakeable;
   let us therefore give thanks to God for it,

6 *and so worship God*
   as he would be worshipped,
   with reverence and with awe;

   giving glory to the Father, and to the Son,
   and to the Holy Spirit,
   one God, glorious for ever.

                                            Amen.

8 APOSTLES' CREED

9 THANKSGIVINGS AND INTERCESSIONS
   LORD'S PRAYER

10 FINAL COLLECT

    God our Father,
    at the first creation
    you set the world's corner-stone in place,
    while the morning stars sang together
    and the angels of God all shouted for joy.

In the new creation
your grace has dawned upon the world
with healing for all.
May Christ, the sun of righteousness,
shine in our hearts for ever
and draw us to that light
where you live in radiant glory;
through the same Jesus Christ our Lord.

Amen.

11   CONCLUSION

The grace of our Lord Jesus Christ,
and the love of God,
and the fellowship of the Holy Spirit,
be with *us* all.   *Amen.*

Sunday
Evening

1 SCRIPTURE SENTENCE

Stay with us, for evening approaches,
and the day is almost over.

·   *St Luke 24: 29*

2 COLLECT OF THE DAY

3 SONG OF PRAISE

Your light has come   *Isaiah 60: 2 - 3, 18 - 20*

1 Though darkness covers the earth
   and dark night the nations,

2 **on you the Lord shines**
   and over you his glory will appear;

3 nations will journey towards your light
   and kings to your radiance.

4 **No longer will the sound of violence**
   be heard in your land,
   nor havoc and ruin within your borders;

5 but you will name your walls Deliverance
   and your gates Praise.

6 ***The sun will no longer be your light by day,***
   nor the moon shine on you by night;

7 the Lord will be your everlasting light,
   your God will be your splendour.

8 ***Never again will your sun set***
   nor your moon withdraw her light;

9 but the Lord will be your everlasting light
   and your days of mourning will be ended.

   Glory to the Father, and to the Son,
   and to the Holy Spirit:
   as it was in the beginning, is now,
   and will be for ever.   ***Amen.***

4 PSALM(S) *said or sung*

5 SCRIPTURE READING(S)

6 SILENCE

7 SONG OF PRAISE

   The mystery of our religion
                                     1 Timothy 3: 16; 6: 15, 16

1 Jesus Christ was manifested in flesh,
   vindicated in spirit.

2 ***He was seen by angels***
   and proclaimed among the nations.

3 He was believed in throughout the world
   and raised to heavenly glory.

4 *He will appear in God's own good time.*
He is the blessed and only Sovereign,
King of kings and Lord of lords.

5 He alone possesses immortality,
dwelling in unapproachable light;

6 *him no one has ever seen or can ever see;*
to him be honour and dominion for ever!

Amen.

Glory to the Father, and to the Son,
and to the Holy Spirit:
as it was in the beginning, is now,
and will be for ever.

Amen.

8 APOSTLES' CREED

9 THANKSGIVINGS AND INTERCESSIONS
LORD'S PRAYER

10 FINAL COLLECT

Loving creator of all,
watch over us this night
and keep us always in the light of your presence.
May our praise continually blend
with the song of all creation,
until we come to those eternal joys
which eye has not seen nor ear heard,
all prepared for those who love you;
through Jesus Christ our Lord.

Amen.

11 CONCLUSION

May God himself, the God of peace,
make *us* holy through and through,
and keep *us* sound in spirit, soul, and body,
free of any fault
when our Lord Jesus Christ comes.

The grace of our Lord Jesus Christ be with *us*.
                                          Amen.

Monday
Morning

1   SCRIPTURE SENTENCE

My help comes only from the Lord,
maker of heaven and earth.   *Psalm 121: 2*

2   COLLECT OF THE DAY

3   SONG OF PRAISE

Benedicite   *The Song of the Three 35 - 37, 60 - 65*

1   Let his whole creation bless the Lord,
     sing his praise and exalt him for ever.

2   ***Bless the Lord, you heavens;***
     sing his praise and exalt him for ever.

3   Bless the Lord, you that are his angels;
     sing his praise and exalt him for ever.

4   ***Let all mankind bless the Lord;***
     sing his praise and exalt him for ever.

5   Israel, bless the Lord;
     sing his praise and exalt him for ever.

6   ***Bless the Lord, you that are his priests;***
     sing his praise and exalt him for ever.

7   Bless the Lord, you that are his servants;
    sing his praise and exalt him for ever.

8   Bless the Lord,
    spirits and souls of the righteous;
    sing his praise and exalt him for ever.

9   Bless the Lord,
    you that are devout and humble in heart;
    sing his praise and exalt him for ever.

10 Give thanks to the Lord, for he is gracious,
    for his mercy endures for ever.

    Let us bless the Father,
    the Son and the Holy Spirit;
    sing out God's praise and exalt him for ever.

4   PSALM(S) *said or sung*

5   SCRIPTURE READING(S)

6   SILENCE

7   SONG OF PRAISE

    The Song of Judith   *Judith 16: 13 - 15*

1   I will sing a new hymn to my God:
    O Lord, you are great and glorious,
    you are marvellous in your strength, invincible.

2   Let your whole creation serve you;
    for you spoke, and all things came to be;

3   you sent out your spirit, and it gave them form;
    none can oppose your word.

*4   Mountains will shake to their depths
    like water,
    rocks melt like wax at your presence;*

5   but you still show compassion
    to those who fear you.

*Glory to the Father, and to the Son,
and to the Holy Spirit:
as it was in the beginning, is now,
and will be for ever.*   *Amen.*

8 APOSTLES' CREED

9 THANKSGIVINGS AND INTERCESSIONS
    LORD'S PRAYER

10 FINAL COLLECT

God of work and rest and pleasure,
may all that we do this week
be an offering of love as well as of duty.
Keep us, this day and every day,
in the spirit of kindness, simplicity, and joy;
through Jesus Christ our Lord.   *Amen.*

11 CONCLUSION

The peace of God,
which is beyond all understanding,
guard *our* hearts and thoughts in Christ Jesus.
    Amen.

Monday
Evening

1   S<small>CRIPTURE</small>   S<small>ENTENCE</small>

> God's love has flooded our hearts
> through the Holy Spirit he has given us.
>
> *Romans 5: 5*

2   C<small>OLLECT</small> <small>OF THE</small> D<small>AY</small>

3   S<small>ONG</small> <small>OF</small> P<small>RAISE</small>

> *The Prologue of St John's Gospel*
>
> *St John 1: 1 - 5, 10 - 14, 16*

1 In the beginning the Word already was.
   The Word was in God's presence,

2 ***and what God was, the Word was.***
   He was with God at the beginning,

3 and through him all things came to be;
   without him no created thing came into being.

4 ***In him was life,***
   and that life was the light of mankind.

5 The light shines in the darkness,
   and the darkness has never mastered it.

6   *He was in the world;*
    but the world, though it owed its being to him,
    did not recognize him.

7   He came to his own,
    and his own people would not accept him.

8   *But to all who did accept him,*
    to those who put their trust in him,
    he gave the right to become children of God.

9   They were not born of human stock,
    nor by the physical desire of a human father,
    but of God.

10 *So the Word became flesh;*
    he made his home among us.

11 We saw his glory,
    such glory as befits the Father's only Son,
    full of grace and truth.

12 *From his full store*
    we have all received grace upon grace.

    Glory to the Father, and to the Son,
    and to the Holy Spirit:
    as it was in the beginning, is now,
    and will be for ever.   *Amen.*

4   PSALM(S) *said or sung*

5   SCRIPTURE READING(S)

6   SILENCE

7   SONG OF PRAISE

The song of our adoption   *Ephesians 1: 3 - 6*

1   Blessed be the God and Father
of our Lord Jesus Christ,
who has conferred on us in Christ
every spiritual blessing in the heavenly realms.

2   Before the foundation of the world
he chose us in Christ to be his people,
to be without blemish in his sight,
to be full of love;

3   he predestined us to be adopted
as his children through Jesus Christ.

4   This was his will and pleasure
in order that the glory of his gracious gift,
so graciously conferred on us in his Beloved,
might redound to his praise.

Glory to the Father, and to the Son,
and to the Holy Spirit:
as it was in the beginning, is now,
and will be for ever.   *Amen.*

8   APOSTLES' CREED

9   THANKSGIVINGS AND INTERCESSIONS
LORD'S PRAYER

10   FINAL COLLECT

Eternal God,
shed your light on those who watch for you.

May our lips always praise you,
our hearts bless you,
and our lives give you glory;
through Jesus Christ our Lord.   ***Amen.***

11 CONCLUSION

God be in my head, and in my understanding;
God be in mine eyes, and in my looking;
God be in my mouth, and in my thinking;
God be at mine end, and at my departing.
                                                                Amen.

May God make *our* hearts firm,
so that *we* may stand before our God and Father
holy and faultless when our Lord Jesus comes
with all those who are his own.
                                                                Amen.

Tuesday
Morning

Lord, I have heard of your fame;
Lord, I am in awe of what you have done.
Through all generations
you have made yourself known,
and in your wrath you did not forget mercy.

Habakkuk 3: 2

2   COLLECT OF THE DAY

3   SONG OF PRAISE

God is my deliverer   *Isaiah 12: 2 - 6*

1   God is my deliverer.
I am confident and unafraid,
for the Lord is my refuge and defence
and has shown himself my deliverer.

**2   With joy you will all draw water
from the wells of deliverance.**

3   On that day you will say:
'Give thanks to the Lord, invoke him by name.

4   *'Make known among the peoples*
    what he has done,
    proclaim that his name is exalted.

5   'Sing psalms to the Lord, for he has triumphed;
    let this be known in all the world.

6   *'Cry out, shout aloud, you dwellers in Zion,*
    for the Holy One of Israel
    is among you in majesty.'

    We praise you, we bless you,
    we worship you, we glorify you,
    strong deliverer, Father, Son, and Holy Spirit,
    almighty and eternal God, glorious for ever.
                                        Amen.

4   PSALM(S) *said or sung*

5   SCRIPTURE READING(S)

6   SILENCE

7   SONG OF PRAISE

    Hannah's Prayer   *1 Samuel 2: 1, 2, 4, 7 - 8*

1   My heart exults in the Lord,
    in the Lord I now hold my head high;
    I rejoice because you have saved me.

2   *There is none but you,*
    none so holy as the Lord,
    none so righteous as our God.

3   Strong men stand in mute dismay,
      but those who faltered put on new strength.

4   Poverty and riches both come from the Lord;
      he brings low and he raises up.

5   He lifts the weak out of the dust
      and raises the poor from the refuse heap

6   to give them a place among the great,
      to assign them seats of honour.

7   The foundations of the earth are the Lord's,
      and he has set the world upon them.

      Glory to the Father, and to the Son,
      and to the Holy Spirit:
      as it was in the beginning, is now,
      and will be for ever.   *Amen.*

8   APOSTLES' CREED

9   THANKSGIVINGS AND INTERCESSIONS
     LORD'S PRAYER

10   FINAL COLLECT

      O God,
      you are the author of peace
      and lover of concord.
      To know you is eternal life,
      to serve you is perfect freedom.
      Defend your servants in every stress and danger,
      that we may trust in your defence
      and not fear the power of any adversaries;
      through Jesus Christ our Redeemer.   *Amen.*

11 CONCLUSION

Always be joyful;
pray continually;
give thanks whatever happens;
for this is what God wills for you in Christ Jesus.

And the blessing of God almighty,
Father, Son, and Holy Spirit,
be with *us* all.   ***Amen.***

Tuesday
Evening

1 SCRIPTURE SENTENCE

No one has ever seen God;
God's only Son,
he who is nearest to the Father's heart,
has made him known. *St John 1: 18*

2 COLLECT OF THE DAY

3 SONG OF PRAISE

Great and marvellous *Revelation 15: 3, 4*

1 Great and marvellous are your deeds,
O Lord God, sovereign over all;

2 *just and true are your ways,*
O King of the ages.

3 Who shall not fear you, Lord,
and do homage to your name?
For you alone are holy.

4 *All nations shall come and worship before you,*
for your just decrees stand revealed.

Glory to the Father, and to the Son,
and to the Holy Spirit:

as it was in the beginning, is now,
and will be for ever.   *Amen.*

4   PSALM(S) *said or sung*

5   SCRIPTURE READING(S)

6   SILENCE

7   SONG OF PRAISE

The Song of Mary   *St Luke 1: 46 - 55*

1   My soul tells out the greatness of the Lord,
    my spirit has rejoiced in God my Saviour;

2   *for he has looked with favour on his servant,*
    lowly as she is.

3   From this day forward
    all generations will count me blessed,
    for the Mighty God has done great things for me.

4   *His name is holy,*
    his mercy sure from generation to generation
    toward those who fear him.

5   He has shown the might of his arm,
    he has routed the proud and all their schemes;

6   *he has brought down monarchs*
    from their thrones,
    and raised on high the lowly.

7   He has filled the hungry with good things,
    and sent the rich away empty.

**8   He has come to the help of Israel his servant,
      as he promised to our forefathers;**

9   he has not forgotten to show mercy
     to Abraham and his children's children for ever.

**Glory to the Father, and to the Son,
and to the Holy Spirit:
as it was in the beginning, is now,
and will be for ever.   Amen.**

8   APOSTLES' CREED

9   THANKSGIVINGS AND INTERCESSIONS
     LORD'S PRAYER

10   FINAL COLLECT

          O divine Master,
          grant that we may not so much
          seek to be consoled,
          as to console;
          to be understood, as to understand;
          to be loved, as to love.
          For it is in giving that we receive;
          in pardoning that we are pardoned;
          in dying that we are born to eternal life.   *Amen.*

11   CONCLUSION

          May the Lord of peace himself give *us* peace
          at all times and in all ways.

          The grace of our Lord Jesus Christ,
          and the love of God,
          and the fellowship of the Holy Spirit
          be with *us* all.   *Amen.*

Wednesday
Morning

1 SCRIPTURE SENTENCE

> The Lord gave the sun for a light by day
> and the moon and stars in their courses
> for a light by night.
> The Lord cleft the sea and its waves roared;
> the Lord of Hosts is his name.   *Jeremiah 31: 35*

2 COLLECT OF THE DAY

3 SONG OF PRAISE

> *The Song of Moses and the Israelites*
> *Exodus 15: 1, 2, 11, 13, 17 - 18*

1 I shall sing to the Lord,
  for he has risen up in triumph.

*2 The Lord is my refuge and my defence;
  he has shown himself my deliverer.*

3 He is my God, and I shall glorify him;
  my father's God, and I shall exalt him.

*4 Lord, who is like you among the gods?
  Who is like you, majestic in holiness.
  worthy of awe and praise,
  worker of wonders?*

5   In your constant love you led the people
    whom you had redeemed:

*6   you guided them by your strength
    to your holy dwelling-place.*

7   You will bring them in and plant them
    in the mount that is your possession,
    the sanctuary
    which your own hands established.

8   The Lord will reign for ever and for ever.

*Glory to the Father, and to the Son,
and to the Holy Spirit:
as it was in the beginning, is now,
and will be for ever.*   *Amen.*

4   PSALM(S) *said or sung*

5   SCRIPTURE READING(S)

6   SILENCE

7   SONG OF PRAISE

    King David's Prayer   *2 Samuel 7: 22 - 24*

1   Lord God, you are great.
    There is none like you;

*2   there is no God but you,
    as everything we have heard bears witness.*

3   And your people Israel,
    to whom can they be compared?

Is there any other nation on earth
whom you, God,
have set out to redeem from slavery
to be your people?

**4 You have won renown for yourself
by great and awesome deeds,
driving out other nations and their gods
to make way for your people
whom you redeemed from Egypt.**

5 You have established your people Israel
as your own for ever,
and you, Lord, have become their God.

**Glory to the Father, and to the Son,
and to the Holy Spirit:
as it was in the beginning, is now,
and will be for ever.**

Amen.

8 APOSTLES' CREED

9 THANKSGIVINGS AND INTERCESSIONS
LORD'S PRAYER

10 FINAL COLLECT

Ever present God,
this day enfolds us and surrounds us:
be in our speaking and in our thinking;
be in our life and on our lips;
be in our hearts and in our souls;
today and for ever.

Amen.

11   CONCLUSION

May the Lord bless *us*
and guard *us*;
may the Lord make his face shine on *us*
and be gracious to *us*;
may the Lord look kindly on *us*
and give *us* peace.

Amen.

Wednesday
Evening

1   SCRIPTURE SENTENCE

> Jesus said:
> 'Ask, and you will receive;
> seek, and you will find;
> knock, and the door will be opened to you.
> For everyone who asks receives,
> those who seek find,
> and to those who knock,
> the door will be opened.'   *St Matthew 7: 7, 8*

2   COLLECT OF THE DAY

3   SONG OF PRAISE

> *Christ, the image of the invisible God*
> *Colossians 1: 13 - 20*

1   God rescued us from the domain of darkness
    and brought us into the kingdom
    of his dear Son.

2   Through him our release is secured
***   and our sins are forgiven.***

3   He is the image of the invisible God;
    his is the primacy over all creation.

4   In him everything in heaven

and on earth was created,
not only things visible
but also the invisible orders
of thrones, sovereignties,
authorities and powers:

5   the whole universe has been created
    through him and for him.
    He exists before all things,
    and all things are held together in him.

6   *He is the head of the body, the church.*
    He is its origin,
    the first to return from the dead,
    to become in all things supreme.

7   For in him God in all his fullness chose to dwell,
    and through him to reconcile
    all things to himself.

8   *He made peace*
    through the shedding of his blood on the cross,
    bringing back to himself all things
    whether on earth or in heaven.

    Glory to the Father, and to the Son,
    and to the Holy Spirit:
    as it was in the beginning, is now,
    and will be for ever.   *Amen.*

4   PSALM(S) *said or sung*

5   SCRIPTURE READING(S)

6   SILENCE

7   SONG OF PRAISE

The Song of Simeon   *St Luke 2: 29 - 32*

1 Now, Lord,
   you are releasing your servant in peace,
   according to your promise.

2 *For I have seen with my own eyes*
   the deliverance you have made ready
   in full view of all nations:

3 a light that will bring revelation to the Gentiles
   and glory to your people Israel.

   Glory to the Father, and to the Son,
   and to the Holy Spirit:
   as it was in the beginning, is now,
   and will be for ever.   *Amen.*

8   APOSTLES' CREED

9   THANKSGIVINGS AND INTERCESSIONS
    LORD'S PRAYER

10 FINAL COLLECT

    God,
    you were before us at our life's beginning;
    be so again at our journey's end.
    You were beside us at our soul's shaping;
    be so again at our life's finishing.   *Amen.*

11 CONCLUSION

    God's grace be with all
    who love our Lord Jesus Christ
    with undying love.   *Amen.*

Thursday
Morning

1 Scripture Sentence

Let all mortals be silent
in the presence of the Lord!
For he has bestirred himself
and come out from his holy dwelling-place.

Zechariah 2: 13

2 Collect of the Day

3 Song of Praise

Isaiah's vision of world peace

Isaiah 2: 2 - 5; 9: 3

1 In days to come
the mountain of the Lord's house
will be set over all other mountains,
raised high above the hills.

2 ***All the nations will stream towards it,
and many peoples will go and say:***

3 'Let us go up to the mountain of the Lord,
to the house of the God of Jacob,

4 ***'that he may teach us his ways
and that we may walk in his paths.'***

5 For instruction comes from Zion,
    and the word of the Lord from Jerusalem.

6 *He will be judge between the nations*
    as arbiter among many peoples.

7 They will beat their swords into mattocks
    and their spears into pruning-knives;

8 *nation will not lift sword against nation*
    nor ever again be trained for war.

9 Come, people of Jacob.
    let us walk in the light of the Lord.

10 *God, you have increased our joy*

11 and given us great gladness.
    To you be glory for ever and ever.   ***Amen.***

4 PSALM(S) *said or sung*

5 SCRIPTURE READING(S)

6 SILENCE

7 SONG OF PRAISE

      God's time of favour   *Isaiah 49: 8 - 10, 13, 26*

1 In the time of my favour I answered you;
    on the day of deliverance I came to your aid.

2 *I have formed you,*
    and destined you to be a light for peoples,

restoring the land
and allotting once more its desolate holdings.

3   I said to the prisoners, 'Go free',
     and to those in darkness,
     'Come out into the open.'

4   Along every path they will find pasture
     and grazing in all the arid places.

5   They will neither hunger nor thirst,
     nor will scorching heat or sun distress them;

6   for the one who loves them will guide them
     and lead them by springs of water.

7   Shout for joy, you heavens; earth rejoice;
     break into songs of triumph, you mountains.

8   For the Lord has comforted his people
     and has had pity on them in their distress.

9   Lord, you are our Deliverer, our Redeemer;

10   Lord, you are the Mighty One of Jacob.
     to you be all glory for ever and ever.

                                Amen.

8   APOSTLES' CREED

9   THANKSGIVINGS AND INTERCESSIONS
    LORD'S PRAYER

10 FINAL COLLECT

Eternal God,
you have set before us the great hope
that your kingdom will come on earth,
and have taught us to pray for its coming.
Make us ready to thank you
for the signs of its dawning,
and to pray and work for the perfect day
when your will shall be done on earth
as it is in heaven;
through Jesus Christ our Lord.   *Amen.*

11 CONCLUSION

May the High God shield *us* all the day long.
May *we* dwell under his protection
today and for ever.   *Amen.*

Thursday
Evening

1   SCRIPTURE SENTENCE

> All that is true, all that is noble,
> all that is just and pure,
> all that is lovable and attractive,
> whatever is excellent and admirable –
> fill your thoughts with these things.
>
> *Philippians 4: 8*

2   COLLECT OF THE DAY

3   SONG OF PRAISE

Zechariah's Song   *Luke 1: 68 - 79*

1   Praise to the Lord, the God of Israel!
For he has turned to his people
and set them free.

2   ***He has raised for us a strong deliverer
from the house of his servant David.***

3   So he promised:
age after age he proclaimed
by the lips of his holy prophets,

4   ***that he would deliver us from our enemies,
out of the hands of all who hate us;***

5 that, calling to mind his solemn covenant,
 he would deal mercifully with our fathers.

6 *This was the oath he swore*
 to our father Abraham,
 to rescue us from enemy hands
 and set us free from fear,

7 so that we might worship in his presence
 in holiness and righteousness
 our whole life long.

8 *And you, my child,*
 will be called Prophet of the Most High,
 for you will be the Lord's forerunner,
 to prepare his way

9 and lead his people to a knowledge of salvation
 through the forgiveness of their sins:

10 *for in the tender compassion of our God*
 the dawn of heaven will break upon us,

11 to shine on those who live in darkness,
 under the shadow of death,
 and to guide our feet into the way of peace.

 Glory to the Father, and to the Son,
 and to the Holy Spirit:
 as it was in the beginning, is now,
 and will be for ever.

       Amen.

4 PSALM(S) *said or sung*

5 SCRIPTURE READING(S)

6   SILENCE

7   SONG OF PRAISE

> *The New Jerusalem*
> *Revelation 21: 1, 2, 22 - 27; 22: 3 - 5; 7: 12*

1   I saw a new heaven and a new earth,
for the first heaven
and the first earth had vanished
and there was no longer any sea.

2   *I saw the Holy City, new Jerusalem,*
coming down out of heaven from God,
made ready like a bride
adorned for her husband.

3   I saw no temple in the city,
for its temple was the sovereign Lord God
and the Lamb.

4   *The city did not need*
the sun or the moon to shine on it,
for the glory of God gave it light,
and its lamp was the Lamb.

5   By its light shall the nations walk,
and to it the kings of the earth
shall bring their splendour.

6   *The gates of the city shall never be shut by day,*
nor will there be any night there.

7   The splendour and wealth of the nations
shall be brought into it,
but nothing unclean shall enter,

nor anyone whose ways are foul or false;
only those shall enter
whose names are inscribed
in the Lamb's book of life.

 8 *The throne of God and of the Lamb
will be there,
and his servants shall worship him;*

 9 they shall see him face to face
and bear his name on their foreheads.

 10 *There shall be no more night,
nor will they need the light of lamp or sun,*

 11 for the Lord God will give them light;
and they shall reign for ever.

 12 *Amen! Praise and glory and wisdom,
thanksgiving and honour,*

 13 power and might,
be to our God for ever!   *Amen.*

 8 APOSTLES' CREED

 9 THANKSGIVINGS AND INTERCESSIONS
    LORD'S PRAYER

10 FINAL COLLECT

Lighten our darkness, we pray, Lord;
and by your mercy defend us
from all perils and dangers of this night;
for the love of your only Son,
our Saviour, Jesus Christ.   *Amen.*

11 CONCLUSION

Praise and honour, glory and might,
to him who sits on the throne
and to the Lamb for ever and ever!

Amen.

Friday
Morning

1   SCRIPTURE SENTENCE

> Zion lifted her hands in prayer,
> but there was no one to comfort her.
>
> *Lamentations 1: 17*

2   COLLECT OF THE DAY

3   SONG OF PRAISE

> *Zion's hope of relief*
>
> *Lamentations 3: 1 - 9, 22 - 24, 31 - 33*

1   I am the one who has known affliction
under the rod of the wrath of the Lord.

2   *It was I whom he led away*
and left to walk in darkness,
where no light is.

3   Against me alone he has turned his hand,
and so it is all day long.

4   *He has wasted away my flesh and my skin*
and broken my bones;
he has built up as walls around me
bitterness and hardship;

5   he has cast me into a place of darkness
like those long dead.

*6   He has hemmed me in so that I cannot escape;
he has weighed me down with fetters.*

7   Even when I cry out and plead for help
he rejects my prayer.

*8   He has barred my road with blocks of stone
and entangled my way.*

9   The Lord's love is surely not exhausted,
nor has his compassion failed;

*10   they are new every morning,
so great is his constancy.*

11   'The Lord,' I say, 'is all that I have;
therefore I shall wait for him patiently.'

*12   Rejection by the Lord does not last for ever.
He may punish, yet he will have compassion
in the fullness of his unfailing love;*

13   he does not willingly afflict
or punish any mortal.
Thanks be to God! Alleluia!

Amen.

4   PSALM(S) *said or sung*

5   SCRIPTURE READING(S)

6   SILENCE

7   SONG OF PRAISE

verses may be omitted

The Suffering Servant   *Isaiah 53: 1 - 11; 54: 5*

1   Who could have believed what we have heard?
To whom has the power of the Lord
been revealed?

2   *He grew up before the Lord like a young plant*
whose roots are in parched ground;
he had no beauty,
no majesty to catch our eyes,
no grace to attract us to him.

3   He was despised, shunned by all,
pain-racked and afflicted by disease;
we despised him, we held him of no account,
an object from which
people turn away their eyes.

4   *Yet it was our afflictions he was bearing,*
our pain he endured,
while we thought of him as smitten by God,
struck down by disease and misery.

5   But he was pierced for our transgressions,
crushed for our iniquities;
the chastisement he bore restored us to health
and by his wounds we are healed.

6*   *We had all strayed like sheep,*
each of us going his own way,
but the Lord laid on him the guilt of us all.

7* He was maltreated,
   yet he was submissive
   and did not open his mouth;
   like a sheep led to the slaughter,
   like a ewe that is dumb before the shearers,
   he did not open his mouth.

8* *He was arrested and sentenced*
   and taken away,
   and who gave a thought to his fate –

9* how he was cut off from the world of the living,
   stricken to death for my people's transgression?

10* *Yet the Lord took thought*
    for his oppressed servant
    and healed him who had given himself
    as a sacrifice for sin.

11* He will enjoy long life
    and see his children's children,
    and in his hand the Lord's purpose will prosper.

12 *By his humiliation*
   my servant will justify many;
   after his suffering he will see light
   and be satisfied;
   it is their guilt he bears.

13 Glory to the Lord of Hosts,
   glory to the God of all the earth,
   glory to the Holy One of Israel, our Redeemer.
                                              Amen.

8 APOSTLES' CREED

9   THANKSGIVINGS AND INTERCESSIONS
    LORD'S PRAYER

10   FINAL COLLECT

O Christ, the Master Carpenter,
who at the last, through wood and nails,
purchased our whole salvation,
wield well your tools
in the workshop of your world,
so that we who come rough-hewn to your bench
may here be fashioned
to a truer beauty of your hand.
We ask it for your own name's sake.

Amen.

11   CONCLUSION

Attend, Lord my God,
to the prayer and supplication of your servant;
listen to the cry and the prayer
which your servant makes before you this day.
Hear in heaven your dwelling
and, when you hear, forgive.   *Amen.*

Friday
Evening

1   SCRIPTURE SENTENCE

> Christ died for us while we were yet sinners,
> and that is God's proof of his love towards us.
>
> *Romans 5: 8*

2   COLLECT OF THE DAY

3   SONG OF PRAISE

> *Jesus, Saviour of the world*   *Salvator Mundi*

1   Jesus, Saviour of the world,
    come to us in your mercy:
    we look to you to save and help us.

2   *By your cross and life laid down*
    you set your people free:
    we look to you to save and help us.

3   When they were on the point of perishing
    you saved your disciples:
    we look to you to come to our help.

4   *In your great mercy*
    set us free from all that imprisons us:
    forgive the sins of all your people.

5   Make yourself known
     as our Saviour and our mighty deliverer:
     save us and help us that we may praise you.

6   Come now and make your home among us,
     Lord Christ Jesus:
     hear our prayer and be with us always.

7   When you come in your glory,
     make us one with you:
     share with us the life of your kingdom.

8   Thanks be to you, O Lord:
     Alleluia!

                                                  Amen.

4   PSALM(S) *said or sung*

5   SCRIPTURE READING(S)

6   SILENCE

7   SONG OF PRAISE

     In Christ the Godhead Dwells
                         Colossians 2: 9 - 10; 12; 14 - 15

1   It is in Christ
     that the Godhead in all its fullness
     dwells embodied,
     it is in him you have been brought to fulfilment.

2   Every power and authority in the universe
     is subject to him as head.

3   You were buried with him in baptism,
     and in that baptism
     you were also raised to life with him,

*4   through your faith in the active power of God,
      who raised him from the dead.*

5   He has cancelled the bond
     which was outstanding against us
     with all its legal demands;
     he has set it aside, nailing it to the cross.

*6   There he disarmed
      the cosmic powers and authorities
      and made a public spectacle of them,*

7   leading them as captives
     in his triumphal procession.

     *Glory to the Father, and to the Son,
     and to the Holy Spirit:
     as it was in the beginning, is now,
     and will be for ever.*   *Amen.*

8   APOSTLES' CREED

9   THANKSGIVINGS AND INTERCESSIONS
     LORD'S PRAYER

10   FINAL COLLECT

     Loving God,
     your Son willingly endured
     agony and shame for us.
     Give us grace
     to take up our cross and follow him,

till at the last we come with him to glory,
where he lives and reigns
with you in the unity of the Spirit,
one God, for ever and ever.

Amen.

11   CONCLUSION

Preserve us, O God, while waking,
and guard us while sleeping,
that awake we may watch with Christ,
and asleep may rest in peace.

Amen.

Saturday
Morning

1   SCRIPTURE SENTENCE

> The Lord God says:
> 'I shall put my spirit into you
> and you will come to life,
> and I shall settle you on your own soil,
> and you will know that I the Lord have spoken
> and I shall act.'
>
> *Ezekiel 37: 14*

2   COLLECT OF THE DAY

3   SONG OF PRAISE

> *The delivering and redeeming God*
> *Isaiah 63: 7 - 14, 16*

1   I shall recount the Lord's unfailing love,
    the prowess of the Lord,
    according to all he has done for us,
    his great goodness to the house of Israel,

2   what he has done for them in his tenderness
    and by his many acts of faithful love.

3   He said, 'Surely they are my people,
    children who will not play me false';
    and he became their deliverer

in all their troubles.

4 *No envoy, no angel,*
but he himself delivered them,
redeemed them in his love and pity;

5 he lifted them up and carried them
through all the days of old.

6 *Yet they rebelled and grieved his holy spirit;*
so he turned hostile to them
and himself fought against them.

7 Then they recalled days long past
and him who drew out his people:

8 *where is he who brought up from the Nile*
the shepherd of his flock?

9 Where is he who put within him his holy spirit,
who sent his glorious power
to walk at Moses' right hand?

10 *Where is he*
who divided the waters before them,
to win for himself everlasting renown,

11 who brought them through the deep
sure-footed as horses in open country,

12 *like cattle moving down into a valley*
guided by the spirit of the Lord?

13 Thus you led your people
to win yourself a glorious name.

14 ***You, Lord, are our Father;***
our Redeemer from of old is your name.
Glory to you, our God, for ever and ever.

Amen.

4 PSALM(S) *said or sung*

5 SCRIPTURE READING(S)

6 SILENCE

7 SONG OF PRAISE

> *Sing a new song to the Lord*
>> *Isaiah 42: 10 - 12; 43: 1 - 3, 11*

1 Sing a new song to the Lord,
sing his praise throughout the world,

2 ***you that sail the broad seas,***
and you that inhabit the coasts and islands.

3 Let the wilderness and its settlement rejoice,
and the encampments where Kedar lives.

4 ***Let the inhabitants of Sela shout for joy,***
let them cry out from the hilltops.

5 Let the coasts and islands
ascribe glory to the Lord;
let them sing his praise.

6 ***Now, Jacob, this is the word of the Lord,***
the word of your Creator,
of him who fashioned you, Israel:

7   have no fear, for I have redeemed you;
    I call you by name; you are mine.

8   When you pass through water
    I shall be with you;
    when you pass through rivers
    they will not overwhelm you;

9   walk through fire, and you will not be scorched,
    through flames, and they will not burn you.

10 I am the Lord your God,
    the Holy One of Israel, your deliverer.

11 You are the Lord,
    you alone are our deliverer.
    Glory to you for ever and ever.

                                    Amen.

8   APOSTLES' CREED

9   THANKSGIVINGS AND INTERCESSIONS
    LORD'S PRAYER

10 FINAL COLLECT

        God, the well-spring of our life,
        pour into our hearts the living water of your grace
        that, refreshed by you,
        we may live this day
        in steadfast reliance on your strength;
        through Jesus Christ our Lord.

                                    Amen.

11 CONCLUSION

In this place will be heard once more
the sounds of joy and gladness,
the voices of bridegroom and bride;
here too will be heard voices shouting,
'Praise the Lord of Hosts,
for the Lord is good; his love endures for ever.'
Amen.

Saturday
Evening

1 SCRIPTURE SENTENCE

Jesus said:
'I am the resurrection and the life.
Whoever has faith in me shall live,
even though he dies;
and no one who lives and has faith in me
shall ever die.'

St John 11: 25, 26

2 COLLECT OF THE DAY

3 SONG OF PRAISE

The Easter Anthems

1 Corinthians 5: 7, 8
Romans 6: 9 - 11
1 Corinthians 15: 20 - 22

1 Christ our Passover lamb has been sacrificed.

2 *So we who observe the festival*
must not use the old leaven,
the leaven of depravity and wickedness,
but only the unleavened bread
which is sincerity and truth.

3 Christ, once raised from the dead,
   is never to die again:
   he is no longer under the dominion of death.

4 *When he died, he died to sin, once for all,*
   and now that he lives, he lives to God

5 In the same way
   you must regard yourselves as dead to sin
   and alive to God, in union with Christ Jesus.

6 *Christ was raised to life –*
   the firstfruits of the harvest of the dead.

7 For since it was a man
   who brought death into the world,
   a man also brought resurrection of the dead.

8 *As in Adam all die,*
   so in Christ all will be brought to life.

   Glory to the Father, and to the Son,
   and to the Holy Spirit:
   as it was in the beginning, is now,
   and will be for ever.   *Amen.*

4 PSALM(S) *said or sung*

5 SCRIPTURE READING(S)

6 SILENCE

7 SONG OF PRAISE

   The song of God's children

   Romans 8: 2; 14 - 19

1   In Christ Jesus the life-giving law of the Spirit
    has set us free from the law of sin and death.

*2   All who are led by the Spirit of God
    are sons of God.
    The Spirit we have received
    is not a spirit of slavery,*

3   leading us back into a life of fear,
    but a Spirit of adoption,
    enabling us to cry 'Abba! Father!'

*4   The Spirit of God affirms to our spirit
    that we are God's children;
    and if children, then heirs,
    heirs of God*

5   and fellow-heirs with Christ;
    but we must share his sufferings
    if we are also to share his glory.

*6   The sufferings we now endure
    bear no comparison with the glory,
    as yet unrevealed, which is in store for us.*

7   The created universe is waiting
    with eager expectation
    for God's children to be revealed.

*Glory to the Father, and to the Son,
    and to the Holy Spirit:
    as it was in the beginning, is now,
    and will be for ever.*

Amen.

8   APOSTLES' CREED

9   THANKSGIVINGS AND INTERCESSIONS
     LORD'S PRAYER

10   FINAL COLLECT

> Abide with us, Lord,
> for evening approaches
> and the day is almost over.
> Abide with us, Lord,
> for the days are hastening on
> and we hasten on with them.
> Abide with us, Lord,
> and with all your faithful people,
> making yourself known
> in the breaking of the word and of the bread.
> Abide with us, Lord,
> until the day-star rises
> and the morning light appears,
> and we shall live with you for ever and ever.
>> *Amen.*

11   CONCLUSION

> Let us bless the Lord.
>> *Thanks be to God.*

> The God of peace,
> who brought back from the dead our Lord Jesus,
> the great Shepherd of the sheep,
> through the blood of an eternal covenant,
> make *us* perfect in all goodness
> so that *we* may do his will.
> May he create in *us* what is pleasing to him;
> through Jesus Christ,
> to whom be glory for ever and ever!
>> *Amen.*

XI
ASCRIPTIONS
of
GLORY

Ascriptions of Glory

Ascriptions of Glory may be used at different points in services: for example, after a declaration of forgiveness; after the gospel reading; after the sermon, the people standing; immediately after baptism.

1   How deep are the wealth
    and the wisdom
    and the knowledge of God!
    How inscrutable his judgements,
    how unsearchable his ways!
    From God and through God and for God
    all things exist –
    to him be glory for ever!   ***Amen.***

Romans 11: 33, 36

2   To him who has the power
    to make you stand firm,
    to the only wise God through Jesus Christ
    be glory for endless ages!   ***Amen.***

Romans 16: 25, 27

3   To God the Father and our Lord Jesus Christ,
    who gave himself for our sins,
    to rescue us out of the present wicked age
    as our God and Father willed;
    to him be glory for ever and ever!   ***Amen.***

Galatians 1: 4

4   Now to him
    who is able through the power
    which is at work among us
    to do immeasurably more
    than all we can ask or conceive,
    to him be glory
    in the church and in Christ Jesus
    from generation to generation for evermore!

Amen.

Ephesians 3: 20 - 21

5   To the King eternal, immortal, invisible,
    the only God,
    be honour and glory for ever and ever!   *Amen.*

1 Timothy 1: 17

6   God is the blessed and only Sovereign,
    King of kings and Lord of lords;
    he alone possesses immortality,
    dwelling in unapproachable light;
    him no one has ever seen or can ever see;
    to him be honour and dominion for ever!   *Amen.*

1 Timothy 6: 15 -16

7   The God of all grace who called you
    to his eternal glory in Christ,
    restore, establish, and strengthen you.
    All power belongs to him for ever and ever!

Amen.

based on 1 Peter 5: 10 - 11

8   Now to the One who can keep you from falling
    and set you in the presence of his glory,
    jubilant and above reproach,
    to the only God our Saviour,
    be glory and majesty, power and authority,
    through Jesus Christ our Lord,
    before all time, now, and for evermore.

    Amen.

    Jude 24 - 25

9   To Jesus Christ,
    who loves us
    and has set us free from our sins with his blood,
    who has made of us a royal house
    to serve as the priests of his God and Father –
    to him be the glory and dominion for ever!

    Amen.

    Revelation 1: 5 - 6

10 To the Lord our God
    who created all things,
    by whose will they were created
    and have their being,
    to him who alone is worthy to receive them,
    be glory and honour and power.

    Amen.

    based on Revelation 4: 11

11 Worthy is the Lamb who was slain,
    to receive power and wealth,
    wisdom and might,
    honour and glory and praise!   *Amen.*

    Revelation 5: 12

12   Praise and honour, glory and might,
      to him who sits on the throne
      and to the Lamb for ever!   **Amen.**

Revelation 5: 13

13   Praise and glory and wisdom,
      thanksgiving and honour, power and might,
      be to our God for ever!   **Amen.**

Revelation 7: 12

14   Glory to the Father, and to the Son,
      and to the Holy Spirit:
      as it was in the beginning, is now,
      and will be for ever.   **Amen.**

15   And now to God, Father, Son, and Holy Spirit,
      be ascribed by us and by the whole Church,
      the kingdom, the power, and the glory,
      for ever and ever.   **Amen.**

16   And now to the Father, and to the Son,
      and to the Holy Spirit,
      be ascribed in the Church
      all honour and glory, might and majesty,
      dominion and power, now and for ever.

                                                   Amen.

17   To the holy, blessed and glorious Trinity,
      three persons and one God,
      be all glory and praise, dominion and power,
      now and for evermore.

                                                   Amen.

18   Blessing and honour, thanksgiving and praise,
      more than we can express,
      be accorded to you, most glorious Trinity,
      Father, Son, and Holy Spirit,
      by all angels, all people, all creatures,
      for ever and ever.   ***Amen.***

19   To God the Father, who first loved us,
      and made us accepted in the Beloved;
      to God the Son who loved us,
      and washed us from our sins in his own blood;
      to God the Holy Spirit,
      who sheds the love of God abroad in our hearts
      be all love and all glory for time and for eternity.
                                                Amen.

20   To our God and Father be glory for ever and ever!
                                                Amen.

21   To God alone be the glory.   ***Amen.***

XII
BENEDICTIONS

Benedictions

Benedictions may be preceded by a Dismissal, such as one of the following:

a. Go in the peace of God.

b. Go in the love of Christ.

c. Go in the power of the Spirit.

d. Go in the power of the Holy Spirit
   to fulfil your calling as servants of Christ.

e. Go in peace to serve the Lord.

f. Go in peace to love and serve the Lord.

1 May the Lord bless you and guard you;
   may the Lord make his face shine on you
   and be gracious to you;
   may the Lord look kindly on you
   and give you peace.   ***Amen.***

   Numbers 6: 24 - 26

2 May God, the source of all perseverance
   and all encouragement,
   grant that you may agree with one another

after the manner of Christ Jesus,
and so with one mind and one voice
may praise the God and Father
of our Lord Jesus Christ. *Romans 15: 5 - 6*

And the blessing of God almighty,
the Father, the Son, and the Holy Spirit
be among you and remain with you. **Amen.**

3 May God, who is the ground of hope,
fill you with all joy and peace
as you lead the life of faith
until, by the power of the Holy Spirit,
you overflow with hope. *Romans 15: 13*

And the blessing of God almighty . . . **Amen.**

4 Live in peace,
and the God of love and peace will be with you.
Amen.

5 The grace of the Lord Jesus Christ,
and the love of God,
and the fellowship of the Holy Spirit,
be with you all. **Amen.**
2 Corinthians 13: 14

6 Find your strength in the Lord,
in his mighty power. *Ephesians 6: 10*

And the blessing of God almighty . . .
Amen.

7   Peace to the community and love with faith,
from God the Father and the Lord Jesus Christ.
God's grace be with all
who love our Lord Jesus Christ
with undying love.   *Ephesians 6: 23*

And the blessing of God almighty . . .   **Amen.**

8   The peace of God,
which is beyond all understanding,
guard your hearts and your thoughts in Christ Jesus.
         Philippians 4: 7

And the blessing of God almighty . . .   **Amen.**

9   Live in union with Christ Jesus as Lord,
be rooted in him, be built in him,
grow strong in the faith;
let your hearts overflow with thankfulness.
         Colossians 2: 6, 7

And the blessing of God almighty . . .   **Amen.**

10   Keep hold of what is good
and avoid all forms of evil.
May God himself, the God of peace,
make you holy through and through,
and keep you sound in spirit, soul, and body,
free of any fault when our Lord Jesus Christ comes.
         1 Thessalonians 5: 21 - 23

And the blessing of God almighty . . .

         Amen.

11   May our Lord Jesus Christ himself,
and God our Father, who has shown us such love,
and in his grace has given us
such unfailing encouragement and so sure a hope,
still encourage and strengthen you
in every good deed and word.

2 Thessalonians 2: 16

And the blessing of God almighty . . .   **Amen.**

12   May the Lord of peace himself
give you peace at all times and in all ways.
The Lord be with you all.   **Amen.**

2 Thessalonians 3:16

13   May the God of peace,
who brought back from the dead our Lord Jesus,
the great Shepherd of the sheep,
through the blood of an eternal covenant,
make you perfect in all goodness
so that you may do his will;
and may he create in us what is pleasing to him,
through Jesus Christ,
to whom be glory for ever and ever!

Hebrews 13: 20 - 21

And the blessing of God almighty . . .   **Amen.**

14   Mercy, peace, and love in fullest measure,
to you whom God has called,
who live in the love of God the Father
and are kept safe for the coming of Jesus Christ.

Amen.

Jude 1, 2

15   To the mercy and protection of God
we commit you.
The blessing of God almighty,
the Father, the Son, and the Holy Spirit
rest upon you and remain with you always.

Amen.

16   Grace and peace be yours in fullest measure,
from God, Father, Son, and Holy Spirit,
now and for ever.   *Amen.*

17   Go in peace.
God the Father,
God the Son,
God the Holy Spirit
bless, preserve, and keep you,
this *day* and for ever.   *Amen.*

18   God grant to the living, grace;
to the departed, rest;
to the Church, the Queen,
the commonwealth, and all people,
peace and concord;
and to us and all his servants, life everlasting.

And the blessing of God almighty,
the Father, the Son, and the Holy Spirit,
be with you and abide with you always.   *Amen.*

19   May the love of the Lord Jesus draw us to himself;
may the power of the Lord Jesus
strengthen us in his service;

may the joy of the Lord Jesus fill our souls;
and may the blessing of God almighty,
the Father, the Son, and the Holy Spirit,
be with you and abide with you always.

Amen.

20   May the Lord bless you,
and preserve you from all evil,
and bring you to everlasting life.   *Amen.*

21   The peace of God be with you,
the peace of Christ be with you,
the peace of the Holy Spirit be with you
and with your children,
for an hour, for ever, for eternity.   *Amen.*

22   The blessing of God and the Lord be yours,
the blessing of the perfect Spirit be yours,
the blessing of the Three be poured on you
mildly and generously.   *Amen.*

23   The guarding of the God of life be on you,
the guarding of the loving Christ be on you,
the guarding of the Holy Spirit be on you
to aid you and enfold you
each day and night of your lives.   *Amen.*

24   May the eye of the great God be on you,
the eye of the God of glory,
the eye of the Virgin's Son,
the eye of the gentle Spirit,

the kindly eye of the Three be on you,
to aid you and to shepherd you. *Amen.*

25 May God's blessing be yours,
and well may it befall you. *Amen.*

26 May God shield you in the valleys,
may Christ aid you on the mountains,
may the Holy Spirit bathe you on the slopes,
in hollow, on hill, on plain,
mountain, valley, and plain. *Amen.*

27 May God make safe to you each steep,
may God make open to you each pass,
may God make clear to you each road,
and may he take you
in the clasp of his own two hands. *Amen.*

28 May God's goodness be yours,
and well and seven times well
may you spend your lives. *Amen.*

29 God's blessing be yours,
and well may it befall you;
Christ's blessing be yours,
and well may you be treated;
the Spirit's blessing be yours,
and well may you spend your lives,
each day that you rise up,
each night that you lie down.

Amen.

30   My own blessing be with you;
     the blessing of God be with you;
     the blessing of saints be with you
     and the peace of the life eternal.   *Amen.*

31   The compassing of the saints be upon you;
     the compassing of the angels be upon you;
     the compassing of the saints and the angels
     be upon you,
     and the love of your creator be with you.   *Amen.*

FOR THE CHRISTIAN YEAR

   Advent
        Look forward in hope
        to the coming of your Saviour,
        prepare the way for Christ your Lord;
        welcome him with love and faith
        when he comes in glory.
        And the blessing of God almighty,
        the Father, the Son, and the Holy Spirit,
        be among you and remain with you always.
                                               Amen.

   Christmas
        May the joy of the angels,
        the humility of the shepherds,
        and the peace of the Christ-Child
        be God's gift to you and to all people
        this Christmas (Day), and always.
        And the blessing of God almighty . . .   *Amen.*

        or

The peace and joy of Christmas
fill your hearts and homes.
And the blessing of God almighty . . .   *Amen.*

Epiphany

May the light of the glorious Gospel of Christ
shine in your hearts, transform your lives,
and brighten the world.
And the blessing of God almighty . . .   *Amen.*

Lent

Be bold to share the life of Christ,
and show his love.
And the blessing of God almighty . . .   *Amen.*

or

Grow in grace
and in the knowledge
of our Lord and Saviour Jesus Christ.
And the blessing of God almighty . . .   *Amen.*

or

Secure in God's love,
be steadfast in his service.
And the blessing of God almighty . . .   *Amen.*

Good Friday

Save us, O Lord, waking,
and guard us sleeping;
that awake we may watch with Christ,
and asleep we may rest in peace.

The Lord almighty grant you
a quiet night and a perfect end.　　　　*Amen.*

Easter

　Christ was raised from the dead
　by the glorious power of the Father.
　Set out, then, on a new life with Christ.
　And the blessing of God almighty . . .　*Amen.*

Ascension

　Christ our King make you faithful
　and strong to do his will,
　and bring you to reign with him in glory.
　And the blessing of God almighty . . .　*Amen.*

Pentecost

　With unflagging zeal, aglow with the Spirit,
　serve the Lord.
　And the blessing of God almighty . . .　*Amen.*

Trinity

　God the Holy Trinity make you strong
　in faith, and hope, and love.
　And the blessing of God almighty . . .　*Amen.*

All Saints

　God give you grace to follow the saints
　in faith, hope, and love.
　And the blessing of God almighty . . .　*Amen.*

St Andrew
>Proclaim the message, press it home,
>work to spread the gospel,
>and so discharge the duties of your calling.
>And the blessing of God almighty . . .   **Amen.**

in the absence of a minister,
one of these prayers may be said by all:

1   **The grace of the Lord Jesus Christ,**
     and the love of God,
     and the fellowship of the Holy Spirit,
     be with us all.   **Amen.**

                                        2 Corinthians 13: 14

2   **May the blessing of God almighty,**
     the Father, the Son, and the Holy Spirit,
     rest upon us
     and upon all our work and worship
     done in his name.
     May he give us light to guide us,
     courage to support us,
     and love to unite us,
     now and for evermore.   **Amen.**

3   **May the love of the Father enfold us,**
     the wisdom of the Son enlighten us,
     the fire of the Spirit inflame us;
     and may the blessing of God rest upon us
     and abide with us, now and evermore.

                                               Amen.

4   *May the grace of Christ attend us,*
    the love of God surround us,
    the Holy Spirit keep us,
    this day and for ever.   *Amen.*

5   *May God the Father make us holy in his love;*
    God the Son enrich us with his grace;
    God the Holy Spirit strengthen us with joy;
    may the Lord bless us
    and keep us in eternal life.   *Amen.*

XIII
READINGS
for
PASTORAL
VISITATION

PASTORAL READINGS

Two series of readings are provided, both of which may be used for regular parish visitation and for pastoral visits to those in need.

Listening to God	*St Luke 8: 4 - 15* The sower	*St Luke 10: 38 - 42* Martha and Mary
God's creation	*Psalm 95: 1 - 7* His people	*Psalm 100* The flock he shepherds
God's providence	*Psalm 23* The Shepherd	*St Matthew 6: 25 - 34* God so clothes
God's searching	*St Luke 15: 1 - 10* Lost sheep, lost coin	*St Luke 15: 11 - 24* Lost son
God above all	*St Mark 12: 28 - 34* Which commandment is first?	*Deuteronomy 30: 15 - 20* What is life for you?
New strength	*Isaiah 40: 21 - 31* Vigour to the weary	*Psalm 103: 1 - 5, 8 - 18* Youth ever new
Searching for God	*St Luke 11: 1 - 13* Ask and receive	*St Matthew 13: 44 - 46* Buried treasure, finest pearl
Prayer to God	*St Matthew 6: 1 - 15* The secret place	*Psalm 42: 1 - 8* Laid aside
For forgiveness	*Psalm 130* Out of the depths	*Psalm 32: 1 - 7* Happy the one
The sin-bearer	*1 Peter 2: 19 - 25* By his wounds	*Isaiah 53: 1 - 9* Laid upon him

605

Forgiven	*St Luke 23: 32 - 43* Penitent thief	*St Luke 18: 9 - 14* Pharisees and tax gatherers
Made whole	*Psalm 126* We rejoiced	*St Mark 2: 1 - 12* Healing of the paralytic
Resurrection	*St Matthew 28: 1 - 10* Nothing to fear	*St John 20: 1 - 18* From the dead
New life	*St John 1: 1 - 14* Children of God	*St John 3: 1 - 8* Born from water and Spirit
Peace of God	*Romans 5: 1 - 11* At peace	*Philippians 4: 6 - 9* Beyond understanding
Communion	*St Luke 24: 13 - 35* He broke the bread	*St Matthew 26: 17 - 29* My body
Prepared for God	*St Matthew 25: 1 - 13* Keep awake, then	*1 Thessalonians 5: 1 - 11* Hearten one another
Suffering	*St Mark 14: 32 - 42* The flesh is weak	*Hebrews 4: 14 - 16* Timely help
Sure foundation	*St Matthew 7: 21 - 29* The wise and the foolish	*Romans 8: 31 - 39* Nothing can separate
With the Lord	*1 Thessalonians 4: 13 - 18* Console one another	*Revelation 21: 1 - 7* God himself with them

XIV
LECTIONARY

The Lectionary

The Revised Common Lectionary was prepared by The Consultation on Common Texts (CCT), and consists of a table of readings which gives the liturgical day or date and the Scripture references for the texts to be read.

It is arranged in a three-year cycle: year A, the year of Matthew; year B, the year of Mark; and year C, the year of Luke. John is read each year, especially around Christmas, Lent and Easter, and also in the year of Mark, whose Gospel is shorter than the others. The sequence of Gospel readings is meant to lead God's people to a deeper knowledge of Christ and a stronger faith in him.

Along with the Gospel, there is a rich provision of Old Testament material, chosen to illuminate the Gospel and to include important narratives of faith. Acts and the Epistles highlight not only apostolic authority, but Christian experience of and reflection on the grace of God in Christ.

Much of the material is offered in semi-continuous form, which allows a larger variety of passages of the Bible to be read. This return to a greater selection of readings of the Bible is not only a means of combating the decline of biblical literacy, among adults as much as among young Christians, but is a recovery of a liturgical way to lead the followers of Christ through his birth, baptism, ministry, death, and resurrection.

The Lectionary presented here is *The Revised Common Lectionary* with some adjustments. The calendar upon which it is based, and the principles it pursues, are explained in *The Revised Common Lectionary* (The Canterbury Press, 1992).

FINDING THE APPROPRIATE SUNDAY

The heading of the Lectionary shows the appropriate cycle, A, B, or C for each Advent-to-Advent year.

The Lectionary provides readings for more Sundays than there are in any one calendar year, and not every set of readings will be used in any one year. This is because Easter is a moveable feast, and the calendar of the Christian Year is also therefore moveable, with only Christmas (25 December) and Epiphany (6 January) fixed to particular dates. As the date of Easter varies from year to year, dates which depend on Easter also vary: for example, Ash Wednesday, and Pentecost. When Easter is early, it encroaches on the nine Sundays after Epiphany, reducing their number from as many as nine to as few as four; but the number of Sundays after Pentecost expands to compensate for the deficit. A table of moveable dates is given below.

Wherever possible, particular dates, between which the readings may occur, have been given in the Lectionary. The dates are inclusive.

When Easter falls as early as March 22, the readings for the Sunday following *Trinity Sunday* are those given for the Eighth Sunday after *Epiphany*.

MOVABLE DATES TO THE YEAR 2025

Year	Ash Wednesday	Easter	Ascension	Pentecost	Sundays after Pentecost	Advent Sunday
1994	16 February	3 April	12 May	22 May	21	27 November
1995	1 March	16 April	25 May	4 June	20	3 December
1996	21 February	7 April	16 May	26 May	21	1 December
1997	12 February	30 March	8 May	18 May	22	30 November
1998	25 February	12 April	21 May	31 May	20	29 November
1999	17 February	4 April	13 May	23 May	21	28 November
2000	8 March	23 April	1 June	11 June	19	3 December
2001	28 February	15 April	24 May	31 May	20	2 December
2002	13 February	31 March	9 May	19 May	22	1 December
2003	5 March	20 April	29 May	8 June	19	30 November
2004	25 February	11 April	20 May	30 May	20	28 November
2005	9 February	27 March	5 May	15 May	22	27 November
2006	1 March	16 April	25 May	4 June	20	3 December
2007	21 February	8 April	17 May	27 May	21	2 December
2008	6 February	23 March	1 May	11 May	23	30 November
2009	25 February	12 April	21 May	31 May	20	29 November
2010	17 February	4 April	13 May	23 May	21	28 November
2011	9 March	24 April	2 June	12 June	18	27 November
2012	22 February	8 April	17 May	27 May	21	2 December
2013	13 February	31 March	9 May	19 May	22	1 December
2014	5 March	20 April	29 May	8 June	19	30 November
2015	18 February	5 April	14 May	24 May	21	29 November
2016	10 February	27 March	5 May	15 May	22	27 November
2017	1 March	16 April	25 May	4 June	20	3 December
2018	14 February	1 April	10 May	20 May	22	2 December
2019	6 March	21 April	30 May	9 June	19	1 December
2020	26 February	12 April	21 May	31 May	20	29 November
2021	17 February	4 April	13 May	23 May	21	28 November

Year	Ash Wednesday	Easter	Ascension	Pentecost	Sundays after Pentecost	Advent Sunday
2022	2 March	17 April	26 May	5 June	19	27 November
2023	22 February	9 April	18 May	28 May	21	3 December
2024	14 February	31 March	9 May	19 May	22	1 December
2025	5 March	20 April	29 May	8 June	19	30 November

NOTES

– *Ash Wednesday* (first day in Lent) can fall at earliest on 4 February and at latest on 10 March.
– *Easter Day* can fall at earliest on 22 March and at latest on 25 April.
– When Easter is early, it encroaches on the Sundays after Epiphany, reducing their number, as necessary, from as many as nine to as few as four.
– *Pentecost (Whit Sunday)* is seven weeks after Easter and can fall at earliest on 10 May and at latest on 13 June.
– *Trinity Sunday* is the Sunday after Whit Sunday.
– *Advent Sunday* is the Sunday nearest to 30 November.

NOTE ON COLOURS

In many churches, a white pulpit fall and Bible markers are used at Holy Baptism and Holy Communion.

Colours may also be used to recognize the movements and moods of the Christian Year: purple for preparation and penance; white or gold for celebration and rejoicing; green for re-commitment and growth in Christ; red for the fire and power of the Holy Spirit.

Colours appropriate to the season are:

Advent	*purple*
Christmas season (beginning Christmas Eve)	*white*
The Epiphany of our Lord	*white*
Sundays after Epiphany	*green*
(but Last Sunday,	
Transfiguration Sunday, *white*)	
Lent	*purple*
(but no colour on Good Friday, Saturday)	
Easter season	
(Easter Day to Sunday after Ascension)	*white*
Pentecost	*red*
Sundays after Pentecost	*green*
(but First Sunday [Trinity]	
and Reign of Christ the King, *white*)	

Other occasions may be marked by appropriate colours:

marriage	*white*
funeral	*purple* or *white*
ordination and induction of a minister	*red*
ordination and admission of an elder	*red*
confirmation	*red*

	YEAR A Beginning on the First Sunday of Advent in 1992, 1995, 1998, 2001, 2004, 2007, 2010, 2013, 2016		YEAR B Beginning on the First Sunday of Advent in 1993, 1996, 1999, 2002, 2005, 2008, 2011, 2014, 2017		YEAR C Beginning on the First Sunday of Advent in 1994, 1997, 2000, 2003, 2006, 2009, 2012, 2015, 2018	
SEASON OF ADVENT						
First Sunday of Advent *between November 27* *and December 3*	Isaiah Psalm Romans St Matthew	2 : 1 - 5 122 13 : 11 - 14 24 : 36 - 44	Isaiah Psalm 1 Corinthians St Mark	64 : 1 - 9 80 : 1 - 7, 17 - 19 1 : 3 - 9 13 : 24 - 37	Jeremiah Psalm 1 Thessalonians St Luke	33 : 14 - 16 25 : 1 - 10 3 : 9 - 13 21 : 25 - 36
Second Sunday of Advent *between December 4* *and December 10*	Isaiah Psalm Romans St Matthew	11 : 1 - 10 72 : 1 - 7, 18 - 19 15 : 4 - 13 3 : 1 - 12	Isaiah Psalm 2 Peter St Mark	40 : 1 - 11 85 : 1 - 2, 8 - 13 3 : 8 - 15a 1 : 1 - 8	Malachi Psalm *or* St Luke Philippians St Luke	3 : 1 - 4 27 1 : 68 - 79 1 : 3 - 11 3 : 1 - 6
Third Sunday of Advent *between December 11* *and December 17*	Isaiah Psalm *or* St Luke James St Matthew	35 : 1 - 10 146 : 5 - 10 1 : 47 - 55 5 : 7 - 10 11 : 2 - 11	Isaiah Psalm *or* St Luke 1 Thessalonians St John	61 : 1 - 4, 8 - 11 126 1 : 47 - 55 5 : 16 - 24 1 : 6 - 8, 19 - 28	Zephaniah Psalm *or* Isaiah Philippians St Luke	3 : 14 - 20 45 12 : 2 - 6 4 : 4 - 7 3 : 7 - 18
Fourth Sunday of Advent *between December 18* *and December 24*	Isaiah Psalm Romans St Matthew	7 : 10 - 16 80 : 1 - 7, 17 - 19 1 : 1 - 7 1 : 18 - 25	2 Samuel Psalm *or* St Luke Romans St Luke	7 : 1 - 11, 16 89 : 1 - 4, 19 - 26 1 : 47 - 55 16 : 25 - 27 1 : 26 - 38	Micah Psalm *or* St Luke Hebrews St Luke	5 : 2 - 5a 80 : 1 - 7 1 : 47 - 55 10 : 5 - 10 1 : 39 - 45, (46 - 55)

	YEAR A	YEAR B	YEAR C
	Beginning on the First Sunday of Advent in 1992, 1995, 1998, 2001, 2004, 2007, 2010, 2013, 2016	Beginning on the First Sunday of Advent in 1993, 1996, 1999, 2002, 2005, 2008, 2011, 2014, 2017	Beginning on the First Sunday of Advent in 1994, 1997, 2000, 2003, 2006, 2009, 2012, 2015, 2018
SEASON OF CHRISTMAS **Nativity of the Lord (Christmas Day)** Any of the three sets of readings may be used on Christmas Eve/Day.	I Isaiah 9 : 2 - 7 Psalm 96 Titus 2 : 11 - 14 St Luke 2 : 1 - 14, (15 - 20)	I Isaiah 9 : 2 - 7 Psalm 96 Titus 2 : 11 - 14 St Luke 2 : 1 - 14, (15 - 20)	I Isaiah 9 : 2 - 7 Psalm 96 Titus 2 : 11 - 14 St Luke 2 : 1 - 14, (15 - 20)
The readings from II and III for Christmas may be used as alternatives for Christmas Day.	II Isaiah 62 : 6 - 12 Psalm 97 Titus 3 : 4 - 7 St Luke 2 : (1 - 7), 8 - 20	II Isaiah 62 : 6 - 12 Psalm 97 Titus 3 : 4 - 7 St Luke 2 : (1 - 7), 8 - 20	II Isaiah 62 : 6 - 12 Psalm 97 Titus 3 : 4 - 7 St Luke 2 : (1 - 7), 8 - 20
If III is not used on Christmas Day, it should be used at some service during the Christmas cycle because of the significance of St John's prologue.	III Isaiah 52 : 7 - 10 Psalm 98 Hebrews 1 : 1 - 4, (5 - 12) St John 1 : 1 - 14	III Isaiah 52 : 7 - 10 Psalm 98 Hebrews 1 : 1 - 4, (5 - 12) St John 1 : 1 - 14	III Isaiah 52 : 7 - 10 Psalm 98 Hebrews 1 : 1 - 4, (5 - 12) St John 1 : 1 - 14
First Sunday after Christmas Day These readings are used on the First Sunday after Christmas unless the readings for the Epiphany of the Lord are preferred.	Isaiah 63 : 7 - 9 Psalm 148 Hebrews 2 : 10 - 18 St Matthew 2 : 13 - 23	Isaiah 61 : 10 - 62 : 3 Psalm 148 Galatians 4 : 4 - 7 St Luke 2 : 22 - 40	1 Samuel 2 : 18 - 20, 26 Psalm 148 Colossians 3 : 12 - 17 St Luke 2 : 41 - 52

616

	YEAR A Beginning on the First Sunday of Advent in 1992, 1995, 1998, 2001, 2004, 2007, 2010, 2013, 2016	YEAR B Beginning on the First Sunday of Advent in 1993, 1996, 1999, 2002, 2005, 2008, 2011, 2014, 2017	YEAR C Beginning on the First Sunday of Advent in 1994, 1997, 2000, 2003, 2006, 2009, 2012, 2015, 2018
January 1 – **The Naming of Jesus**	Numbers 6 : 22 - 27 Psalm 8 Galatians 4 : 4 - 7 *or* Philippians 2 : 5 - 11 St Luke 2 : 15 - 21	Numbers 6 : 22 - 27 Psalm 8 Galatians 4 : 4 - 7 *or* Philippians 2 : 5 - 11 St Luke 2 : 15 - 21	Numbers 6 : 22 - 27 Psalm 8 Galatians 4 : 4 - 7 *or* Philippians 2 : 5 - 11 St Luke 2 : 15 - 21
January 1 – **when observed as** **New Year's Day**	Ecclesiastes 3 : 1 - 13 Psalm 8 Revelation 21 : 1 - 6a St Matthew 25 : 31 - 46	Ecclesiastes 3 : 1 - 13 Psalm 8 Revelation 21 : 1 - 6a St Matthew 25 : 31 - 46	Ecclesiastes 3 : 1 - 13 Psalm 8 Revelation 21 : 1 - 6a St Matthew 25 : 31 - 46

Second Sunday after
Christmas Day
These readings are provided for use when Epiphany (January 6) is celebrated on a weekday following the Second Sunday after Christmas Day.
	Jeremiah 31 : 7 - 14
	Psalm 147 : 12 - 20
	Ephesians 1 : 3 - 14
	St John 1 : (1 - 9),
	          10 - 18
		Jeremiah 31 : 7 - 14
		Psalm 147 : 12 - 20
		Ephesians 1 : 3 - 14
		St John 1 : (1 - 9),
		          10 - 18
			Jeremiah 31 : 7 - 14
			Psalm 147 : 12 - 20
			Ephesians 1 : 3 - 14
			St John 1 : (1 - 9),
			          10 - 18

SEASON OF EPIPHANY
Epiphany of the Lord
	Isaiah 60 : 1 - 6
	Psalm 72 : 1 - 7,
	          10 - 14
	Ephesians 3 : 1 - 12
	St Matthew 2 : 1 - 12
		Isaiah 60 : 1 - 6
		Psalm 72 : 1 - 7,
		          10 - 14
		Ephesians 3 : 1 - 12
		St Matthew 2 : 1 - 12
			Isaiah 60 : 1 - 6
			Psalm 72 : 1 - 7,
			          10 - 14
			Ephesians 3 : 1 - 12
			St Matthew 2 : 1 - 12

	YEAR A Beginning on the First Sunday of Advent in 1992, 1995, 1998, 2001, 2004, 2007, 2010, 2013, 2016	YEAR B Beginning on the First Sunday of Advent in 1993, 1996, 1999, 2002, 2005, 2008, 2011, 2014, 2017	YEAR C Beginning on the First Sunday of Advent in 1994, 1997, 2000, 2003, 2006, 2009, 2012, 2015, 2018
First Sunday after the Epiphany (Baptism of the Lord) *between January 7 and January 13*	Isaiah 42 : 1 - 9 Psalm 29 Acts 10 : 34 - 43 St Matthew 3 : 13 - 17	Genesis 1 : 1 - 5 Psalm 29 Acts 19 : 1 - 7 St Mark 1 : 4 - 11	Isaiah 43 : 1 - 7 Psalm 29 Acts 8 : 14 - 17 St Luke 3 : 15 - 17, 21 - 22
Second Sunday after the Epiphany *between January 14 and January 20*	Isaiah 49 : 1 - 7 Psalm 40 : 1 - 11 1 Corinthians 1 : 1 - 9 St John 1 : 29 - 42	1 Samuel 3 : 1 - 10, (11 - 20) Psalm 139 : 1 - 6, 13 - 18 1 Corinthians 6 : 12 - 20 St John 1 : 43 - 51	Isaiah 62 : 1 - 5 Psalm 36 : 5 - 10 1 Corinthians 12 : 1 - 11 St John 2 : 1 - 11
Third Sunday after the Epiphany *between January 21 and January 27*	Isaiah 9 : 1 - 4 Psalm 27 : 1, 4 - 9 1 Corinthians 1 : 10 - 18 St Matthew 4 : 12 - 23	Jonah 3 : 1 - 5, 10 Psalm 62 : 5 - 12 1 Corinthians 7 : 29 - 31 St Mark 1 : 14 - 20	Nehemiah 8 : 1 - 3, 5 - 6, 8 - 10 Psalm 19 1 Corinthians 12 : 12 - 31a St Luke 4 : 14 - 21
Fourth Sunday after the Epiphany *between January 28 and February 3* *If this is the Sunday before Ash Wednesday, it is therefore the Last Sunday after the Epiphany. In this event, do not use the readings given here, but instead use those for the **Last Sunday after the Epiphany**.	Micah 6 : 1 - 8 Psalm 15 1 Corinthians 1 : 18 - 31 St Matthew 5 : 1 - 12	Deuteronomy 18 : 15 - 20 Psalm 111 1 Corinthians 8 : 1 - 13 St Mark 1 : 21 - 28	Jeremiah 1 : 4 - 10 Psalm 71 : 1 - 6 1 Corinthians 13 : 1 - 13 St Luke 4 : 21 - 30

	YEAR A Beginning on the First Sunday of Advent in 1992, 1995, 1998, 2001, 2004, 2007, 2010, 2013, 2016	YEAR B Beginning on the First Sunday of Advent in 1993, 1996, 1999, 2002, 2005, 2008, 2011, 2014, 2017	YEAR C Beginning on the First Sunday of Advent in 1994, 1997, 2000, 2003, 2006, 2009, 2012, 2015, 2018

Fifth Sunday after the Epiphany
between February 4 and February 10
*If this is the Sunday before Ash Wednesday, it is there-fore the Last Sunday after the Epiphany. In this event, do not use the readings given here, but instead use those for the **Last Sunday after the Epiphany**.
	Isaiah 58 : 1 - 9a,
	             (9b - 12)
	Psalm 112 : 1 - 9,
	               (10)
	1 Corinthians 2 : 1 - 12,
	             (13 - 16)
	St Matthew 5 : 13 - 20
		Isaiah 40 : 21 - 31
		Psalm 147 : 1 - 11, 20c
		1 Corinthians 9 : 16 - 23
		St Mark 1 : 29 - 39
			Isaiah 6 : 1 - 8,
			           (9 - 13)
			Psalm 138
			1 Corinthians 15 : 1 - 11
			St Luke 5 : 1 - 11

Sixth Sunday after the Epiphany *between February 11 and February 17* *If this is the Sunday before Ash Wednesday, it is there-fore the Last Sunday after the Epiphany. In this event, do not use the readings given here, but instead use those for the **Last Sunday after the Epiphany**.	Deuteronomy 30 : 15 - 20 Psalm 119 : 1 - 8 1 Corinthians 3 : 1 - 9 St Matthew 5 : 21 - 37	2 Kings 5 : 1 - 14 Psalm 30 1 Corinthians 9 : 24 - 27 St Mark 1 : 40 - 45	Jeremiah 17 : 5 - 10 Psalm 1 1 Corinthians 15 : 12 - 20 St Luke 6 : 17 - 26

	YEAR A Beginning on the First Sunday of Advent in 1992, 1995, 1998, 2001, 2004, 2007, 2010, 2013, 2016	YEAR B Beginning on the First Sunday of Advent in 1993, 1996, 1999, 2002, 2005, 2008, 2011, 2014, 2017	YEAR C Beginning on the First Sunday of Advent in 1994, 1997, 2000, 2003, 2006, 2009, 2012, 2015, 2018
Seventh Sunday after the Epiphany *between February 18 and February 24* *If this is the Sunday before Ash Wednesday, it is therefore the Last Sunday after the Epiphany. In this event, do not use the readings given here, but instead use those for the **Last Sunday after the Epiphany**.	Leviticus 19 : 1 - 2, 9 - 18 Psalm 119 : 33 - 40 1 Corinthians 3 : 10 - 11, 16 - 23 St Matthew 5 : 38 - 48	Isaiah 43 : 18 - 25 Psalm 41 2 Corinthians 1 : 18 - 22 St Mark 2 : 1 - 12	Genesis 45 : 3 - 11, 15 Psalm 37 : 1 - 11, 39 - 40 1 Corinthians 15 : 35 - 38, 42 - 50 St Luke 6 : 27 - 38
Eighth Sunday after the Epiphany *between February 25 and February 29* *(See above)	Isaiah 49 : 8 - 16a Psalm 131 1 Corinthians 4 : 1 - 5 St Matthew 6 : 24 - 34	Hosea 2 : 14 - 20 Psalm 103 : 1 - 13, 22 2 Corinthians 3 : 1 - 6 St Mark 2 : 13 - 22	Isaiah 55 : 10 - 13 Psalm 92 : 1 - 4, 12 - 15 1 Corinthians 15 : 51 - 58 St Luke 6 : 39 - 49
Ninth Sunday after the Epiphany *between March 1 and March 9* Whenever this Sunday occurs, it is also the Last Sunday after the Epiphany; the readings for both Sundays are the same.	Exodus 24 : 12 - 18 Psalm 2 *or* 99 2 Peter 1 : 16 - 21 St Matthew 17 : 1 - 9	2 Kings 2 : 1 - 12 Psalm 50 : 1 - 6 2 Corinthians 4 : 3 - 6 St Mark 9 : 2 - 9	Exodus 34 : 29 - 35 Psalm 99 2 Corinthians 3 : 12 - 4 : 2 St Luke 9 : 28 - 36, (37 - 43)

	YEAR A Beginning on the First Sunday of Advent in 1992, 1995, 1998, 2001, 2004, 2007, 2010, 2013, 2016	YEAR B Beginning on the First Sunday of Advent in 1993, 1996, 1999, 2002, 2005, 2008, 2011, 2014, 2017	YEAR C Beginning on the First Sunday of Advent in 1994, 1997, 2000, 2003, 2006, 2009, 2012, 2015, 2018
Last Sunday after the Epiphany (Transfiguration of the Lord)	Exodus 24 : 12 - 18 Psalm 2 2 Peter 1 : 16 - 21 St Matthew 17 : 1 - 9	2 Kings 2 : 1 - 12 Psalm 50 : 1 - 6 2 Corinthians 4 : 3 - 6 St Mark 9 : 2 - 9	Exodus 34 : 29 - 35 Psalm 99 2 Corinthians 3 : 12 - 4 : 2 St Luke 9 : 28 - 36, (37 - 43)
SEASON OF LENT			
Ash Wednesday	Joel 2 : 1 - 2, 12 - 17 *or* Isaiah 58 : 1 - 12 Psalm 51 : 1 - 17 2 Corinthians 5 : 20b - 6 : 10 St Matthew 6 : 1 - 6, 16 - 21	Joel 2 : 1 - 2, 12 - 17 *or* Isaiah 58 : 1 - 12 Psalm 51 : 1 - 17 2 Corinthians 5 : 20b - 6 : 10 St Matthew 6 : 1 - 6, 16 - 21	Joel 2 : 1 - 2, 12 - 17 *or* Isaiah 58 : 1 - 12 Psalm 51 : 1 - 17 2 Corinthians 5 : 20b - 6 : 10 St Matthew 6 : 1 - 6, 16 - 21
First Sunday in Lent	Genesis 2 : 15 - 17; 3 : 1 - 7 Psalm 32 Romans 5 : 12 - 19 St Matthew 4 : 1 - 11	Genesis 9 : 8 - 17 Psalm 25 : 1 - 10 1 Peter 3 : 18 - 22 St Mark 1 : 9 - 15	Deuteronomy 26 : 1 - 11 Psalm 91 : 1 - 2, 9 - 16 Romans 10 : 8b - 13 St Luke 4 : 1 - 13
Second Sunday in Lent	Genesis 12 : 1 - 4a Psalm 121 Romans 4 : 1 - 5, 13 - 17 St John 3 : 1 - 17	Genesis 17 : 1 - 7, 15 - 16 Psalm 22 : 23 - 31 Romans 4 : 13 - 25 Mark 8 : 31 - 38	Genesis 15 : 1 - 12, 17 - 18 Psalm 27 Philippians 3 : 17 - 4 : 1 St Luke 13 : 31 - 35

	YEAR A Beginning on the First Sunday of Advent in 1992, 1995, 1998, 2001, 2004, 2007, 2010, 2013, 2016	YEAR B Beginning on the First Sunday of Advent in 1993, 1996, 1999, 2002, 2005, 2008, 2011, 2014, 2017	YEAR C Beginning on the First Sunday of Advent in 1994, 1997, 2000, 2003, 2006, 2009, 2012, 2015, 2018
Third Sunday in Lent	Exodus 17 : 1 - 7 Psalm 95 Romans 5 : 1 - 11 St John 4 : 5 - 42	Exodus 20 : 1 - 17 Psalm 19 1 Corinthians 1 : 18 - 25 St John 2 : 13 - 22	Isaiah 55 : 1 - 9 Psalm 63 : 1 - 8 1 Corinthians 10 : 1 - 13 St Luke 13 : 1 - 9
Fourth Sunday in Lent	1 Samuel 16 : 1 - 13 Psalm 23 Ephesians 5 : 8 - 14 St John 9 : 1 - 41	Numbers 21 : 4 - 9 Psalm 107 : 1 - 3, 17 - 22 Ephesians 2 : 1 - 10 St John 3 : 14 - 21	Joshua 5 : 9 - 12 Psalm 32 2 Corinthians 5 : 16 - 21 St Luke 15 : 1 - 3, 11b - 32
Fifth Sunday in Lent	Ezekiel 37 : 1 - 14 Psalm 130 Romans 8 : 6 - 11 St John 11 : 1 - 45	Jeremiah 31 : 31 - 34 Psalm 51 : 1 - 12 or Psalm 119 : 9 - 16 Hebrews 5 : 5 - 10 St John 12 : 20 - 33	Isaiah 43 : 16 - 21 Psalm 126 Philippians 3 : 4b - 14 St John 12 : 1 - 8

	YEAR A Beginning on the First Sunday of Advent in 1992, 1995, 1998, 2001, 2004, 2007, 2010, 2013, 2016	YEAR B Beginning on the First Sunday of Advent in 1993, 1996, 1999, 2002, 2005, 2008, 2011, 2014, 2017	YEAR C Beginning on the First Sunday of Advent in 1994, 1997, 2000, 2003, 2006, 2009, 2012, 2015, 2018
HOLY WEEK	*Entry into Jerusalem*	*Entry into Jerusalem*	*Entry into Jerusalem*
Sixth Sunday in Lent (Palm/Passion) Whenever possible, even if readings for the Entry into Jerusalem are used, it is desirable that the complete Passion narrative should be read, as part of the preparation for Easter.	St Matthew 21 : 1 - 11 Psalm 118 : 1 - 2, 19 - 29	St Mark 11 : 1 - 11 *or* St John 12 : 12 - 16 Psalm 118 : 1 - 2, 19 - 29	St Luke 19 : 28 - 40 Psalm 118 : 1 - 2, 19 - 29
	Passion	*Passion*	*Passion*
	Isaiah 50 : 4 - 9a Psalm 31 : 9 - 16 Philippians 2 : 5 - 11 St Matthew 26 : 14 - 27 : 66 *or* St Matthew 27 : 11 - 54	Isaiah 50 : 4 - 9a Psalm 31 : 9 - 16 Philippians 2 : 5 - 11 St Mark 14 : 1 - 15 : 47 *or* St Mark 15 : 1 - 39 (40 - 47)	Isaiah 50 : 4 - 9a Psalm 31 : 9 - 16 Philippians 2 : 5 - 11 St Luke 22 : 14 - 23 : 56 *or* St Luke 23 : 1 - 49

	YEAR A Beginning on the First Sunday of Advent in 1992, 1995, 1998, 2001, 2004, 2007, 2010, 2013, 2016		YEAR B Beginning on the First Sunday of Advent in 1993, 1996, 1999, 2002, 2005, 2008, 2011, 2014, 2017		YEAR C Beginning on the First Sunday of Advent in 1994, 1997, 2000, 2003, 2006, 2009, 2012, 2015, 2018	
Monday in Holy Week	Isaiah Psalm Hebrews St John	42 : 1 - 9 36 : 5 - 11 9 : 11 - 15 12 : 1 - 11	Isaiah Psalm Hebrews St John	42 : 1 - 9 36 : 5 - 11 9 : 11 - 15 12 : 1 - 11	Isaiah Psalm Hebrews St John	42 : 1 - 9 36 : 5 - 11 9 : 11 - 15 12 : 1 - 11
Tuesday in Holy Week	Isaiah Psalm 1 Corinthians St John	49 : 1 - 7 71 : 1 - 14 1 : 18 - 31 12 : 20 - 36	Isaiah Psalm 1 Corinthians St John	49 : 1 - 7 71 : 1 - 14 1 : 18 - 31 12 : 20 - 36	Isaiah Psalm 1 Corinthians St John	49 : 1 - 7 71 : 1 - 14 1 : 18 - 31 12 : 20 - 36
Wednesday in Holy Week	Isaiah Psalm Hebrews St John	50 : 4 - 9a 70 12 : 1 - 3 13 : 21 - 32	Isaiah Psalm Hebrews St John	50 : 4 - 9a 70 12 : 1 - 3 13 : 21 - 32	Isaiah Psalm Hebrews St John	50 : 4 - 9a 70 12 : 1 - 3 13 : 21 - 32
Thursday in Holy Week	Exodus Psalm 1 Corinthians St John	12 : 1 - 14 116 : 1 - 2, 12 - 19 11 : 23 - 26 13 : 1 - 17, 31b - 35	Exodus Psalm 1 Corinthians St John	12 : 1 - 14 116 : 1 - 2, 12 - 19 11 : 23 - 26 13 : 1 - 17, 31b - 35	Exodus Psalm 1 Corinthians St John	12 : 1 - 14 116 : 1 - 2, 12 - 19 11 : 23 - 26 13 : 1 - 17, 31b - 35

	YEAR A Beginning on the First Sunday of Advent in 1992, 1995, 1998, 2001, 2004, 2007, 2010, 2013, 2016	YEAR B Beginning on the First Sunday of Advent in 1993, 1996, 1999, 2002, 2005, 2008, 2011, 2014, 2017	YEAR C Beginning on the First Sunday of Advent in 1994, 1997, 2000, 2003, 2006, 2009, 2012, 2015, 2018
Good Friday	Isaiah 52 : 13 - 53 : 12 Psalm 22 Hebrews 10 : 16 - 25 *or* Hebrews 4 : 14 - 16; 5 : 7 - 9 St John 18 : 1 - 19 : 42	Isaiah 52 : 13 - 53 : 12 Psalm 22 Hebrews 10 : 16 - 25 *or* Hebrews 4 : 14 - 16; 5 : 7 - 9 St John 18 : 1 - 19 : 42	Isaiah 52 : 13 - 53 : 12 Psalm 22 Hebrews 10 : 16 - 25 *or* Hebrews 4 : 14 - 16; 5 : 7 - 9 St John 18 : 1 - 19 : 42
Saturday These readings are for use at services other than an Easter Vigil.	Job 14 : 1 - 14 *or* Lamentations 3 : 1 - 9, 19 - 24 Psalm 31 : 1 - 4, 15 - 16 1 Peter 4 : 1 - 8 St Matthew 27 : 57 - 66 *or* St John 19 : 38 - 42	Job 14 : 1 - 14 *or* Lamentations 3 : 1 - 9, 19 - 24 Psalm 31 : 1 - 4, 15 - 16 1 Peter 4 : 1 - 8 St Matthew 27 : 57 - 66 *or* St John 19 : 38 - 42	Job 14 : 1 - 14 *or* Lamentations 3 : 1 - 9, 19 - 24 Psalm 31 : 1 - 4, 15 - 16 1 Peter 4 : 1 - 8 St Matthew 27 : 57 - 66 *or* St John 19 : 38 - 42
SEASON OF EASTER **Resurrection of the Lord** **Easter Vigil** A minimum of three pairs of Old Testament readings, together with an Epistle and a Gospel, should be chosen. The pair including Exodus 14 should always be used. *(see over)*	Genesis 1 : 1 - 2 : 4a Psalm 136 : 1 - 9, 23 - 26 Genesis 7 : 1 - 5, 11 - 18; 8 : 6 - 18; 9 : 8 - 13 Psalm 46	Genesis 1 : 1 - 2 : 4a Psalm 136 : 1 - 9, 23 - 26 Genesis 7 : 1 - 5, 11 - 18; 8 : 6 - 18; 9 : 8 - 13 Psalm 46	Genesis 1 : 1 - 2 : 4a Psalm 136 : 1 - 9, 23 - 26 Genesis 7 : 1 - 5, 11 - 18; 8 : 6 - 18; 9 : 8 - 13 Psalm 46

	YEAR A Beginning on the First Sunday of Advent in 1992, 1995, 1998, 2001, 2004, 2007, 2010, 2013, 2016	YEAR B Beginning on the First Sunday of Advent in 1993, 1996, 1999, 2002, 2005, 2008, 2011, 2014, 2017	YEAR C Beginning on the First Sunday of Advent in 1994, 1997, 2000, 2003, 2006, 2009, 2012, 2015, 2018
Genesis Psalm	22 : 1 - 18 16	22 : 1 - 18 16	22 : 1 - 18 16
Exodus Exodus	14 : 10 - 31; 15 : 20 - 21 15 : 1b - 13, 17 - 18	14 : 10 - 31; 15 : 20 - 21 15 : 1b - 13, 17 - 18	14 : 10 - 31; 15 : 20 - 21 15 : 1b - 13, 17 - 18
Isaiah Isaiah	55 : 1 - 11 12 : 2 - 6	55 : 1 - 11 12 : 2 - 6	55 : 1 - 11 12 : 2 - 6
Proverbs Psalm	8 : 1 - 8, 19 - 21; 9 : 4b - 6 19	8 : 1 - 8, 19 - 21; 9 : 4b - 6 19	8 : 1 - 8, 19 - 21; 9 : 4b - 6 19
Ezekiel Psalm	36 : 24 - 28 42 and 43	36 : 24 - 28 42 and 43	36 : 24 - 28 42 and 43
Ezekiel Psalm	37 : 1 - 14 143	37 : 1 - 14 143	37 : 1 - 14 143
Zephaniah Psalm	3 : 14 - 20 98	3 : 14 - 20 98	3 : 14 - 20 98

	YEAR A Beginning on the First Sunday of Advent in 1992, 1995, 1998, 2001, 2004, 2007, 2010, 2013, 2016		YEAR B Beginning on the First Sunday of Advent in 1993, 1996, 1999, 2002, 2005, 2008, 2011, 2014, 2017		YEAR C Beginning on the First Sunday of Advent in 1994, 1997, 2000, 2003, 2006, 2009, 2012, 2015, 2018	
	Romans Psalm	6: 3-11 114	Romans Psalm	6: 3-11 114	Romans Psalm	6: 3-11 114
	St Matthew	28: 1-10	St Mark	16: 1-8	St Luke	24: 1-12
Easter Day	Acts or Jeremiah Psalm	10:34-43 31: 1-6 118: 1-2, 14-24	Acts or Isaiah Psalm	10:34-43 25: 6-9 118: 1-2, 14-24	Acts or Isaiah Psalm	10:34-43 65:17-25 118: 1-2, 14-24
	Colossians or Acts	3: 1-4 10:34-43	1 Corinthians or Acts	15: 1-11 10:34-43	1 Corinthians or Acts	15:19-26 10:34-43
	St John or St Matthew	20: 1-18 28: 1-10	St John or St Mark	20: 1-18 16: 1-8	St John or St Luke	20: 1-18 24: 1-12
Easter Evening	Isaiah Psalm 1 Corinthians St Luke	25: 6-9 114 5: 6b-8 24:13-49	Isaiah Psalm 1 Corinthians St Luke	25: 6-9 114 5: 6b-8 24:13-49	Isaiah Psalm 1 Corinthians St Luke	25: 6-9 114 5: 6b-8 24:13-49
Second Sunday of Easter	Acts Psalm or Exodus Psalm 1 Peter St John	2: 14a, 22-32 16 15: 1-11 111 1: 3-9 20:19-31	Acts Psalm or Isaiah Psalm 1 John St John	4:32-35 133 65:17-25 3 1: 1-2:2 20:19-31	Acts Psalm or Psalm or 2 Kings Psalm Revelation St John	5:27-32 118:14-29 150 7: 1-16 2 1: 4-8 20:19-31

	YEAR A Beginning on the First Sunday of Advent in 1992, 1995, 1998, 2001, 2004, 2007, 2010, 2013, 2016	YEAR B Beginning on the First Sunday of Advent in 1993, 1996, 1999, 2002, 2005, 2008, 2011, 2014, 2017	YEAR C Beginning on the First Sunday of Advent in 1994, 1997, 2000, 2003, 2006, 2009, 2012, 2015, 2018
Sixth Sunday of Easter	Acts 17 : 22 - 31 Psalm 66 : 8 - 20 or Ezekiel 43 : 1 - 7a Psalm 115 1 Peter 3 : 13 - 22 St John 14 : 15 - 21	Acts 10 : 44 - 48 Psalm 98 or Genesis 35 : 9 - 15 Psalm 101 1 John 5 : 1 - 6 St John 15 : 9 - 17	Acts 16 : 9 - 15 Psalm 67 or Deuteronomy 34 : 1 - 12 Psalm 109 : 21 - 31 Revelation 21 : 10, 22 - 22 : 5 St John 14 : 23 - 29 or St John 5 : 1 - 9
Ascension of the Lord These readings may also be used on the Seventh Sunday of Easter.	Acts 1 : 1 - 11 Psalm 47 or 93 or Daniel 7 : 9 - 14 Psalm 24 : 7 - 10 Ephesians 1 : 15 - 23 St Luke 24 : 44 - 53	Acts 1 : 1 - 11 Psalm 47 or 93 or Daniel 7 : 9 - 14 Psalm 68 : 15 - 20, 32 - 35 Ephesians 1 : 15 - 23 St Luke 24 : 44 - 53	Acts 1 : 1 - 11 Psalm 47 or 93 or Daniel 7 : 9 - 14 Psalm 113 Ephesians 1 : 15 - 23 St Luke 24 : 44 - 53
Seventh Sunday of Easter	Acts 1 : 6 - 14 Psalm 68 : 1 - 10, 32 - 35 or Isaiah 45 : 1 - 7 Psalm 21 : 1 - 7 1 Peter 4 : 12 - 14; 5 : 6 - 11 St John 17 : 1 - 11	Acts 1 : 15 - 17, 21 - 26 Psalm 1 or Jeremiah 10 : 1 - 10a Psalm 108 1 John 5 : 9 - 13 St John 17 : 6 - 19	Acts 16 : 16 - 34 Psalm 97 or 2 Kings 2 : 1 - 15 Psalm 2 Revelation 22 : 12 - 14, 16 - 17, 20 - 21 St John 17 : 20 - 26

	YEAR A Beginning on the First Sunday of Advent in 1992, 1995, 1998, 2001, 2004, 2007, 2010, 2013, 2016	YEAR B Beginning on the First Sunday of Advent in 1993, 1996, 1999, 2002, 2005, 2008, 2011, 2014, 2017	YEAR C Beginning on the First Sunday of Advent in 1994, 1997, 2000, 2003, 2006, 2009, 2012, 2015, 2018
DAY OF PENTECOST The passage from Acts must be used, either as the first or second reading	Acts 2 : 1 - 21 or Numbers 11 : 24 - 30 Psalm 104 : 24 - 34, 35b 1 Corinthians 12 : 3b - 13 or Acts 2 : 1 - 21 St John 20 : 19 - 23 or St John 7 : 37 - 39	Acts 2 : 1 - 21 or Ezekiel 37 : 1 - 14 Psalm 104 : 24 - 34, 35b Romans 8 : 22 - 27 or Acts 2 : 1 - 21 St John 15 : 26 - 27; 16 : 4b - 15	Acts 2 : 1 - 21 or Genesis 11 : 1 - 9 Psalm 104 : 24 - 34, 35b Romans 8 : 14 - 17 or Acts 2 : 1 - 21 St John 14 : 8 - 17, (25 - 27)
SEASON AFTER PENTECOST **Trinity Sunday (First Sunday after Pentecost)** *If the Sunday between May 24 and 28 inclusive follows Trinity Sunday, the readings for the Eighth Sunday after the Epiphany are used.*	Genesis 1 : 1 - 2 : 4a Psalm 8 2 Corinthians 13 : 11 - 13 St Matthew 28 : 16 - 20	Isaiah 6 : 1 - 8 Psalm 29 Romans 8 : 12 - 17 St John 3 : 1 - 17	Proverbs 8 : 1 - 4, 22 - 31 Psalm 8 Romans 5 : 1 - 5 St John 16 : 12 - 15

	YEAR A — Beginning on the First Sunday of Advent in 1992, 1995, 1998, 2001, 2004, 2007, 2010, 2013, 2016	YEAR B — Beginning on the First Sunday of Advent in 1993, 1996, 1999, 2002, 2005, 2008, 2011, 2014, 2017	YEAR C — Beginning on the First Sunday of Advent in 1994, 1997, 2000, 2003, 2006, 2009, 2012, 2015, 2018
Sunday between May 29 and June 4 **(if after Trinity Sunday)**	Genesis 6 : 9 - 22; 7 : 24; 8 : 14 - 19	1 Samuel 3 : 1 - 10, (11 - 20)	1 Kings 18 : 20 - 21, (22 - 29), 30 - 39
	Psalm 46	Psalm 139 : 1 - 6, 13 - 18	Psalm 96
	or Deuteronomy 11 : 18 - 21, 26 - 28	*or* Deuteronomy 5 : 12 - 15	*or* 1 Kings 8 : 22 - 23, 41 - 43
	Psalm 31 : 1 - 5, 19 - 24	Psalm 81 : 1 - 10	Psalm 96 : 1 - 9
	Romans 1 : 16 - 17; 3 : 22b - 28, (29 - 31)	2 Corinthians 4 : 5 - 12	Galatians 1 : 1 - 12
	St Matthew 7 : 21 - 29	St Mark 2 : 23 - 3 : 6	St Luke 7 : 1 - 10
Sunday between June 5 and June 11 **(if after Trinity Sunday)**	Genesis 12 : 1 - 9	1 Samuel 8 : 4 - 11, (12 - 15), 16 - 20, (11 : 14 - 15)	1 Kings 17 : 8 - 16, (17 - 24)
	Psalm 33 : 1 - 12	Psalm 138	Psalm 146
	or Hosea 5 : 15 - 6 : 6	*or* Genesis 3 : 8 - 15	*or* 1 Kings 17 : 17 - 24
	Psalm 50 : 7 - 15	Psalm 130	Psalm 30
	Romans 4 : 13 - 25	2 Corinthians 4 : 13 - 5 : 1	Galatians 1 : 11 - 24
	St Matthew 9 : 9 - 13, 18 - 26	St Mark 3 : 20 - 35	St Luke 7 : 11 - 17

	YEAR A Beginning on the First Sunday of Advent in 1992, 1995, 1998, 2001, 2004, 2007, 2010, 2013, 2016	YEAR B Beginning on the First Sunday of Advent in 1993, 1996, 1999, 2002, 2005, 2008, 2011, 2014, 2017	YEAR C Beginning on the First Sunday of Advent in 1994, 1997, 2000, 2003, 2006, 2009, 2012, 2015, 2018
Sunday between June 12 and June 18 **(if after Trinity Sunday)**	Genesis 18 : 1 - 15, (21 : 1 - 7) Psalm 116 : 1 - 2, 12 - 19 *or* Exodus 19 : 2 - 8a Psalm 100 Romans 5 : 1 - 8 St Matthew 9 : 35 - 10 : 8, (9 - 23)	1 Samuel 15 : 34 - 16 : 13 Psalm 20 *or* Ezekiel 17 : 22 - 24 Psalm 92 : 1 - 4, 12 - 15 2 Corinthians 5 : 6 - 10, (11 - 13), 14 - 17 St Mark 4 : 26 - 34	1 Kings 21 : 1 - 10, (11 - 14), 15 - 21a Psalm 5 : 1 - 8 *or* 2 Samuel 11 : 26 - 12 : 10, 13 - 15 Psalm 32 Galatians 2 : 15 - 21 St Luke 7 : 36 - 8 : 3
Sunday between June 19 and June 25 **(if after Trinity Sunday)**	Genesis 21 : 8 - 21 Psalm 86 : 1 - 10, 16 - 17 *or* Jeremiah 20 : 7 - 13 Psalm 69 : 7 - 10, (11 - 15), 16 - 18 Romans 6 : 1b - 11 St Matthew 10 : 24 - 39	1 Samuel 17 : (1a, 4 - 11, 19 - 23), 32 - 49 Psalm 9 : 9 - 20 *or* 1 Samuel 17 : 57 - 18 : 5, 10 - 16 Psalm 133 *or* Job 38 : 1 - 11 Psalm 107 : 1 - 3, 23 - 32 2 Corinthians 6 : 1 - 13 St Mark 4 : 35 - 41	1 Kings 19 : 1 - 4, (5 - 7), 8 - 15a Psalm 42 *and* 43 *or* Isaiah 65 : 1 - 9 Psalm 22 : 19 - 28 Galatians 3 : 23 - 29 St Luke 8 : 26 - 39

	YEAR A Beginning on the First Sunday of Advent in 1992, 1995, 1998, 2001, 2004, 2007, 2010, 2013, 2016		YEAR B Beginning on the First Sunday of Advent in 1993, 1996, 1999, 2002, 2005, 2008, 2011, 2014, 2017		YEAR C Beginning on the First Sunday of Advent in 1994, 1997, 2000, 2003, 2006, 2009, 2012, 2015, 2018	

Sunday between June 26 and July 2	Genesis
	Psalm
	or Jeremiah
	Psalm
	
	Romans
	St Matthew
		22 : 1 - 14
		13
		28 : 5 - 9
		89 : 1 - 4,
		  15 - 18
		6 : 12 - 23
		10 : 40 - 42
			2 Samuel
			Psalm
			or Lamentations
			Psalm
			2 Corinthians
			St Mark
				1 : 1, 17 - 27
				130
				3 : 23 - 33
				30
				8 : 7 - 15
				5 : 21 - 43
					2 Kings
					
					Psalm
					
					or 1 Kings
					
					Psalm
					Galatians
					St Luke
						2 : 1 - 2,
						  6 - 14
						77 : 1 - 2,
						  11 - 20
						19 : 15 - 16,
						  19 - 21
						16
						5 : 1, 13 - 25
						9 : 51 - 62

Sunday between July 3 and July 9	Genesis
	
	Psalm
	or Song of Songs
	(*or* Zechariah
	Psalm
	Romans
	St Matthew
		24 : 34 - 38,
		  42 - 49,
		  58 - 67
		45 : 10 - 17
		2 : 8 - 13
		9 : 9 - 12)
		145 : 8 - 14
		7 : 15 - 25a
		11 : 16 - 19,
		  25 - 30
			2 Samuel
			
			Psalm
			or Ezekiel
			Psalm
			2 Corinthians
			St Mark
				5 : 1 - 5,
				  9 - 10
				48
				2 : 1 - 5
				123
				12 : 2 - 10
				6 : 1 - 13
					2 Kings
					Psalm
					or Isaiah
					Psalm
					Galatians
					
					St Luke
						5 : 1 - 14
						30
						66 : 10 - 14
						66 : 1 - 9
						6 : (1 - 6),
						  7 - 16
						10 : 1 - 11,
						  16 - 20

	YEAR A Beginning on the First Sunday of Advent in 1992, 1995, 1998, 2001, 2004, 2007, 2010, 2013, 2016	YEAR B Beginning on the First Sunday of Advent in 1993, 1996, 1999, 2002, 2005, 2008, 2011, 2014, 2017	YEAR C Beginning on the First Sunday of Advent in 1994, 1997, 2000, 2003, 2006, 2009, 2012, 2015, 2018
Sunday between July 10 and July 16	Genesis 25 : 19 - 34 Psalm 119 : 105 - 112 *or* Isaiah 55 : 10 - 13 Psalm 65 : (1 - 8), 9 - 13 Romans 8 : 1 - 11 St Matthew 13 : 1 - 9, 18 - 23	2 Samuel 6 : 1 - 5, 12b - 19 Psalm 24 *or* Amos 7 : 7 - 15 Psalm 85 : 8 - 13 Ephesians 1 : 3 - 14 St Mark 6 : 14 - 29	Amos 7 : 7 - 17 Psalm 82 *or* Deuteronomy 30 : 9 - 14 Psalm 25 : 1 - 10 Colossians 1 : 1 - 14 St Luke 10 : 25 - 37
Sunday between July 17 and July 23	Genesis 28 : 10 - 19a Psalm 139 : 1 - 12, 23 - 24 *or* Isaiah 44 : 6 - 8 Psalm 86 : 11 - 17 Romans 8 : 12 - 25 St Matthew 13 : 24 - 30, 36 - 43	2 Samuel 7 : 1 - 14a Psalm 89 : 20 - 37 *or* Jeremiah 23 : 1 - 6 Psalm 23 Ephesians 2 : 11 - 22 St Mark 6 : 30 - 34, 53 - 56	Amos 8 : 1 - 12 Psalm 52 *or* Genesis 18 : 1 - 10a Psalm 15 Colossians 1 : 15 - 28 St Luke 10 : 38 - 42
Sunday between July 24 and July 30	Genesis 29 : 15 - 28 Psalm 105 : 1 - 11, 45b; (or Psalm 128) *or* 1 Kings 3 : 5 - 12 Psalm 119 : 129 - 136 Romans 8 : 26 - 39 St Matthew 13 : 31 - 33, 44 - 52	2 Samuel 11 : 1 - 15 Psalm 14 *or* 2 Kings 4 : 42 - 44 Psalm 145 : 10 - 18 Ephesians 3 : 14 - 21 St John 6 : 1 - 21	Hosea 1 : 2 - 10 Psalm 85 *or* Genesis 18 : 20 - 32 Psalm 138 Colossians 2 : 6 - 15, (16 - 19) St Luke 11 : 1 - 13

	YEAR A Beginning on the First Sunday of Advent in 1992, 1995, 1998, 2001, 2004, 2007, 2010, 2013, 2016	YEAR B Beginning on the First Sunday of Advent in 1993, 1996, 1999, 2002, 2005, 2008, 2011, 2014, 2017	YEAR C Beginning on the First Sunday of Advent in 1994, 1997, 2000, 2003, 2006, 2009, 2012, 2015, 2018
Sunday between July 31 and August 6	Genesis 32 : 22 - 31 Psalm 17 : 1 - 7, 15 *or* Isaiah 55 : 1 - 5 Psalm 145 : 8 - 9, 14 - 21 Romans 9 : 1 - 5 St Matthew 14 : 13 - 21	2 Samuel 11 : 26 - 12 : 13a Psalm 51 : 1 - 12 *or* Exodus 16 : 2 - 4, 9 - 15 Psalm 78 : 23 - 29 Ephesians 4 : 1 - 16 St John 6 : 24 - 35	Hosea 11 : 1 - 11 Psalm 107 : 1 - 9, 43 *or* Ecclesiastes 1 : 2, 12 - 14; 2 : 18 - 23 Psalm 49 : 1 - 12 Colossians 3 : 1 - 11 St Luke 12 : 13 - 21
Sunday between August 7 and August 13	Genesis 37 : 1 - 4, 12 - 28 Psalm 105 : 1 - 6, 16 - 22, 45b *or* 1 Kings 19 : 9 - 18 Psalm 85 : 8 - 13 Romans 10 : 5 - 15 St Matthew 14 : 22 - 33	2 Samuel 18 : 5 - 9, 15, 31 - 33 Psalm 130 *or* 1 Kings 19 : 4 - 8 Psalm 34 : 1 - 8 Ephesians 4 : 25 - 5 : 2 St John 6 : 35, 41 - 51	Isaiah 1 : 1, 10 - 20 Psalm 50 : 1 - 8, 22 - 23 *or* Genesis 15 : 1 - 6 Psalm 33 : 12 - 22 Hebrews 11 : 1 - 3, 8 - 16 St Luke 12 : 32 - 40
Sunday between August 14 and August 20	Genesis 45 : 1 - 15 Psalm 133 *or* Isaiah 56 : 1, 6 - 8 Psalm 67 Romans 11 : 1 - 2a, 29 - 32 St Matthew 15 : (10 - 20), 21 - 28	1 Kings 2 : 10 - 12; 3 : 3 - 14 Psalm 111 *or* Proverbs 9 : 1 - 6 Psalm 34 : 9 - 14 Ephesians 5 : 15 - 20 St John 6 : 51 - 58	Isaiah 5 : 1 - 7 Psalm 80 : 1 - 2, 8 - 19 *or* Jeremiah 23 : 23 - 29 Psalm 82 Hebrews 11 : 29 - 12 : 2 St Luke 12 : 49 - 56

	YEAR A Beginning on the First Sunday of Advent in 1992, 1995, 1998, 2001, 2004, 2007, 2010, 2013, 2016	YEAR B Beginning on the First Sunday of Advent in 1993, 1996, 1999, 2002, 2005, 2008, 2011, 2014, 2017	YEAR C Beginning on the First Sunday of Advent in 1994, 1997, 2000, 2003, 2006, 2009, 2012, 2015, 2018

Sunday between August 21 and August 27	Exodus 1 : 8 - 2 : 10
	Psalm 124
	    or Isaiah 51 : 1 - 6
	     Psalm 138
	Romans 12 : 1 - 8
	St Matthew 16 : 13 - 20
		1 Kings 8 : (1, 6, 10 - 11),
		             22 - 30,
		             41 - 43
		Psalm 84
		   or Joshua 24 : 1 - 2a,
		           14 - 18
		     Psalm 34 : 15 - 22
		Ephesians 6 : 10 - 20
		St John 6 : 56 - 69
			Jeremiah 1 : 4 - 10
			Psalm 71 : 1 - 6
			    or Isaiah 58 : 9b - 14
			     Psalm 103 : 1 - 8
			Hebrews 12 : 18 - 29
			St Luke 13 : 10 - 17

Sunday between August 28 and September 3	Exodus 3 : 1 - 15
	Psalm 105 : 1 - 6,
	         23 - 26, 45c
	   or Jeremiah 15 : 15 - 21
	     Psalm 26 : 1 - 8
	Romans 12 : 9 - 21
	St Matthew 16 : 21 - 28
		Songs of Songs 2 : 8 - 13
		Psalm 45 : 1 - 2,
		           6 - 9
		   or Deuteronomy 4 : 1 - 2,
		           6 - 9
		     Psalm 15
		James 1 : 17 - 27
		St Mark 7 : 1 - 8,
		           14 - 15,
		           21 - 23
			Jeremiah 2 : 4 - 13
			Psalm 81 : 1, 10 - 16
			   or Proverbs 25 : 6 - 7
			     Psalm 112
			Hebrews 13 : 1 - 8,
			           15 - 16
			St Luke 14 : 1, 7 - 14

	YEAR A Beginning on the First Sunday of Advent in 1992, 1995, 1998, 2001, 2004, 2007, 2010, 2013, 2016	YEAR B Beginning on the First Sunday of Advent in 1993, 1996, 1999, 2002, 2005, 2008, 2011, 2014, 2017	YEAR C Beginning on the First Sunday of Advent in 1994, 1997, 2000, 2003, 2006, 2009, 2012, 2015, 2018
Sunday between September 4 and September 10	Exodus 12 : 1 - 14 Psalm 149 *or* Ezekiel 33 : 7 - 11 Psalm 119 : 33 - 40 Romans 13 : 8 - 14 St Matthew 18 : 15 - 20	Proverbs 22 : 1 - 2, 8 - 9, 22 - 23 Psalm 125 *or* Isaiah 35 : 4 - 7a Psalm 146 James 2 : 1 - 10, (11 - 13), 14 - 17 St Mark 7 : 24 - 37	Jeremiah 18 : 1 - 11 Psalm 139 : 1 - 6, 13 - 18 *or* Deuteronomy 30 : 15 - 20 Psalm 1 Philemon 1 - 21 St Luke 14 : 25 - 33
Sunday between September 11 and September 17	Exodus 14 : 19 - 31 Psalm 114 (*or* Exodus 15 : 1b - 11, 20 - 21) *or* Genesis 50 : 15 - 21 Psalm 103 : (1 - 7), 8 - 13 Romans 14 : 1 - 12 St Matthew 18 : 21 - 35	Proverbs 1 : 20 - 33 Psalm 19 *or* Isaiah 50 : 4 - 9a Psalm 116 : 1 - 9 James 3 : 1 - 12 St Mark 8 : 27 - 38	Jeremiah 4 : 11 - 12, 22 - 28 Psalm 14 *or* Exodus 32 : 7 - 14 Psalm 51 : 1 - 10 1 Timothy 1 : 12 - 17 St Luke 15 : 1 - 10
Sunday between September 18 and September 24	Exodus 16 : 2 - 15 Psalm 105 : 1 - 6, 37 - 45 *or* Jonah 3 : 10 - 4 : 11 Psalm 145 : 1 - 8 Philippians 1 : 21 - 30 St Matthew 20 : 1 - 16	Proverbs 31 : 10 - 31 Psalm 1 *or* Jeremiah 11 : 18 - 20 Psalm 54 James 3 : 13 - 4 : 3, 7 - 8a St Mark 9 : 30 - 37	Jeremiah 8 : 18 - 9 : 1 Psalm 79 : 1 - 9 *or* Amos 8 : 4 - 7 Psalm 113 1 Timothy 2 : 1 - 7 St Luke 16 : 1 - 13

	YEAR A Beginning on the First Sunday of Advent in 1992, 1995, 1998, 2001, 2004, 2007, 2010, 2013, 2016	YEAR B Beginning on the First Sunday of Advent in 1993, 1996, 1999, 2002, 2005, 2008, 2011, 2014, 2017	YEAR C Beginning on the First Sunday of Advent in 1994, 1997, 2000, 2003, 2006, 2009, 2012, 2015, 2018
Sunday between September 25 and October 1	Exodus 17 : 1 - 7 Psalm 78 : 1 - 4, 12 - 16 *or* Ezekiel 18 : 1 - 4, 25 - 32 Psalm 25 : 1 - 9 Philippians 2 : 1 - 13 St Matthew 21 : 23 - 32	Esther 7 : 1 - 6, 9 - 10; 9 : 20 - 22 Psalm 124 *or* Numbers 11 : 4 - 6, 10 - 16, 24 - 29 Psalm 19 : 7 - 14 James 5 : 13 - 20 St Mark 9 : 38 - 50	Jeremiah 32 : 1 - 3a, 6 - 15 Psalm 91 : 1 - 6, 14 - 16 *or* Amos 6 : 1a, 4 - 7 Psalm 146 1 Timothy 6 : 6 - 19 St Luke 16 : 19 - 31
Sunday between October 2 and October 8	Exodus 20 : 1 - 4, 7 - 9, 12 - 20 Psalm 19 *or* Isaiah 5 : 1 - 7 Psalm 80 : 7 - 15 Philippians 3 : 4b - 14 St Matthew 21 : 33 - 46	Job 1 : 1; 2 : 1 - 10 Psalm 26 *or* Genesis 2 : 18 - 24 Psalm 8 Hebrews 1 : 1 - 4; 2 : 5 - 12 St Mark 10 : 2 - 16	Lamentations 1 : 1 - 6 Lamentations 3 : 19 - 26 (*or* Psalm 137) *or* Habakkuk 1 : 1 - 4; 2 : 1 - 4 Psalm 37 : 1 - 9 2 Timothy 1 : 1 - 14 St Luke 17 : 5 - 10

	YEAR A Beginning on the First Sunday of Advent in 1992, 1995, 1998, 2001, 2004, 2007, 2010, 2013, 2016	YEAR B Beginning on the First Sunday of Advent in 1993, 1996, 1999, 2002, 2005, 2008, 2011, 2014, 2017	YEAR C Beginning on the First Sunday of Advent in 1994, 1997, 2000, 2003, 2006, 2009, 2012, 2015, 2018

Sunday between October 9 and October 15	Exodus 32 : 1 - 14
	Psalm 106 : 1 - 6,
	    19 - 23
	or Isaiah 25 : 1 - 9
	Psalm 23
	Philippians 4 : 1 - 9
	St Matthew 22 : 1 - 14
		Job 23 : 1 - 9,
		    16 - 17
		Psalm 22 : 1 - 15
		or Amos 5 : 6 - 7,
		    10 - 15
		Psalm 90 : 12 - 17
		Hebrews 4 : 12 - 16
		St Mark 10 : 17 - 31
			Jeremiah 29 : 1, 4 - 7
			Psalm 66 : 1 - 12
			or 2 Kings 5 : 1 - 3,
			    7 - 15c
			Psalm 111
			2 Timothy 2 : 8 - 15
			St Luke 17 : 11 - 19

Sunday between October 16 and October 22	Exodus 33 : 12 - 23
	Psalm 99
	or Isaiah 45 : 1 - 7
	Psalm 96 : 1 - 9,
	    (10 - 13)
	1 Thessalonians 1 : 1 - 10
	St Matthew 22 : 15 - 22
		Job 38 : 1 - 7,
		    (34 - 41)
		Psalm 104 : 1 - 9,
		    24, 35c
		or Isaiah 53 : 4 - 12
		Psalm 91 : 9 - 16
		Hebrews 5 : 1 - 10
		St Mark 10 : 35 - 45
			Jeremiah 31 : 27 - 34
			Psalm 119 : 97 - 104
			or Genesis 32 : 22 - 31
			Psalm 121
			2 Timothy 3 : 14 - 4 : 5
			St Luke 18 : 1 - 8

Sunday between October 23 and October 29	Deuteronomy 34 : 1 - 12
	Psalm 90 : 1 - 6,
	    13 - 17
	or Leviticus 19 : 1 - 2,
	    15 - 18
	Psalm 1
	1 Thessalonians 2 : 1 - 8
	St Matthew 22 : 34 - 46
		Job 42 : 1 - 6,
		    10 - 17
		Psalm 34 : 1 - 8,
		    (19 - 22)
		or Jeremiah 31 : 7 - 9
		Psalm 126
		Hebrews 7 : 23 - 28
		St Mark 10 : 46 - 52
			Joel 2 : 23 - 32
			Psalm 65
			or Jeremiah 14 : 7 - 10,
			    19 - 22
			Psalm 84 : 1 - 7
			2 Timothy 4 : 6 - 8,
			    16 - 18
			St Luke 18 : 9 - 14

	YEAR A Beginning on the First Sunday of Advent in 1992, 1995, 1998, 2001, 2004, 2007, 2010, 2013, 2016	YEAR B Beginning on the First Sunday of Advent in 1993, 1996, 1999, 2002, 2005, 2008, 2011, 2014, 2017	YEAR C Beginning on the First Sunday of Advent in 1994, 1997, 2000, 2003, 2006, 2009, 2012, 2015, 2018
Sunday between October 30 and November 5	Joshua 3 : 7 - 17	Ruth 1 : 1 - 18	Habakkuk 1 : 1 - 4; 2 : 1 - 4
On Sunday November 1, or on the Sunday after November 1, the readings for All Saints (p 642) may be used.	Psalm 107 : 1 - 7, 33 - 37	Psalm 146	Psalm 119 : 137 - 144
	or Micah 3 : 5 - 12	*or* Deuteronomy 6 : 1 - 9	*or* Isaiah 1 : 10 - 18
	Psalm 43	Psalm 119 : 1 - 8	Psalm 32 : 1 - 7
	1 Thessalonians 2 : 9 - 13	Hebrews 9 : 11 - 14	2 Thessalonians 1 : 1 - 4, 11 - 12
	St Matthew 23 : 1 - 12	St Mark 12 : 28 - 34	St Luke 19 : 1 - 10
Sunday between November 6 and November 12	Joshua 24 : 1 - 3a, 14 - 25	Ruth 3 : 1 - 5; 4 : 13 - 17	Haggai 1 : 15b - 2 : 9
On Sunday November 1, or on the Sunday after November 1, the readings for All Saints (p 642) may be used.	Psalm 78 : 1 - 7	Psalm 127	Psalm 145 : 1 - 5, 17 - 21; (*or* Psalm 98)
	or Amos 5 : 18 - 24	*or* 1 Kings 17 : 8 - 16	*or* Job 19 : 23 - 27a
	Psalm 70	Psalm 146	Psalm 17 : 1 - 9
	1 Thessalonians 4 : 13 - 18	Hebrews 9 : 24 - 28	2 Thessalonians 2 : 1 - 5, 13 - 17
	St Matthew 25 : 1 - 13	St Mark 12 : 38 - 44	St Luke 20 : 27 - 38
Sunday between November 13 and November 19	Judges 4 : 1 - 7	1 Samuel 1 : 4 - 20	Isaiah 65 : 17 - 25
	Psalm 123	1 Samuel 2 : 1 - 10	Isaiah 12
	or Zephaniah 1 : 7, 12 - 18	*or* Daniel 12 : 1 - 3	*or* Malachi 4 : 1 - 2a
	Psalm 90 : 1 - 8, (9 - 11), 12	Psalm 16	Psalm 98
	1 Thessalonians 5 : 1 - 11	Hebrews 10 : 11 - 14, (15 - 18), 19 - 25	2 Thessalonians 3 : 6 - 13
	St Matthew 25 : 14 - 30	St Mark 13 : 1 - 8	St Luke 21 : 5 - 19

	YEAR A Beginning on the First Sunday of Advent in 1992, 1995, 1998, 2001, 2004, 2007, 2010, 2013, 2016	YEAR B Beginning on the First Sunday of Advent in 1993, 1996, 1999, 2002, 2005, 2008, 2011, 2014, 2017	YEAR C Beginning on the First Sunday of Advent in 1994, 1997, 2000, 2003, 2006, 2009, 2012, 2015, 2018
Sunday between November 20 and November 26 **(Reign of Christ the King)**	Ezekiel 34 : 11 - 16, 20 - 24 Psalm 100 *or Ezekiel* 34 : 11 - 16, 20 - 24 Psalm 95 : 1 - 7a Ephesians 1 : 15 - 23 St Matthew 25 : 31 - 46	2 Samuel 23 : 1 - 7 Psalm 132 : 1 - 12, (13 - 18) *or Daniel* 7 : 9 - 10, 13 - 14 Psalm 93 Revelation 1 : 4b - 8 St John 18 : 33 - 37	Jeremiah 23 : 1 - 6 Luke 1 : 68 - 79 *or Jeremiah* 23 : 1 - 6 Psalm 46 Colossians 1 : 11 - 20 St Luke 23 : 33 - 43
SPECIAL DAYS			
Christian Unity	Ezekiel 37 : 15 - 24 Psalm 122 1 Corinthians 3 : 1 - 11 St Matthew 28 : 16 - 20	Jeremiah 33 : 6 - 9 Psalm 102 : 13 - 22 Ephesians 4 : 1 - 6 St John 17 : 11b - 23	Ezekiel 47 : 1 - 12 Psalm 133 *and* 134 Revelation 21 : 9 - 14, 22 - 27 St Luke 13 : 22 - 30
Presentation of the Lord *(February 2)*	Malachi 3 : 1 - 4 Psalm 24 Hebrews 2 : 14 - 18 St Luke 2 : 22 - 40	1 Samuel 2 : 1 - 11 Psalm 29 Galatians 4 : 1 - 7 St Luke 2 : 22 - 40	Haggai 2 : 1 - 9 Psalm 8 1 John 3 : 1 - 8 St Luke 2 : 22 - 40
Springtime	Genesis 8 : 15 - 22 Psalm 65 : 9 - 13 Galatians 6 : 7 - 10 St Matthew 6 : 24 - 30	Song of Songs 2 : 8 - 13 Psalm 104 : 1, 10 - 24 2 Corinthians 9 : 6 - 15 St John 12 : 20 - 26	Isaiah 5 : 1 - 7 Psalm 126 James 3 : 13 - 18 St Luke 12 : 23 - 31

	YEAR A Beginning on the First Sunday of Advent in 1992, 1995, 1998, 2001, 2004, 2007, 2010, 2013, 2016	YEAR B Beginning on the First Sunday of Advent in 1993, 1996, 1999, 2002, 2005, 2008, 2011, 2014, 2017	YEAR C Beginning on the First Sunday of Advent in 1994, 1997, 2000, 2003, 2006, 2009, 2012, 2015, 2018
Harvest Festival	Deuteronomy 26 : 1 - 11 Psalm 145 : 8 - 21 Revelation 14 : 14 - 18 St Matthew 13 : 24 - 33	Deuteronomy 8 : 1 - 10 Psalm 67 Acts 14 : 13 - 17 St John 6 : 24 - 35	Ruth 2 Psalm 144 Galatians 5 : 16 - 25 St Luke 12 : 13 - 21
Michaelmas *(September 29)*	2 Kings 6 : 8 - 17 Psalm 103 : 19 - 22 Revelation 12 : 7 - 12a St Matthew 18 : 1 - 6, 10	Daniel 10 : 4 - 11 : 2 Psalm 91 Revelation 12 : 7 - 12a St Mark 13 : 21 - 27	Genesis 23 : 20 - 33 Psalm 148 Revelation 12 : 7 - 12a St Luke 9 : 23 - 27
All Saints *(November 1)*	Revelation 7 : 9 - 17 *or* Isaiah 51 : 1 - 6 Psalm 34 : 1 - 10, 22 1 John 3 : 1 - 3 St Matthew 5 : 1 - 12	Isaiah 25 : 6 - 9 Psalm 24 Revelation 21 : 1 - 6a St John 11 : 32 - 44	Daniel 7 : 1 - 3 15 - 18 Psalm 149 Ephesians 1 : 11 - 23 St Luke 6 : 20 - 31
Remembrance Day	Isaiah 25 : 1 - 9 Psalm 20 Revelation 22 : 1 - 5 St Matthew 5 : 38 - 48	Deuteronomy 4 : 9 - 14 Psalm 46 Romans 8 : 31 - 35 St John 15 : 9 - 17	Micah 4 : 1 - 8 Psalm 9 : 9 - 20 2 Thessalonians 2 : 13 - 3 : 5 St Luke 1 : 68 - 79
St Andrew's Day *(November 30)*	Zechariah 8 : 20 - 23 Psalm 87 Romans 10 : 8b - 15 St Matthew 4 : 12 - 20	Isaiah 49 : 1 - 12 Psalm 40 : 1 - 11 Philemon 3 - 11 St John 1 : 35 - 42	Isaiah 55 Psalm 1 1 Corinthians 4 : 1 - 16 St John 12 : 20 - 36

	YEAR A Beginning on the First Sunday of Advent in 1992, 1995, 1998, 2001, 2004, 2007, 2010, 2013, 2016		YEAR B Beginning on the First Sunday of Advent in 1993, 1996, 1999, 2002, 2005, 2008, 2011, 2014, 2017		YEAR C Beginning on the First Sunday of Advent in 1994, 1997, 2000, 2003, 2006, 2009, 2012, 2015, 2018	
Dedication/Anniversary	Genesis Psalm 1 Corinthians St Matthew	28 : 10 - 22 48 : (1 - 8), 9 - 14 3 : 9 - 17 12 : 1 - 8	2 Chronicles Psalm Romans St John	6 : 12 - 21 84 12 4 : 19 - 26	2 Samuel Psalm 2 Peter St Luke	24 : 18 - 25 122 2 : 1 - 10 4 : 16 - 30

XV
SCRIPTURE
SENTENCES
and
COLLECTS
of the
DAY

The heading shows the appropriate cycle, A, B, or C for each Advent-to-Advent year.

Scripture sentences and collects are provided for more Sundays than there are in any one calendar year, and not every set of readings will be used in any one year. This is because Easter is a moveable feast, and the calendar of the Christian Year is also therefore moveable, with only Christmas (25 December) and Epiphany (6 January) fixed to particular dates. As the date of Easter varies from year to year, dates which depend on Easter also vary: for example, Ash Wednesday, and Pentecost. When Easter is early, it encroaches on the nine Sundays after Epiphany, reducing their number from as many as nine to as few as four; but the number of Sundays after Pentecost expands to compensate for the deficit. A table of moveable dates is given at the beginning of the Lectionary.

Wherever possible, particular dates, between which the readings may occur, have been given in the Lectionary. The dates are inclusive.

When Easter falls as early as March 22, the readings for the Sunday following *Trinity Sunday* are those given for the Eighth Sunday after *Epiphany*.

Calendar	Sentence		Collect

SEASON OF ADVENT
First Sunday of Advent
between November 27
and December 3

A Stand upright and hold your heads high, because your liberation is near.
St Luke 21: 28

B Awake sleeper, rise from the dead, and Christ will shine upon you.
Ephesians 5: 14

C The watchmen raise their voices and shout together in joy; for with their own eyes they see the Lord return to Zion.
Isaiah 52: 8

Almighty God,
give us grace to cast away
the works of darkness
and put on the armour of light,
now in the time of this mortal life,
in which your Son Jesus Christ
came to us in great humility;
that on the last day,
when he shall come again in his glorious majesty
to judge both the living and the dead,
we may rise to the life immortal;
through him who lives and reigns
with you and the Holy Spirit,
one God, now and for ever.

Second Sunday of Advent
between December 4
and December 10

A The Lord God had warned them time and again through his messengers, for he took pity on his people and on his dwelling-place.
2 Chronicles 36: 15

B They will know that they have a prophet among them, whether they listen or whether in their rebelliousness they refuse to listen.
Ezekiel 2: 5

C The Prophet of the Most High will be the Lord's forerunner, to prepare his way and lead his people to a knowledge of salvation through the forgiveness of their sins.
St Luke 1: 76 - 77

Almighty God,
you sent your servant John the Baptist
to prepare your people to welcome the Messiah.
Inspire the ministers and stewards of your truth
to turn our disobedient hearts to you,
that when the Christ shall come again
to be our judge
we may stand with confidence before his glory;
who is alive and reigns
with you and the Holy Spirit,
one God, now and for ever.

Calendar	Sentence		Collect
Third Sunday of Advent *between December 11* *and December 17*	**A**	I wait for the Lord with longing; I put my hope in his word. My soul waits for the Lord more eagerly than watchmen for the morning. *Psalm 130: 5 - 6*	God of power and mercy, you call us once again to celebrate the coming of your Son. Remove those things which hinder love of you, that when he comes he may find us waiting in awe and wonder for him; who lives and reigns with you and the Holy Spirit, one God, now and for ever.
	B	The Lord is good to those who look to him, to anyone who seeks him; it is good to wait in patience for deliverance by the Lord. *Lamentations 3: 25 - 26*	
	C	I shall stand at my post, I shall take up my position on the watchtower, keeping a look-out to learn what the Lord says to me. *Habakkuk 2: 1*	
Fourth Sunday of Advent *between December 18* *and December 24*	**A**	'A virgin will conceive and bear a son, and he shall be called Emmanuel', a name which means 'God is with us'. *St Matthew 1: 23*	Heavenly Father, you chose the Virgin Mary, full of grace, to be the mother of our Lord and Saviour. Fill us with your grace, that in all things we may embrace your will, and with her rejoice in your salvation; through Jesus Christ our Lord, who lives and reigns with you and the Holy Spirit, one God, now and for ever.
	B	'My soul tells out the greatness of the Lord, my spirit has rejoiced in God my Saviour.' *St Luke 1: 46b - 47*	
	C	Rejoice, daughter of Zion! I am coming, I shall make my dwelling among you, says the Lord. *Zechariah 2: 10*	

Calendar	Sentence	Collect
SEASON OF CHRISTMAS	*these sentences may be used after midnight*	Eternal God,
Nativity of the Lord		this holy night is radiant
	A The kindness and generosity of God our Saviour has dawned upon the world.	with the brilliance of your one true light.
Christmas Day		Grant that we who have known
	Titus 3: 4	the revelation of that light on earth
eve of Christmas		may come to see the splendour
	B The grace of God has dawned upon the world with healing for all mankind.	of your heavenly glory;
		through Jesus Christ our Lord,
		who is alive and reigns
	Titus 2: 11	with you and the Holy Spirit,
		one God, now and for ever.
	C Arise, shine, for your light has come; and over you the glory of the Lord has dawned.	
		or
	Isaiah 60: 1	Almighty God,
		you wonderfully created
		and yet more wonderfully restored
		our human nature.
		Grant that we may share the divine life
		of your Son Jesus Christ,
		who humbled himself
		to share our humanity,
		and now lives and reigns
		with you and the Holy Spirit,
		one God, now and for ever.
in the early morning	**A** I bring you good news, news of great joy for the whole nation. Today there has been born to you in the city of David a deliverer – the Messiah, the Lord. *St Luke 2: 10b - 11*	Heavenly Father,
		you sent your Son into the world
		to take our nature upon him
		and to be born of a pure virgin.
		Grant that, as we are born again in him,

651

B God has caused his light to shine in our hearts, the light which is knowledge of the glory of God in the face of Jesus Christ.   *2 Corinthians 4: 6*

he may continually dwell in us
and reign on earth
as he reigns in heaven,
with you and the Holy Spirit,
one God, now and for ever.

C Thanks be to God for his gift which is beyond all praise!
        2 Corinthians 9: 15

during the day

ABC The Word became flesh; he made his home among us, and we saw his glory, such glory as befits the Father's only Son, full of grace and truth.
        St John 1: 14

God our Father,
your Word has come among us
in the Holy Child of Bethlehem.
Grant that the light of faith
may illumine our hearts
and shine in our words and deeds;
through him who is Christ our Lord,
who lives and reigns
with you and the Holy Spirit,
one God, now and for ever.

First Sunday after Christmas
*between December 26
and January 1*

A This is how he showed his love among us: he sent his only Son into the world that we might have life through him.
        1 John 4: 9

Almighty God,
you have shed upon us the new light
of your incarnate Word.
Grant that this light, enkindled in our hearts,
may shine forth in our lives;
through Jesus Christ our Lord,
who lives and reigns with you,
in the unity of the Holy Spirit,
one God, now and for ever.

B Christ Jesus came into the world to save sinners.
        1 Timothy 1: 15

Calendar	Sentence	Collect

January 1
The naming of Jesus

C When the appointed time came, God
sent his Son, born of a woman.
Galatians 4: 4

ABC God bestowed on him the name above
all names, that at the name of Jesus
every knee should bow, and every
tongue acclaim, 'Jesus Christ is Lord'.
Philippians 2: 9 - 11

Eternal Father,
we give thanks for your incarnate Son,
whose name is our salvation.
Plant in every heart, we pray,
the love of him
who is the Saviour of the world,
our Lord Jesus Christ;
who lives and reigns
with you and the Holy Spirit,
one God, in glory everlasting.

January 1
when observed as
New Year's Day

ABC In times past God spoke through the
prophets; but in this the final age he
has spoken to us in his Son.
Hebrews 1: 1 - 2

Eternal God,
you sent your Son to be born among us
that we might be born again
to newness of life.
Fill us with the gladness
of your great redemption,
that as we begin this new year
with your blessing,
we may continue it in your favour,
and live all our days
as your dear children;
through Jesus Christ our Lord,
who is alive and reigns
with you and the Holy Spirit,
one God, now and for ever.

Calendar	Sentence	Collect
Second Sunday after Christmas Day *between January 2 and January 5*	**A** Pay heed to me, my people, and listen to me, for instruction will shine forth from me and my judgement will be a light to peoples. *Isaiah 51: 4*	God of power and life, you are the glory of all who believe in you. Fill the world with your splendour and show the nations the light of your truth; through Jesus Christ your Son our Lord, who is alive and reigns with you and the Holy Spirit, one God, now and for ever.
	B God the Lord has spoken and summoned the world from the rising of the sun to its setting. God shines out of Zion, perfect in beauty. *Psalm 50: 1 - 2*	
	C From the west the Lord's name will be feared, and his glory revered from the rising of the sun. His glory will come like a swift river on which the wind of the Lord moves. *Isaiah 59: 19*	
SEASON OF EPIPHANY **Epiphany of the Lord** *January 6 or First Sunday in January*	**A** Where is the new-born king of the Jews? We observed the rising of his star, and have come to pay him homage. *St Matthew 2: 2*	Eternal God, by a star you led wise men to the worship of your Son. Guide by your light the nations of the earth, that the whole world may know your glory; through Jesus Christ our Lord, who lives and reigns with you and the Holy Spirit, one God, now and for ever.
	B On you the Lord shines and over you his glory will appear; nations will journey to your light and kings to your radiance. *Isaiah 60: 2a - 3*	

654

Calendar	Sentence	Collect
	C By the light of the Lamb shall the nations walk, and to it the kings of the earth shall bring their splendour. *Revelation 21: 24*	
First Sunday after the Epiphany (**Baptism of the Lord**) *between January 7 and January 13*	**A** There came a voice came from heaven, saying, 'This is my beloved Son, in whom I take delight'. *St Matthew 3: 17*	Eternal Father, at the baptism of Jesus you revealed him to be your Son, and anointed him with the Holy Spirit. Keep all who are born of water and the Spirit faithful to their calling as your people; through Jesus Christ our Lord, who lives and reigns with you and the Holy Spirit, one God, now and for ever.
	B The Lord is strength to his people, a safe refuge for his anointed one. Save your people and bless those who belong to you, shepherd them and carry them for ever. *Psalm 28: 8 - 9*	
	C Because God was merciful, he saved us through the water of rebirth and the renewing power of the Holy Spirit, which he lavished upon us through Jesus Christ our Saviour. *Titus 3: 5*	
Second Sunday after the Epiphany *between January 14 and January 20*	**A** God has caused his light to shine in our hearts, the light which is knowledge of the glory of God in the face of Jesus Christ. *2 Corinthians 4: 6*	Almighty God, your Son our Saviour Jesus Christ is the light of the world.

655

Calendar	Sentence		Collect
	B	Arise, shine, for your light has come; and over you the glory of the Lord has dawned. *Isaiah 60: 1*	Grant that your people, may shine with the radiance of his glory, that he may be known, worshipped, and obeyed to the ends of the earth; who lives and reigns with you and the Holy Spirit, one God, now and for ever.
	C	Live lives worthy of the God who calls you into his kingdom and glory. *1 Thessalonians 2: 12*	
Third Sunday after the Epiphany *between January 21 and January 27*	A	As God has called you, live up to your calling. *Ephesians 4: 1*	Almighty God, by grace alone you call us and accept us in your service. Strengthen us by your Spirit, and make us worthy of your call; through Jesus Christ our Lord, who lives and reigns with you and the Holy Spirit, one God, now and for ever.
	B	The time has arrived; the kingdom of God is upon you. Repent, and believe the gospel. *St Mark 1: 15*	
	C	Consider how great is the love which the Father has bestowed on us in calling us his children! *1 John 3: 1*	
Fourth Sunday after the Epiphany *between January 28 and February 3*	A	You know the generosity of our Lord Jesus Christ: he was rich, yet for your sake he became poor, so that through his poverty you might become rich. *2 Corinthians 8: 9*	Living God, in Christ you make all things new. Transform the poverty of our nature by the riches of your grace, and in the renewal of our lives show forth your glory;

Calendar		Sentence	Collect
	B	Blessed are the poor in spirit; the kingdom of Heaven is theirs. *St Matthew 5: 3*	through Jesus Christ our Lord, who is alive and reigns with you and the Holy Spirit, one God, now and for ever.
	C	You must be renewed in mind and spirit, and put on the new nature created in God's likeness. *Ephesians 4: 23 - 24*	
Fifth Sunday after the Epiphany *between February 4 and February 10*	**A**	Jesus said, 'I am the light of the world. No follower of mine shall walk in darkness; he shall have the light of life'. *St John 8: 12*	Merciful Lord, grant to your faithful people pardon and peace, that we may be cleansed from all our sins and serve you with a quiet mind; through Jesus Christ our Lord, who is alive and reigns with you and the Holy Spirit, one God, now and for ever.
	B	The Lord will give strength to his people; the Lord will bless his people with peace. *Psalm 29: 11*	
	C	God is a forgiving God, gracious and compassionate, long-suffering and ever constant, and he did not abandon us. *Nehemiah 9: 17*	
Sixth Sunday after the Epiphany *between February 11 and February 17*	**A**	The Lord's love is surely not exhausted, nor has his compassion failed; they are new every morning, so great is his constancy. *Lamentations 3: 22 - 23*	Almighty and ever-living God, your Son Jesus Christ healed the sick and restored them to wholeness of life. Look with compassion on the anguish of the world,

657

Calendar	Sentence	Collect

B
The earth is filled with the Lord's unfailing love. *Psalm 33: 5b*

and by your power make whole
all peoples and nations;
through Jesus Christ our Lord,
who lives and reigns
with you and the Holy Spirit,
one God, now and for ever.

C
The Lord your God is in your midst.
He will rejoice over you and be glad;
he will show you his love once more.
Zephaniah 3: 17

Seventh Sunday after the Epiphany
between February 18 and February 24

A
Whoever is obedient to his word, in him the love of God is truly made perfect.
1 John 2: 5

Almighty God,
your Son revealed in signs and miracles
the wonder of your saving love.
Renew your people with your heavenly grace,
and in all our weakness
sustain us by your mighty power;
through Jesus Christ our Lord,
who is alive and reigns
with you and the Holy Spirit,
one God, now and for ever.

B
Grow in grace and in the knowledge of our Lord and Saviour Jesus Christ.
2 Peter 3: 18

C
Lord, who is like you, majestic in holiness, worthy of awe and praise, worker of wonders?
Exodus 15: 11

Eighth Sunday after the Epiphany
between February 25 and February 29

A
Dwell in me, as I in you. Apart from me you can do nothing.
St John 15: 4, 5

Almighty God,
grant us the Spirit to think and do always
those things that are right,
that we who can do nothing good without you,
may live according to your holy will;
through Jesus Christ our Lord,
who lives and reigns
with you and the Holy Spirit,
one God, now and for ever.

B
I am able to face anything through Christ Jesus who gives me strength.
Philippians 4: 13

Calendar	Sentence	Collect

C From his full store we have all received grace upon grace. *St John 1: 16*

Ninth Sunday after the Epiphany
between March 1 and March 7

A The Lord is my light and my salvation. Whom shall I fear? *Psalm 27: 1*

B The course of the righteous is like morning light, growing ever brighter till it is broad day. *Proverbs 4: 18*

C I am the light of the world. No follower of mine shall walk in darkness; he shall have the light of life. *St John 8: 12*

Almighty God,
you have revealed your will to all people
and promised us your saving help.
May we hear and do what you command,
that the darkness may be overcome
by the power of your light;
through your Son Jesus Christ our Lord,
who lives and reigns
with you and the Holy Spirit,
one God, now and for ever.

Last Sunday after the Epiphany
(Transfiguration of the Lord)

A The Son of man must be lifted up, in order that everyone who has faith may in him have eternal life. *St John 3: 14 - 15*

B God forbid that I should boast of anything but the cross of our Lord Jesus Christ, through which the world is crucified to me and I to the world! *Galatians 6: 14*

C When Christ appears we shall be like him, because we shall see him as he is. *1 John 3: 2*

God of light and truth,
open our eyes to the glory of your presence
in the world around us,
but chiefly in the face
of Jesus Christ your Son our Lord;
that we may grow into his likeness,
and attain the happy fulfilment of our hope
when the splendour of the Saviour
will be revealed;
through the same Jesus Christ our Lord,
who lives and reigns
with you and the Holy Spirit,
one God, now and for ever.

Calendar	Sentence		Collect
SEASON OF LENT			
Ash Wednesday	A	I thirst for God, the living God; when shall I come to appear in his presence? *Psalm 42: 2*	Almighty and everlasting God, you despise nothing you have made and forgive the sins of all who are penitent. Create and make in us new and contrite hearts. Give us grace worthily to lament our sins and acknowledge our brokenness, that we may receive from you, the God of all mercy, perfect remission and forgiveness; through Jesus Christ our Lord.
	B	God so loved the world that he gave his only Son, that everyone who has faith in him may not perish but have eternal life. *St John 3: 16*	
	C	Repent, for the kingdom of Heaven is upon you. *St Matthew 4: 17*	
First Sunday in Lent	A	Because Jesus himself has passed through the test of suffering, he is able to help those who are in the midst of their test. *Hebrews 2: 18*	Almighty God, your Son Jesus Christ fasted forty days in the wilderness, and was tempted as we are but did not sin. Give us grace to discipline ourselves in obedience to your Spirit; and, as you know our weakness, so may we know your power to save; through Jesus Christ our Lord.
	B	God keeps faith and will not let you be tested beyond your powers. *1 Corinthians 10: 13*	
	C	Trials come so that your faith may prove itself worthy of all praise, glory, and honour when Jesus Christ is revealed. *1 Peter 1: 7*	

Calendar	Sentence	Collect

Second Sunday in Lent

A   Let your face shine on your servants;
save us in your unfailing love.
Psalm 31: 1b

B   When Christ appears we shall be like
him, because we shall see him as he is.
1 John 3: 2

C   Come to me and listen to my words,
hear me and you will have life.
Isaiah 55: 3

Almighty God,
whose most dear Son went not up to joy
but first he suffered pain,
and entered not into glory
before he was crucified:
mercifully grant that we,
walking in the way of the cross,
may find it none other
than the way of life and peace;
through Jesus Christ our Lord.

or

Almighty God,
your Son was revealed in majesty
before he suffered death upon the cross.
Give us faith to perceive his glory,
that being strengthened by his grace
we may be changed into his likeness,
from glory to glory;
through Jesus Christ our Lord.

Third Sunday in Lent

A   Frail mortals are filled with the rich
plenty of your house, and you give
them to drink from the stream of your
delights; for with you is the fountain of
life.
Psalm 36: 7, 8

A   Almighty God,
you give the water of eternal life
through Jesus Christ your Son.
May we always thirst for you,
the spring of life and source of goodness;
through the same Jesus Christ our Lord.

Calendar	Sentence		Collect	

B The Lord is in his holy temple; let all the earth be silent in his presence.
Habakkuk 2: 20

BC Almighty God,
of ourselves we have no power to help ourselves.
Keep us outwardly in our bodies
and inwardly in our souls;
that we may be defended from all adversities
which may happen to the body,
and from all evil thoughts
which may assault and hurt the soul;
through Jesus Christ our Lord.

C Prove your repentance by the fruit you bear.
St Luke 3: 8

Fourth Sunday in Lent

A Send out your light and your truth to be my guide; let them lead me to your holy hill, to your dwelling-place.
Psalm 43: 3

A Almighty God,
you have delivered us from the death of sin
and raised us to new life in your love,
through our Saviour Jesus Christ;
and in baptism you have made us one with him
so that now we are the children of light.
Grant that we may walk in his light
and show forth your glory in the world;
through the same Jesus Christ our Lord.

B Those who live on the level of the spirit have the spiritual outlook, and that is life and peace.
Romans 8: 6

C Satisfy us at daybreak with your love, that we may sing for joy and be glad all our days.
Psalm 90: 14

BC Gracious Father,
your blessed Son Jesus Christ came from heaven
to be true bread which gives life to the world.
Evermore give us this bread,
that he may live in us, and we in him,
who lives and reigns
with you and the Holy Spirit,
one God, now and for ever.

Calendar	Sentence	Collect

Fifth Sunday in Lent

A Our God is a God who saves; to the
Lord God belongs all escape from death.
Psalm 68: 20

B Jesus died for all so that those who live
should cease to live for themselves, and
should live for him who for their sake
died and was raised to life.
2 Corinthians 5: 15

C Whoever wants to save his life will
lose it, but whoever loses his life for
my sake will find it.
St Matthew 16: 26

A Almighty God,
your Son came into the world
to free us all from sin and death.
Breathe upon us with the power of your Spirit,
that we may be raised to new life in Christ,
and serve you in holiness and righteousness
all our days;
through the same Jesus Christ, our Lord.

BC Most merciful God,
by the death and resurrection
of your Son Jesus Christ,
you created humanity anew.
Grant that by faith in him
who suffered on the cross,
we may triumph in the power of his victory;
through Jesus Christ our Lord.

HOLY WEEK

This Collect may be used on each day of Holy Week:
Almighty God,
in your great love you gave your only Son
to die for our sins
and for the sins of the whole world.
Help us by your Holy Spirit
to worship you with reverence,
and to enter with joy
into the celebration of those mighty acts
whereby you bring us life and immortality;
through the same Jesus Christ our Lord.

Calendar	Sentence		Collect

Sixth Sunday in Lent (Passion Sunday or Palm Sunday)

A We proclaim Christ nailed to the cross. He is the power of God and the wisdom of God.
1 Corinthians 1: 23, 24

B Now is the hour of judgement for this world; now shall the prince of this world be driven out. And when I am lifted up from the earth I shall draw everyone unto myself.
St John 12: 31, 32

C Jesus wept over the city and said, 'If only you had known this day the way that leads to peace! But no; it is hidden from your sight'.
St Luke 19: 41, 42

Lord Jesus Christ,
on the first Palm Sunday
you entered the rebellious city
where you were to die.
Enter our hearts, we pray,
and subdue them to yourself.
And as your disciples blessed your coming
and spread garments and branches in your way,
make us ready to lay at your feet
all that we have and are,
that we too may bless your coming
in the name of the Lord.

or

Almighty and ever-living God,
in tender love for all our human race
you sent your Son our Saviour Jesus Christ
to take our flesh
and suffer death upon a cross.
Grant that we may follow
the example of his great humility,
and share in the glory of his resurrection;
through Jesus Christ our Lord.

Monday in Holy Week

A Those who choose to do my will, will receive from me a memorial and a name in my own house and within my walls; for my house will be called a house of prayer for all nations. *Isaiah 56: 4, 5, 7*

Almighty God,
your Son Jesus Christ
cleared the temple
of those who desecrated the holy place.
Cleanse our hearts from greed and selfishness,

B

Let us strive to know the Lord, whose coming is as sure as the sunrise. He will come to us like the rain, like spring rains that water the earth.

Hosea 6: 3

that we may become the temple of the living God, the dwelling-place of your Holy Spirit; through the same Jesus Christ our Lord.

or

C

One thing I ask of the Lord, it is the one thing that I seek: that I may dwell in the house of the Lord all the days of my life, to gaze on the beauty of the Lord and to seek him in his temple.

Psalm 27: 4

Almighty and ever-living God, in tender love for all our human race you sent your Son our Saviour Jesus Christ to take our flesh and suffer death upon a cross. Grant that we may follow the example of his great humility, and share in the glory of his resurrection; through Jesus Christ our Lord.

Tuesday in Holy Week

A

Let the gospel of Christ dwell among you in all its richness: teach and instruct one another with all the wisdom it gives you.

Colossians 3: 16

Almighty God, your Son Jesus Christ taught the people the way of righteousness and judgement. Grant us a ready mind and willing spirit to learn from him all that you would teach us, and keep us watchful for his coming and diligent in his work; through the same Jesus Christ our Lord.

B

A great prophet has arisen among us. God has shown his care for his people.

St Luke 7: 16

C

The word of God is alive and active. It cuts more keenly than any two-edged sword.

Hebrews 4: 12

or

Almighty and ever-living God, in tender love for all our human race

Calendar

Sentence

Collect

you sent your Son our Saviour Jesus Christ
to take our flesh
and suffer death upon a cross.
Grant that we may follow
the example of his great humility,
and share in the glory of his resurrection;
through Jesus Christ our Lord.

Wednesday in Holy Week

A God, hear my cry; listen to my prayer.
From the end of the earth I call to you
with fainting heart; lift me up and set
me high on a rock. *Psalm 61: 1 - 2*

B The Lord is strength to his people, a safe
refuge for his anointed one.
Psalm 28: 8

C My close companions abhor me, and
those whom I love have turned against
me.
Job 19: 19

Almighty God,
your Son Jesus Christ
withdrew to the quietness of Bethany
to prepare himself for his passion.
In the fellowship of his suffering,
strengthen us to be more than conquerors
in our trials and temptations,
that whether betrayed by friends
or hurt by enemies,
we may remain steadfast in our faith unto the end;
through the same Jesus Christ our Lord.

or

Almighty and ever-living God,
in tender love for all our human race
you sent your Son our Saviour Jesus Christ
to take our flesh
and suffer death upon a cross.
Grant that we may follow
the example of his great humility,
and share in the glory of his resurrection;
through Jesus Christ our Lord.

Calendar	Sentence		Collect

Thursday in Holy Week

A We must not use the old leaven, the leaven of depravity and wickedness, but only the unleavened bread which is sincerity and truth.

1 Corinthians 5: 8

B You desire faithfulness in the inmost being. Wash me and I shall be whiter than snow.

Psalm 51: 6, 7

C I give you a new commandment: love one another; as I have loved you, so you are to love one another.

St John 13: 34

A God our Father,
your Son Jesus Christ
has left to us this meal of bread and wine
in which we share his body and his blood.
As we keep the feast of his redeeming love
may we feed on him by faith,
receive his grace,
and find fullness of life;
through the same Jesus Christ our Lord.

BC Holy God, source of all love,
on the night before he died
Jesus gave his disciples a new commandment
to love one another as he loved them.
Write this commandment in our hearts.
Give us the will to be the servant of others
as he was the servant of all,
who gave up his life and died for us,
Jesus Christ our Lord.

Good Friday

A Joy has vanished from our hearts; our dancing is turned to mourning. Woe to us, sinners that we are!

Lamentations 5: 15, 16

B Is it nothing to you, you passers-by? If only you would look and see: is there any agony like mine?

Lamentations 1: 12

A Almighty God,
look graciously, we pray, on this your family
for whom our Lord Jesus Christ
was willing to be betrayed
and given up into the hands of sinners
and to suffer death upon the cross;
who is alive and glorified with you
and the Holy Spirit,
one God, now and for ever.

Calendar	Sentence		Collect
		C	*or* Almighty God, your Son Jesus Christ endured the cross for our sake. Remove from us all coldness and cowardice of heart, and give us courage to take up our cross and follow him; through the same Jesus Christ our Lord.
	Who is this coming from Edom, from Bozrah with his garments stained red, one splendidly attired, striding along with mighty power? *Isaiah 63: 1*		
Saturday in Holy Week	Give light to my eyes lest I sleep the sleep of death, lest my enemies say, 'I have overthrown him'. *Psalm 13: 3, 4*	A	O God, creator of heaven and earth, as the crucified body of your dear Son was laid in the tomb and rested on this holy Sabbath, so may we await with him the coming of the third day and rise with him to newness of life; through the same Jesus Christ our Lord.
	Unless a grain of wheat falls into the ground and dies, it remains that and nothing more; but if it dies it bears a rich harvest. *St John 12: 24*	B	*or*
	One who has been in prison may well rise to be king. *Ecclesiastes 4: 14*	C	Grant, Lord, that we who are baptized into the death of your Son our Saviour Jesus Christ may continually put to death our evil desires and be buried with him; that through the grave and gate of death we may pass to our joyful resurrection, through his merits, who died, was buried, and rose again for us, your Son Jesus Christ our Lord.

Calendar	Sentence	Collect

SEASON OF EASTER
Resurrection of the Lord

Easter Vigil

A Awake, sleeper, rise from the dead,
and Christ will shine upon you.
Ephesians 5: 14

Eternal Giver of life and light,
you make this holy night shine
with the radiance of the risen Christ.
Renew your Church
with the joy and gladness of his presence,
that we may worship you in sincerity and truth,
and shine as lights in the world,
offering the word of life;
through Jesus Christ our Lord
who is alive and reigns
with you and the Holy Spirit,
one God, now and for ever.

B With all my heart I long for you in the
night, at dawn I seek for you.
Isaiah 26: 9

C The darkness is passing away and the
true light is already shining.
1 John 2: 8

Easter Day

A We are here to give you the good news,
that God has fulfilled the promise by
raising Jesus from the dead.
Acts 13: 32, 33

Lord of life and power,
through the mighty resurrection of your Son,
you have overcome death
and opened the gate of everlasting life.
Grant that we, being dead to sin
and alive to you in Jesus Christ,
may reign with him in glory,
who with you and the Holy Spirit is alive,
one God, now and for ever.

B I am the living One; I was dead, and
now I am alive for evermore.
Revelation 1: 18

C God not only raised our Lord from the
dead; he will also raise us by his
power.
1 Corinthians 6: 14

Easter Evening

A By the resurrection of Jesus Christ
from the dead, God gave us new birth
into a living hope.
1 Peter 1: 3

Almighty Father,
in your great mercy
you made glad the disciples

669

Calendar	Sentence		Collect
	B	You are in our midst, Lord, and we bear your name. *Jeremiah 14: 9*	with the sight of the risen Lord. Give us such knowledge of his presence with us
	C	Because I live, you too will live. *St John 14: 19*	that we may be strengthened and sustained by his risen life, and serve you continually in righteousness and truth; through Jesus Christ our Lord.
Second Sunday of Easter	**A**	Scripture speaks of 'things beyond our seeing, prepared by God for those who love him'; and these are what God has revealed to us through the Spirit. *1 Corinthians 2: 9 - 10*	Almighty and eternal God, the strength of those who believe and the hope of those who doubt, may we, who have not seen, have faith and receive the fullness of Christ's blessing, who is alive and reigns
	B	I pray that your inward eyes may be enlightened, so that you may know how vast are the resources of his power open to us who have faith. *Ephesians 1: 18, 19*	with you and the Holy Spirit, one God, now and for ever.
	C	They who look to God are radiant with joy; they will never be put out of countenance. *Psalm 34: 5*	
Third Sunday of Easter	**A**	When they asked, he gave them bread of heaven in plenty. *Psalm 105: 40*	God of life and love, your Son made himself known to his disciples in the breaking of bread.

Calendar	Sentence	Collect
	B I am the bread of life. Whoever comes to me will never be hungry, and whoever believes in me will never be thirsty *St John 6: 35*	Open the eyes of our faith, that we may see him in his redeeming work, who is alive and reigns with you and the Holy Spirit, one God, now and for ever.
	C Blessed are those who hunger and thirst to see right prevail; they shall be satisfied. *St Matthew 5: 6*	
Fourth Sunday of Easter	**A** Acknowledge that the Lord is God; he made us, and we are his, his own people, the flock which he shepherds. *Psalm 100: 3*	God of peace, who brought back from the dead our Lord Jesus, the great Shepherd of the sheep, through the blood of an eternal covenant, make us perfect in goodness so that we may do your will; and create in us what is pleasing to you; through the same Jesus Christ our Lord.
	B Like a shepherd he will tend his flock, and with his arm keep them together. *Isaiah 40: 11*	
	C Look after the flock of God whose shepherds you are. So when the chief shepherd appears, you will receive glory, a crown that never fades. *1 Peter 5: 2, 4*	
Fifth Sunday of Easter	**A** I shall run the course made known in your commandments, for you set free my heart. *Psalm 119: 32*	Almighty God, your Son Jesus Christ is the way, the truth, and the life.

B

The Lord has told you mortals what is good, and what it is that the Lord requires of you: only to act justly, to love loyalty, to walk humbly with your God.
Micah 6: 8

Give us grace to love one another and walk in the way of his commandments, who lives and reigns with you and the Holy Spirit, one God, now and for ever.

or

C

Make your paths known to me, Lord; teach me your ways. Lead me by your faithfulness and teach me, for you are God my saviour.
Psalm 25: 4 - 5

Living God, so teach us to know you through your Son Jesus Christ, that we may walk in harmony with his will, and share the power of his eternal life; through the same Jesus Christ our Lord.

Sixth Sunday of Easter

A

If you, bad as you are, know how to give good things to your children, how much more will your heavenly Father give good things to those who ask him!
St Matthew 7: 11

Merciful God, you have prepared for those who love you such good things as pass all understanding. Pour into our hearts such love toward you, that we, loving you above all things, may obtain your promises, which exceed all that we can desire; through Jesus Christ our Lord, who is alive and reigns with you and the Holy Spirit, one God, now and for ever.

B

Bless the Lord, my soul, and forget none of his benefits.
Psalm 103: 2

C

Without God who can eat with enjoyment? He gives wisdom and knowledge and joy.
Ecclesiastes 2: 25, 26

Ascension of the Lord

A

We see Jesus, who for a short while was made subordinate to the angels, crowned now with glory and honour.

Hebrews 2: 9

Almighty God,
your Son our Saviour Jesus Christ
ascended far above all heavens
that the might fill all things.
Grant that your Church on earth
may be filled with his presence
and that he may remain with us always,
to the end of the world;
through the same Jesus Christ our Lord,
who is alive and reigns
with you and the Holy Spirit,
one God, now and for ever.

B

Since we have a great high priest who has passed through the heavens, Jesus the Son of God, let us hold fast to the faith we profess.

Hebrews 4: 14

C

Christ has entered heaven itself, to appear now before God on our behalf.

Hebrews 9: 24

Seventh Sunday of Easter

A

God's mighty strength was seen at work when he raised Christ from the dead, and enthroned him at his right hand in the heavenly realms.

Ephesians 1: 20

Almighty God,
you have raised your only Son
to the right hand of your glory,
and bestowed on him the name above all names.
Assure us that as he reigns with you in heaven
so he abides with us on earth to the end of time;
through the same Jesus Christ our Lord
who lives and is glorified
with you and the Holy Spirit,
one God, now and for ever.

B

If I go and prepare a place for you, I shall come again and take you to myself, so that where I am you may be also.

St John 14: 3

C

I will be with you always, to the end of time.

St Matthew 28: 20

Calendar	Sentence		Collect
DAY OF PENTECOST	A	Through the Holy Spirit he has given us, God's love has flooded our hearts. *Romans 5: 5*	Almighty and ever-living God, you fulfilled the promises of Easter by sending your Holy Spirit and opening the way of life eternal to every race and nation. Keep us in the unity of your Spirit, that every tongue may tell of your glory; through Jesus Christ our Lord, who lives and reigns with you and the Holy Spirit, one God, now and for ever.
	B	I am going to put breath into you, and you will live. *Ezekiel 37: 5*	
	C	You will receive power when the Holy Spirit comes upon you; and you will bear witness for me. *Acts 1: 8*	
SEASON AFTER PENTECOST			
First Sunday after Pentecost (Trinity Sunday)	A	Through Christ we have access to the Father in the one Spirit. *Ephesians 2: 18*	Almighty and eternal God, through your Word and Spirit you created all things. In Jesus Christ, the Word made flesh, you reveal your salvation in all the world. Through your Holy Spirit, you give us a share in your life and love. Keep us firm in this faith, and fill us with the vision of your glory, that we may serve and praise you all our days; through Jesus Christ our Lord, who is alive and reigns with you and the Holy Spirit, one God, now and for ever.
	B	Can you fathom the mystery of God, or attain to the limits of the Almighty? *Job 11: 7*	
	C	The grace of the Lord Jesus Christ, and the love of God, and the fellowship of the Holy Spirit, be with you all. *2 Corinthians 13: 14*	

Calendar	Sentence	Collect
Sunday *between May 29 and June 4* (**if after Trinity Sunday**)	**A** You are a people claimed by God as his own, to proclaim the glorious deeds of him who has called you out of darkness into his marvellous light. *1 Peter 2: 9*	God of the nations, you have revealed your will to all people and promised us your saving help. Grant us your grace, both to hear and to do what you command, that darkness may be overcome by the power of your light; through your Son Jesus Christ our Lord, who lives and reigns with you and the Holy Spirit, one God, now and for ever.
	B Let every word and action, every thing you do, be in the name of the Lord Jesus, and give thanks through him to God the Father. *Colossians 3: 17*	
	C Stand firm and immovable, and work for the Lord always, work without limit, since you know that in the Lord your labour cannot be lost. *1 Corinthians 15: 58*	
Sunday *between June 5 and June 11* (**if after Trinity Sunday**)	**A** The victory by which the world is overcome is our faith. *1 John 5: 4*	Almighty and merciful God, you have assured the human family of eternal life through Jesus Christ our Saviour. Deliver us from the death of sin and raise us to new life in him, who lives and reigns with you and the Holy Spirit, one God, now and for ever.
	B If the Spirit of him who raised Jesus from the dead dwells in you, then the God who raised Christ Jesus from the dead will also give new life to you through his indwelling Spirit. *Romans 8: 11*	

Calendar	Sentence		Collect

Sunday *between June 12* *and June 18* **(if after Trinity Sunday)**

C — You have not seen Christ, yet you love him; and trusting in him now without seeing him, you are filled with a glorious joy too great for words. *1 Peter 1: 8*

A — The Spirit of God affirms to our spirit that we are God's children. He comes to the aid of our weakness. *Romans 8: 16, 26*

B — If Christ is in you, the Spirit is your life. *Romans 8: 10*

C — By your gracious spirit guide me. Revive me, Lord, for the honour of your name. *Psalm 143: 10, 11*

Almighty God,
without you we are not able to please you.
Mercifully grant that your Holy Spirit
may in all things direct and rule our hearts;
through Jesus Christ our Lord,
who is alive and reigns
with you and the Holy Spirit,
one God, now and for ever.

Sunday *between June 19* *and June 25* **(if after Trinity Sunday)**

A — Take heart, you seekers after God. For the Lord listens to the poor and does not despise his captive people. *Psalm 69: 32, 33*

B — Have no fear, for I have redeemed you; I call you by your name; you are mine. *Isaiah 43: 1*

C — We can take courage and say, 'The Lord is my helper. I will not fear; what can man do to me?' *Hebrews 13: 6*

O God our defender,
when storms rage about us
and cause us to be afraid,
rescue your people from despair,
deliver your sons and daughters from fear,
and preserve us all from unbelief;
through your Son, Jesus Christ our Lord,
who lives and reigns
with you and the Holy Spirit,
one God, now and for ever.

Calendar	Sentence		Collect

Sunday *between June 26 and July 2*

A   Be generous to one another, tender-hearted, forgiving one another as God in Christ forgave you.

Ephesians 4: 32

B   Blessed be the Lord whose unfailing love for me was wonderful.

Psalm 31: 21

C   There is nothing love cannot face; there is no limit to its faith, its hope, its endurance.

1 Corinthians 13: 7

Almighty God,
you have taught us through your Son
that love fulfils the law.
Grant us grace to love you
with all our heart,
all our soul,
all our mind,
all our strength,
and to love our neighbour as ourselves;
through Jesus Christ our Lord,
who lives and reigns
with you and the Holy Spirit, one God,
now and for ever.

Sunday *between July 3 and July 9*

A   Serve one another in love.

Galatians 5: 13

B   The greatest among you must bear himself like the youngest, the one who rules like one who serves. I am among you like a servant.

St Luke 22: 26, 27

C   With unflagging zeal, aglow with the Spirit, serve the Lord.

Romans 12: 11

Almighty God,
your Son Jesus Christ has taught us
that what we do
for the least of your children
we do also for him.
Give us the will to serve others
as he was the servant of all,
who gave up his life and died for us,
but lives and reigns
with you and the Holy Spirit,
one God, now and for ever.

Calendar	Sentence		Collect

Sunday *between July 10 and July 16*

A The grass may wither, the flower fade, but the word of our God will endure for ever. *Isaiah 40: 8*

Almighty God,
you have made us for yourself,
and our hearts are restless
till they find their rest in you.
Give us peace in your service,
and in the world to come
the joy of seeing you face to face;
through Jesus Christ our Lord,
who lives and reigns
with you and the Holy Spirit,
one God, now and for ever.

B The Son of man did not come to be served but to serve, and to give his life as a ransom for many. *St Mark 10: 45*

C I have come that they may have life, and may have it in all its fullness. *St John 10: 10*

Sunday *between July 17 and July 23*

A Be rooted in Christ, be built in him, grow strong in the faith; let your hearts overflow with thankfulness. *Colossians 2: 7*

Almighty God,
your Son has opened for us
a new and living way into your presence.
Give us pure hearts and constant wills
to worship you in spirit and in truth;
through Jesus Christ our Lord,
who lives and reigns
with you and the Holy Spirit,
one God, now and for ever.

B May you, in company with all God's people, be strong to grasp what is the breadth and length and height and depth of Christ's love. *Ephesians 3: 18, 19*

C Out of the treasure of his glory God grant you inward strength and power through his Spirit, that through faith Christ may dwell in your hearts in love. *Ephesians 3: 16, 17*

Calendar	Sentence		Collect
Sunday *between July 24 and July 30*	A	My one desire is to know Christ and the power of his resurrection. *Philippians 3: 10*	O God, the protector of all who trust in you, without you nothing is strong, nothing is holy. Increase and multiply upon us your mercy, that with you as our ruler and guide, we may so pass through things temporal, that we lose not the things eternal; through Jesus Christ our Lord, who lives and reigns with you and the Holy Spirit, one God, now and for ever and ever.
	B	I am able to face anything through Christ who gives me strength. *Philippians 4: 13*	
	C	Jesus is able to save completely those who approach God through him, since he is always alive to plead on their behalf. *Hebrews 7: 25*	
Sunday *between July 31 and August 6*	A	Never again shall they feel hunger or thirst; because the Lamb who is at the centre of the throne will be their shepherd and will guide them to springs of the water of life. *Revelation 7: 16, 17*	Almighty God, your Son Jesus Christ fed the hungry with the bread of his life and the word of his kingdom. Renew your people with your heavenly grace, and in all our weakness sustain us by the true and living bread, Jesus Christ your Son our Lord, who lives and reigns with you and the Holy Spirit, one God, now and for ever.
	B	The Lord will be your guide continually and will satisfy your needs in the bare desert. *Isaiah 58: 11*	
	C	Do not store up for yourselves treasure on earth, but store up for yourselves treasure in heaven. For where your treasure is there will your heart be also. *St Matthew 6: 19, 20, 21*	

Calendar	Sentence		Collect
Sunday *between August 7 and August 13*	A	The life I now live is not my life, but the life which Christ lives in me. *Galatians 2: 20*	Almighty God, you sent your Holy Spirit to be the life and light of your Church. Open our hearts to the riches of your grace, that we may bring forth the fruit of the Spirit in love, joy, and peace; through Jesus Christ our Lord, who is alive and reigns with you and the Holy Spirit, one God, now and for ever.
	B	Here I stand knocking at the door; if any one hears my voice and opens the door, I will come in and he and I will eat together. *Revelation 3: 20*	
	C	If the Spirit is the source of our life, let the Spirit also direct its course. *Galatians 5: 25*	
Sunday *between August 14 and August 20*	A	It was not to judge the world that God sent his Son into the world, but that the through him the world might be saved. *St John 3: 17*	Almighty God, you have broken the tyranny of sin and sent into our hearts the Spirit of your Son. Give us grace to dedicate our freedom to your service, that all people may know the glorious liberty of the children of God; through Jesus Christ our Lord, who lives and reigns with you and the Holy Spirit, one God, now and for ever.
	B	He who possesses the Son of God possesses life. *1 John 5: 12*	
	C	Live as those who are free; not however as though your freedom provided a cloak for wrongdoing, but as slaves in God's service. *1 Peter 2: 16*	

Calendar	Sentence	Collect

Sunday between *August 21 and August 27*

A We know that the Son of God has come and given us understanding to know the true God.
1 John 5: 20

B Let us love one another because the source of love is God. Everyone who loves is a child of God and knows God, for God is love.
1 John 4: 7, 8

C Love is patient and kind, never quick to take offence. Love keeps no score of wrongs, takes no pleasure in the sins of others, but delights in the truth.
1 Corinthians 13: 4, 5, 6

Almighty God,
you have taught us
that without love
all our doings are worth nothing.
Send your Holy Spirit,
and pour into our hearts
that most excellent gift of love,
the true bond of peace and of all virtues;
through Jesus Christ our Lord,
who lives and reigns
with you and the Holy Spirit,
one God, now and for ever.

Sunday between *August 28 and September 3*

A Offer your very selves to God: a living sacrifice, dedicated and fit for his acceptance.
Romans 12: 1

B Blessed are those whose hearts are pure; they shall see God.
St Matthew 5: 8

C Humble yourselves under God's mighty hand, and he will lift you up.
1 Peter 5: 6

Almighty and ever-living God,
you are the author and giver of all good things.
Graft in our hearts the love of your name,
increase in us true religion,
nourish us with all goodness,
and of your great mercy keep us in the same;
through Jesus Christ our Lord,
who lives and reigns
with you and the Holy Spirit,
one God, now and for ever.

Calendar	Sentence		Collect
Sunday *between September 4 and September 10*	**A**	Cry out, shout aloud, for the Holy One of Israel is among you in majesty. *Isaiah 12: 6*	Stir up, O Lord, the wills of your faithful people, that richly bearing the fruit of good works, we may by you be richly rewarded; through Jesus Christ our Lord, who is alive and reigns with you and the Holy Spirit, one God, now and for ever.
	B	Stand firm in the faith; be valiant, be strong. Let everything you do be done in love. *1 Corinthians 16: 13, 14*	
	C	We have set our hope on the living God, who is the Saviour of all. *1 Timothy 4: 10*	
Sunday *between September 11 and September 17*	**A**	Bless the Lord, my soul. He pardons all my wrongdoing, and crowns me with love and compassion. *Psalm 103: 1, 3, 4*	Almighty God, you call your Church to witness that in Christ we are reconciled to you. Help us so to proclaim the good news of your love, that all who hear it may turn to you; through Jesus Christ our Lord, who lives and reigns with you and the Holy Spirit, one God, now and for ever.
	B	Take strength from the grace of God which is ours in Christ Jesus. *2 Timothy 2: 1*	
	C	This is what love really is: not that we have loved God, but that he loved us and sent his Son as a sacrifice to atone for our sins. *1 John 4: 10*	

Calendar	Sentence	Collect

Sunday *between September 18 and September 24*

A
To the Lord belong the earth and everything in it, the world and all its inhabitants.

Psalm 24: 1

Almighty God,
you created the heavens and the earth,
and made us in your image.
Teach us to discern your hand
in all your works
and to serve you
with reverence and thanksgiving;
through Jesus Christ our Lord,
who is alive and reigns
with you and the Holy Spirit,
one God, now and for ever.

B
No place is left for any human pride in the presence of God. If any one must boast, let him boast of the Lord.

1 Corinthians 1: 29, 31

C
The Lord is gracious and compassion-ate, long-suffering and ever faithful. The Lord is good to all; his compassion rests upon all his creatures.

Psalm 145: 8 - 9

Sunday *between September 25 and October 1*

A
Look to the Lord and be strong; at all times seek his presence.

Psalm 105: 4

Grant, O merciful God,
that your Church,
being gathered by your Holy Spirit into one,
may show forth your power among all peoples,
to the glory of your name;
through Jesus Christ our Lord,
who lives and reigns
with you and the Holy Spirit,
one God, now and for ever.

B
Send out your light and your truth to be my guide; let them lead me to your holy hill, to your dwelling-place.

Psalm 43: 3

C
Your word is everlasting, Lord; it is firmly fixed in heaven. Your faithful-ness endures for all generations.

Psalm 119: 89 - 90

Calendar	Sentence		Collect
Sunday *between October 2 and October 8*	**A**	How good and how pleasant it is to live together in unity! *Psalm 133: 1*	Almighty God, you have built your Church on the foundation of the apostles and prophets, Jesus Christ himself being the chief cornerstone. Join us together in unity of spirit by their teaching, that we may become a holy temple, acceptable to you; through Jesus Christ our Lord, who lives and reigns with you and the Holy Spirit, one God, now and for ever.
	B	Spare no effort to make fast with bonds of peace the unity which the Spirit gives. *Ephesians 4: 3*	
	C	Join in the struggle for that faith which God entrusted to his people once and for all. *Jude 3*	
Sunday *between October 9 and October 15*	**A**	Happy are those whom you choose and bring near to remain in your courts. Grant us in abundance the bounty of your house. *Psalm 65: 4*	Almighty God, in our baptism you adopted us for your own. Quicken your Spirit within us, that we, being renewed both in body and mind, may worship you in sincerity and truth and serve you with thankfulness of heart; through Jesus Christ our Lord, who lives and reigns with you and the Holy Spirit, one God, now and for ever.
	B	If we belong to Christ, it is all God's doing; it is God also who has set his seal upon us, and given the Spirit to dwell in our hearts. *2 Corinthians 1: 21, 22*	
	C	It is good to give thanks to the Lord, for his love endures for ever. *Psalm 106: 1*	

Calendar	Sentence		Collect
Sunday *between October 16 and October 22*	**A**	What does the Lord your God ask of you? Only this: to fear the Lord your God, to conform to all his ways, to love him, and to serve him with all your heart and soul. *Deuteronomy 10: 12*	Almighty and ever-living God, increase in us your gift of faith, that forsaking what lies behind and reaching out to what is before, we may run the way of your commandments and win the crown of everlasting joy; through Jesus Christ our Lord, who lives and reigns with you and the Holy Spirit, one God, now and for ever.
	B	God will show us the path of life; in his presence is the fullness of joy, at his right hand are pleasures for evermore. *Psalm 16: 11*	
	C	Ask, and you will receive; seek, and you will find; knock, and the door will be opened to you. *St Matthew 7: 7*	
Sunday *between October 23 and October 29*	**A**	The law was given through Moses, but grace and truth came through Jesus Christ. *St John 1: 17*	O God our redeemer, you heard the cry of your people, and sent your servant Moses to lead them out of slavery. Free us from the tyranny of sin and death, and by the leading of your Spirit bring us to our promised land; through Jesus Christ our Lord, who lives and reigns with you and the Holy Spirit, one God, now and for ever.
	B	If I fixed my eyes on all your commandments, I should never be put to shame. *Psalm 119: 6*	
	C	The Lord is kind and forgiving, full of love towards all who cry to him. *Psalm 86: 5*	

Calendar		Sentence	Collect
Sunday *between October 30 and November 5 inclusive*	A	We have put our faith in Jesus Christ, in order that we might be justified through this faith, and not through actions dictated by the law. *Galatians 2: 16*	Almighty God, your servant Abraham obeyed your call, rejoicing in your promise that in him all the families of the earth should be blessed. Give us faith like his, that in us your promises may be fulfilled; through Jesus Christ our Lord, who lives and reigns with you and the Holy Spirit, one God, now and for ever.
	B	Has not God chosen those who are poor in the eyes of the world to be rich in faith, and to possess the kingdom he has promised to those who love him? *St James 2: 5*	
	C	You are reaping the harvest of your faith, that is, salvation for your souls. *1 Peter 1: 9*	
Sunday *between November 6 and November 12*	A	Lead me by your faithfulness and teach me, for you are God my saviour; in you I put my hope all day long. *Psalm 25: 5*	Eternal God, you caused all holy scriptures to be written for our learning. Grant us so to hear them, read, mark, learn, and inwardly digest them, that we may embrace and ever hold fast the blessed hope of everlasting life, which you have given us in our Saviour Jesus Christ, who lives and reigns with you and the Holy Spirit, one God, for ever and ever.
	B	The Lord is waiting to show you his favour. Happy are all who wait for him! *Isaiah 30: 18*	
	C	God who is the ground of hope, fill you with all joy and peace as you lead the life of faith until, by the power of the Holy Spirit, you overflow with hope. *Romans 15: 13*	

Calendar	Sentence		Collect

Sunday *between November 13 and November 19*

A How long, Lord, will you hide yourself from sight? Remember how fleeting is our life!
Psalm 89: 46, 47

B Look forward to the coming of the day of God, and work to hasten it on.
2 Peter 3: 12

C Obey your orders without fault or failure until the appearance of our Lord Jesus Christ which God will bring about in his own good time.
1 Timothy 6: 14, 15

Almighty God,
you sent your Son Jesus Christ
to be the light of the world.
Free us from all that darkens and ensnares us,
and bring us to eternal light and joy;
through the power of him
who is alive and reigns
with you and the Holy Spirit,
one God, now and for ever.

Sunday *between November 20 and November 26*
(Reign of Christ the King)

A The Lord has become King, clothed with majesty; the Lord is robed, girded with might.
Psalm 93: 1

B The Lord has established his throne for judgement. He it is who will judge the world with justice, who will try the cause of peoples with equity.
Psalm 9: 7, 8

C From you, Bethlehem, will come a king for me, one whose origins are far back in the past. He will rise up to lead Israel in the strength of the Lord, in the majesty of the name of the Lord.
Micah 5: 2, 4

Almighty and everlasting God,
it is your will to restore all things
in your well-beloved Son,
our Lord and King.
Grant that the peoples of the earth,
now divided and enslaved by sin,
may be freed and brought together
under his gentle and loving rule;
who lives and reigns
with you and the Holy Spirit,
one God, now and for ever.

Calendar	Sentence	Collect

SPECIAL DAYS
Christian Unity

A
God has reconciled us to himself
through Christ, and has enlisted us in
this ministry of reconciliation.
2 Corinthians 5: 18

B
How good and how pleasant it is to live
together in unity!
Psalm 133: 1

C
Through the Holy Spirit God has given
us, God's love has flooded our hearts.
Romans 5: 5

Creator of all,
by your Holy Spirit
you have made a diversity of peoples one
in the confession of your name.
Lead them, by the same Spirit,
to show to the whole earth
one mind in belief
and one passion for righteousness;
through Jesus Christ our Lord.

Presentation of the Lord
(February 2)

A
One thing I ask of the Lord, it is the
one thing I seek: that I may dwell in
the house of the Lord all the days of
my life, to gaze on the beauty of the
Lord and to seek him in his temple.
Psalm 27: 4

B
God, within your temple, we meditate
on your steadfast love.
Psalm 48: 9

C
Bring an offering and enter his courts;
tremble before him, all the earth.
Psalm 96: 8, 9

Gracious God,
your Son Jesus Christ
was presented in the temple
and acclaimed the light of the nations.
Grant that in him
we may be presented to you,
and in the world
may shine as lights
reflecting his glory;
through Jesus Christ our Lord,
who lives and reigns
with you and the Holy Spirit,
one God, now and for ever.

Calendar	Sentence		Collect

Springtime

A As the earth puts forth her blossom or plants in the garden burst into flower, so will the Lord God make his victory and renown blossom before all nations.
Isaiah 61: 11

Almighty God,
you have promised
that seedtime and harvest will never cease.
Bless this land with seasonable weather
and a fruitful harvest,
and so direct the labours
of those who manage the land
that they may employ
the resources of nature to your glory,
for our well-being
and the relief of those in need;
through Jesus Christ our Lord,
who lives and reigns
with you and the Holy Spirit,
one God, now and for ever.

B The Lord has sent me to comfort all who mourn, to give them garlands instead of ashes. They will be called trees of righteousness, planted by the Lord for his adornment.
Isaiah 61: 1, 2, 3

C Blessed is anyone who trusts in the Lord, and rests his confidence on him. He will be like a tree planted by the waterside that sends out its roots along a stream. When the heat comes it has nothing to fear; its foliage stays green.
Jeremiah 17: 7 - 8

Harvest Festival

A The earth has yielded its harvest. May God, our God, bless us.
Psalm 67: 6

Almighty God,
we offer you hearty thanks
for your goodness and care
in giving to us the fruits of the earth
in their seasons.
Give us grace to use them rightly,
to your glory,
for the relief of those in need,
and our own well-being;

B God cares for the earth and makes it fruitful. He crowns the year with his good gifts.
Psalm 65: 9, 11

Calendar	Sentence		Collect
	C	There are many who say, 'If only we might see good times! Let the light of your face shine on us, Lord'. But you have put into my heart a greater happiness than others had from grain and wine in plenty. *Psalm 4: 6 - 7*	through Jesus Christ, the living Bread, who came down from heaven and gives life to the world, and who lives and reigns with you and the Holy Spirit, one God, now and for ever.
Michaelmas (*September 29*)	A	You have made the Most High your dwelling-place. He will charge his angels to guard you wherever you go. *Psalm 91: 9, 11*	Eternal God, you have appointed both angels and people to worship and serve you in your kingdom. As your holy angels stand before you in heaven, so may they help and defend us here on earth; through Jesus Christ our Lord, who is alive and reigns with you and the Holy Spirit, one God, now and for ever.
	B	Bless the Lord, you his angels, mighty in power, who do his bidding and obey his command. *Psalm 103: 20*	
	C	Do not neglect to show hospitality; by doing this, some have entertained angels unawares. *Hebrew 13: 2*	
All Saints (*November 1*)	A	Give joyful thanks to the Father, who has made you fit to share the heritage of God's people, in the realm of light. *Colossians 1: 12*	Almighty God, you have knit together your elect in one communion and fellowship in the mystical body of your Son.

Calendar	Sentence	Collect
	B You have come to Mount Zion, the city of the living God, the heavenly Jerusalem, to God the judge of all, and to the spirits of good men made perfect, and to Jesus the mediator of a new covenant. *Hebrews 12: 22, 23, 24*	Give us grace to follow your blessed saints in all virtuous and godly living, that we may come to those inexpressible joys which you have prepared for those who perfectly love you; through Jesus Christ our Lord, who lives and reigns with you and the Holy Spirit, one God, now and for ever.
	C They will be called the Holy People, the Redeemed of the Lord. *Isaiah 62: 12*	
Remembrance Day	**A** Not to us, Lord, not to us, but to your name give glory for your love, for your faithfulness! *Psalm 115: 1*	Almighty God, keep us mindful of all your benefits and heedful of our high calling, that we may yield ourselves in new obedience to your holy will, and live henceforth as those who are not their own, but are bought with a price; through Jesus Christ our Lord, who lives and reigns with you and the Holy Spirit, one God, now and for ever.
	B Some boast of chariots and some of horses, but our boast is the name of the Lord our God. *Psalm 20: 7*	
	C God is our refuge and our stronghold, a timely help in trouble; so we are not afraid though the earth shakes. *Psalm 46: 1, 2*	
St Andrew's Day (*November 30*)	**A** One of the two who followed Jesus was Andrew. The first thing he did was to find his brother Simon, and say to him, 'We have found the Messiah'. He brought Simon to Jesus. *St John 1: 40 - 42*	Almighty God, you gave such grace to your apostle Saint Andrew that he readily obeyed the calling of your Son Jesus Christ and followed him without delay,

B   Jesus said to Simon and Andrew,
'Come with me, and I will make you
fishers of men'.

St Matthew 4: 19

bringing his brother with him.
Grant us the same spirit of cheerful obedience,
that we may give ourselves willingly
to share in the witness of your Church
to the whole world;
through Jesus Christ our Lord,
who lives and reigns
with you and the Holy Spirit,
one God, now and for ever.

C   A harvest of light has arisen for the
righteous, and joy for the upright in
heart.

Psalm 97: 11

Dedication/Anniversary

A   Come, bless the Lord, all you his servants. Lift up your hands towards the
sanctuary and bless the Lord.

Psalm 134: 1, 2

Almighty God,
as we celebrate
the *dedication* of this house of prayer,
we praise you for the many blessings
you have given those who worship here.

B   My eyes will be open and my ears
attentive to the prayers which are made
in this place. I have chosen and consecrated this house.

2 Chronicles 7: 15 - 16

We pray that all
who seek you in this place
may find you.
Fill us with your Holy Spirit,
that we may become
the living temple of your glory;
through Jesus Christ our Lord,
who lives and reigns
with you and the Holy Spirit,
one God, now and for ever.

C   Who may go up the mountain of the
Lord? Who may stand in his holy place?
One who has clean hands and a pure
heart.

Psalm 24: 3 - 4

INDEX

Index

The LORD'S PRAYER

FIRST FORM

Our Father in heaven
hallowed be your name,
your kingdom come,
your will be done,
on earth as in heaven.
Give us today our daily bread.
Forgive us our sins
as we forgive those who sin against us.
Save us from the time of trial
and deliver us from evil.
For the kingdom, the power,
and the glory are yours
now and for ever.   Amen.

SECOND FORM

Our Father, who art in heaven,
hallowed be thy name.
Thy kingdom come.
Thy will be done, on earth as it is in heaven.
Give us this day our daily bread.
And forgive us our debts, as we forgive our debtors.
And lead us not into temptation, but deliver us from evil.
For thine is the kingdom, and the power,
and the glory, for ever.   Amen.

or

   And forgive us our trespasses,
   as we forgive those who trespass against us.
   And lead us not into temptation,
   but deliver us from evil.
   For thine is the kingdom, the power, and the glory,
   for ever and ever.   Amen.

A STATEMENT *of* CHRISTIAN FAITH

We believe in one God:
  Father, Son and Holy Spirit.
  God is love.

We praise God the Father:
  who created the universe and keeps it in being.
  He has made us his sons and daughters
  to share his joy,
  living together in justice and peace,
  caring for his world and for each other.

We proclaim Jesus Christ, God the Son:
  born of Mary,
  by the power of the Holy Spirit,
  he became one of us,
  sharing our life and our death.
  He made known God's compassion and mercy,
  giving hope and declaring forgiveness of sin,
  offering healing and wholeness to all.
  By his death on the cross and by his resurrection,
  he has triumphed over evil.
  Jesus is Lord of life and of all creation.